CULTURE & TEXT

CULTURE & TEXT

Discourse and Methodology in Social Research and Cultural Studies

edited by

Alison Lee and Cate Poynton

ROWMAN & LITTLEFIELD PUBLISHERS, INC.
Lanham • Boulder • New York • Oxford

ROWMAN & LITTLEFIELD PUBLISHERS, INC.

Published in the United States of America
by Rowman & Littlefield Publishers, Inc.
4720 Boston Way, Lanham, Maryland 20706
http://www.rowmanlittlefield.com

12 Hid's Copse Road
Cumnor Hill, Oxford OX2 9JJ, England

Editorial arrangement copyright © 2000 by Alison Lee
and Cate Poynton
Copyright © in individual chapters remains with the authors

ISBN 0-7425-0058-6 (cloth)
ISBN 0-7425-0059-4 (pbk)

Printed in Malaysia

Foreword

In my view, the provenance and problematic of this timely collection is best understood by working back from its conclusion. In the final paragraph of the final chapter, Alison Lee writes:

> In drawing the threads of this discussion together . . . the project of engaging in the search for method is both necessary and inevitable. The need for 'responsibility' in research brings a corresponding requirement for systematicity, of some kind or another. Yet the search for method, of itself, is never sufficient to produce or account for the texts of analysis. Discourse analysts need to be able to account reflexively for the textuality of their own texts.

In Lee's view, discourse analysts (of most persuasions) have been surprisingly unreflexive about their own language. In contrast, questions about the power, politics and practices of representation by the academic community have been pivotal in critical anthropology for some years. Lee speaks clearly and pointedly about this 'methodology/performativity' tension, and of the associated need for discourse analysts to consider together the questions of respondent 'agency' and analyst 'advocacy' which too often are kept separate.

Inevitably, given this belief in a need to be both 'expert' (in terms of 'systematicity, of one kind or another') and 'lay' (as some kind of 'responsible' conduit for the voices of others), a book that aims to be an introduction to and summary of discourse analysis will move between these positions. We can see this at work if we continue backwards from Lee's concluding piece to Jennifer Biddle's account of Warlpiri use of the alphabet and Jan Wright's analysis of school phys.ed's disciplining of the female body. Biddle's is an 'anti-authoritarian' analysis which is deeply suspicious of the editors' brief to 'make explicit the methods I've used in order that these might be repeated'. But, she worries, 'Is there a method here? What if there isn't? . . . Method. An ugly word'—made all the more troublesome by her dictionary's conjuncture between 'method, methodical and Methodist. "Procedure for gaining an object" . . . "Excessive regard for methods"'. In this account 'methodology' may be as imperialist as white culture's instrumentalist strategies of naming. But then Biddle proceeds to give us both an exciting and systematic account of the way in which Warlpiri recourse to written initialling usurps Western written authority for their own purposes (in avoiding speaking aloud the name of a recently deceased person). So, Biddle asks herself, 'can refusal be a method? Does irreverence count?'. Well, yes, except that Biddle's own method is an excellent example of local, situated research, where Warlpiri voices and practices intermesh with the academic intertextualities accessed by the researcher's own theoretical choices: here (most convincingly) Butler's 'performativity', Derrida's 'iteration' and de Certeau's 'tactics'. Possibly it is in that performative *staging* of 'lay' and 'expert' voices that Lee's call for both 'method' and 'rewriting' in discourse analysis can best be served. The heteroglossia here is of a sustained but also empirically 'grounded' reflexive meeting of Warlpiri and academic voices.

Jan Wright's 'Disciplining the body' takes the opposite tack. Here we hear about the intertexts (of medicine, law, technocratic rationality, human movement, fitness and health etc.) that augment the power of the teacher, and of those other discourses and gazes (of male students) that account for the girls being analysed doing their physical education separately from the boys. But this analysis is achieved by way of a Foucauldian grid (via Jennifer Gore) of 'surveillance', 'normalisation', 'exclusion', classification', 'distribution', 'individualisation', 'totalisation', 'regulation'. This is a 'governmentality' approach, which draws on systemic functional linguistics to show how the teacher 'is embodied as the expert . . . to assist others through . . . moving bodies', while at the same time inviting the girls to regulate their own behaviour via competence in technologies of the self. There is little here (as Lee would point out) about the power of the Foucauldian expert accessing teachers and classes via professional-quality Walkmans. But one point of this book is to invite the reader to make those digressions herself: to contemplate, for example, the shape of that more reflexive account, or, alternatively, to contemplate an approach that might take a more feminist/psychoanalytical direction in seeking the girls' own pleasures and risks in their displayed bodies.

A related analysis to this, emphasising questions of corporeality via 'discourteous feminist readings' is central to Pether and Threadgold's discourse analysis of 'sex, property, equity'. Here 'experts' are again at the centre of things—indeed different (male) centres within the high judiciary—as the authors divest themselves of 'evidence' and 'authority' (and deconstruct such truth-claims in their male judges) and explore 'some of the repressed investments, desires and subjectivities that haunt the legal imagination'. Just like their new historicist model for this piece, Marjorie Levinson, who locates other intertexts and her own 'corporeality and habitus' in 'intervening between Wordsworth and his text' of *Tintern Abbey,* so Pether and Threadgold are acknowledgedly discourteous feminists who do 'not ignore dominant reading practices' in the Australian legal story but who 'produce the scene of writing differently'. Here the 'advocacy' is clear and not unexpected. But it reveals itself analytically (via the new historicist model) by deconstructing the way in which powerful expert men do (and do not) *determine* the agency of women before the law.

Reflexivity, in Pether and Threadgold's piece, is an assertive wager; whereas in Scheeres and Solomon's analysis of methodological dilemmas they themselves have faced in collaborative research practice it is more agonised and self-critical. As successful consultants in the booming (economic rationalist) field of workplace restructuring and training, the authors honestly faced the problems of many of their colleagues in being stretched between their own expertise as academics and the expert demands of managerialism. But, as Scheeres and Solomon remind us, academics work in a managerialist industry too: so how then to develop 'methodological processes that open up, challenge, incite and disrupt what might be regarded as inevitable non-negotiables or closures'? Of the three stages of the consultancy project that they discuss—the tender document, the final report and the 'follow-up' training manuals—it is the last that gave them space for some 'disruption'. Sometimes academics operate the opposite way: writing a submission that acknowledges (at least in part) their own position (even politics), and then watching in disappointment as the 'open door' the successful bid seemed to promise is closed off by the time of the final report or of the advertising campaign around it. Scheeres and Solomon seem more street-wise here in being reflexively silent in the first two stages about the 'methodology of the significance of local site-specific factors', and then later helping training participants to consider the power relationships in their workplace. Like the Warlpiri use of naming, here the researchers both conformed to the linear, instrumentalist desires of the 'bosses' (thus providing 'validity' for further consultancies within their own economically rationalist industry) and challenged this in a minor way. But they are dissatisfied with so little. Perhaps, they argue, the methodology of hybrid research, of intersecting modern and postmodern approaches, would provide both the agreed 'contract' and 'training participants' explorations and disruptions disturbing the prescriptive single outcome'.

As we work back then from Lee's (for me) defining statement about 'method' and 'rewriting' (or 'performance', in Terry Threadgold's materialist formulation) we can readily trace the richness of a book that asks questions repeatedly about 'expertise': the researcher's, the designated power holder's (the teacher, the white lawyer and bureaucrat, the consultancy agent), and the respondent's. I do not have the space here to detail each chapter's response to Lee's problematic; but there is valuable work from Carolyn Baker on the 'culture-in-action' approach of membership categorisation analysis in opposing decontextualised, non-local schema approaches to talk (here among schoolchildren, parents and teachers); Gillian Fuller in bringing (systemic) linguistics and (motivated) critical theory together in analysing the sites, intertexts and specific texts of science-popularising material (again here 'prestigious sources of authority', both Western and Native, are given voices that only seem to allow 'people to speak for themselves'); and Jackie Cook's analysis of talkback radio in terms of a set of mobile relationships—between masculinist 'ratings' demands from 'enterprise culture', and the micro-politics of dual 'conversational exchange' (within the studio, and between host and caller). Here, too, Cook insists on some space for resistance, particularly of the kind where one macho male engaging on-air with another draws attention to the whole procedure.

Early in the book parallel chapters by Cate Poynton and Terry Threadgold tell their different (Anglo-American and European) stories concerning discourse analysis. Poynton adopts a Foucauldian genealogical approach in locating discourse analysis in terms of its conditions of emergence and its effects: the legacy of Saussure and Chomsky (with attendant losses in relation to the analysis of the materiality of speech); discourse analysis as technological tool for description and interpretation (including the meticulous descriptions of Conversation Analysis); text as social semiotic (the radical nature of Halliday's emphasis on 'text' as social action); Foucauldian and feminist emphases on power, corporeality and 'context'; and critical, multi-modal work developing within the semiotic tradition (van Dijk, Kress, van Leeuwen). But, echoing the concerns of Scheeres and Solomon, Poynton worries at the increasing usage of linguistics at the end of the twentieth century as part of the economic rationalist 'technologisation' of discourse, and about the future possibilities for an oppositional stance. Terry Threadgold's emphasis is poststructuralist ('Saussure under erasure' via Jakobson's poetic, Derrida's deconstruction, Foucault's reversals and discontinuities, Kristeva's writing-as-analysis, Butler's performativity). Her question (to radical academics) is: 'whether "making visible" what iteration does and then allowing iteration to do its work is actually enough to effect a change, to radically alter the system of gender hierarchy and compulsory heterosexuality.' Returning to Lee's issues of agency and advocacy, systematicity against reflexivity, Threadgold argues that academics' emphasis on iteration is, indeed, not enough. 'I do not think this is enough and I do think Butler's account in the end is limited to a linguistic rewriting which fails to understand the way oppression may actually craft and shape the materiality of the body through, for example, starvation, torture, long hours of lowly paid and exploited labour and so on.' At the time of writing, that 'and so on' includes the daily representation on television of the plight of Kosovar refugees, which draws our attention, urgently, to Threadgold's point (via Spivak and Derrida) that we should not 'simply wait for iterativity to do its work' but rethink 'the matter of bodies' in the 'mechanics of disciplinarization and institutionalization . . . of the colonizer'. As Threadgold says, it is in the poststructuralist 'unpredictabilities'—between 'the dangers of believing we can know and do' (the lure of 'expert' methodology) and 'the constant need to know and do more' (the politics of advocacy)—that reside 'the most immediate and challenging aspects of work in feminist discourse analysis and in postlinguistics as we approach the millenium'.

I have worked back from the conclusion of the book but, in what follows, Cate Poynton and Alison Lee establish their own introduction to *Culture & Text*, and their own sense of the logics contained in their collection. On the one hand, they speak of structuring the book around the 'linguistics/poststructuralism "divide" ' (insisting on an approach that gives equal weighting to the inter-relatedness of theory with 'political and institutional dimensions' and to 'their inevitable imbrication with the methodological'). On the other hand, they emphasise the 'thematics' logic of the collection: 'situated knowledges, the body, writing'. Whether you start from introduction or conclusion, enough has been said here, I hope, to vindicate Poynton and Lee's claim 'for the value of a variety of forms of attending to the detail of texts, spoken and written, in carrying out discourse analysis within a broader poststructuralist framework'.

JOHN TULLOCH,
CARDIFF UNIVERSITY, APRIL 1999

Contents

Acknowledgements

We would like to acknowledge the contributions of a number of people and institutions to the project that became this book, from initial conception to final product. We thank all of our contributors for their creative participation in its conceptualisation and execution, especially at the working symposium at which we presented and worked on the draft chapters. In particular, we thank Terry Threadgold who, as joint Cultural Studies Series Editor for Allen & Unwin, enthusiastically supported the idea of this book from its inception and provided much valuable advice.

We thank the Faculty of Education at the University of Technology, Sydney and the Women's Research Centre and the School of Communication and Media at the University of Western Sydney, Nepean. The financial support they provided for the development of the collection, through sponsorship of the working symposium and assistance in the preparation of the manuscript, has been invaluable. We particularly thank Dianne Dickenson and Jill Molan, who worked on the manuscript before it went to the publisher, copy-editing and checking references.

Contributors

Carolyn Baker is Associate Professor in the Graduate School of Education at the University of Queensland. Her expertise is in ethnomethodology and she draws on its various analytic traditions in her research into questions of literacy and schooling. Her books include *Children's First School Books* (with Peter Freebody) and the edited collection *Towards a Critical Sociology of Reading Pedagogy* (with Allan Luke).

Jennifer Biddle is an anthropologist, teaching at Macquarie University in Sydney. She has spent considerable fieldwork time with the Warlpiri people of Central Australia. She is co-editor (with Elspeth Probyn) of the forthcoming collection *Shame And Other Impossible Emotions.* Her work uses anthropology, social theory and linguistics inflected by feminist, poststructuralist, psychoanalytic and postcolonial theory in order to reflect on anthropology's—and the individual anthropologist's—relation to the object of its gaze.

Jackie Cook is a professional radio broadcaster and academic who teaches journalism, media and cultural studies in the School of Communication and Information Studies at the University of South Australia. She has substantial publications on radio and on other media. She is currently completing a major study on radio, drawing on critical discourse analysis, feminist and cultural studies perspectives and the technical knowledges of her professional expertise.

Gillian Fuller teaches multimedia in the School of Media and Communications at the University of New South Wales. Her academic expertise crosses critical, feminist and postcolonial theory and linguistics. She has worked and published in the areas of museums, science education and multimedia. Her current research is concerned with notions of the miraculous and technology within contemporary colonialist practice.

Alison Lee's work with writing encompasses school and academic literacies, writing as research for postgraduate researchers, and critical and ethnographic understandings of writing as cultural production. She is an Associate Professor in the Faculty of Education at the University of Technology, Sydney. Her publications include *Gender, Literacy, Curriculum: rewriting school geography, Postgraduate Studies/ Postgraduate Pedagogy* (co-edited with Bill Green) and numerous articles and chapters. She is currently writing a book titled *The Rise of the Professional Doctorate: changing doctoral education in Australia* (with Bill Green and Marie Brennan).

Penny Pether has taught law and English studies in Australia and the United States, where she is currently an Assistant Professor of Law and Director of Lawyering Skills at Southern Illinois University School of Law. Her interdisciplinary poststructuralist legal scholarship has most recently focused on constitutional theory and national identity, legal pedagogy and sexual assault. Her work in English studies has encompassed Victorian and modernist literature, restoration drama and feminist crime fiction.

Cate Poynton teaches and researches in language and discourse studies in the School of Communication and Media at the University of Western Sydney, Nepean, where she is Director of the Women's Research Centre. Her first book, *Language and Gender: making the difference* (1985), was located within feminist linguistics. Her ongoing engagement with poststructuralist theories, and her current research on voice, with its particular focus on radio, locate her work in media and cultural studies and in the arts. She is co-editor (with Sally Macarthur) of *Musics and Feminisms* (1999) and is currently writing *A Civilisation of Speech: voice, modernity and the speaking subject*.

Hermine Scheeres is a researcher, consultant and teacher in culture, language and literacy in the Faculty of Education at the University of Technology, Sydney. She has been a member of numerous government and industry committees related to language, literacy and professional development. She has written extensively in the area of workplace communication and training, both government-commissioned reports and textbooks. Her books include *Communication Skills* and (with

Helen Joyce et al.) *Effective Communication in the Restructured Worlplace.* Her current research is concerned with worker subjectivities in the restructuring workplace.

Nicky Solomon is a senior academic in the Faculty of Education at the University of Technology, Sydney, and Program Manager for Work-based Learning across the University. Her current writing and research interests focus on the relationship between workplaces and universities and on the pedagogical and epistemological implications of this relationship. Recent relevant publications include papers in the following collections: *Understanding Workplace Learning, Making Space: reframing practice in adult education* (with John Garrick), and *Studies in the Education of Adults* (with Robin Usher).

Terry Threadgold is Professor of Media and Cultural Studies Research in the School of Media, Journalism and Cultural Studies at Cardiff University. She is well known for her interdisciplinary research in semiotics, poststructuralist feminism, performance studies, critical linguistics, feminist legal studies and feminist pedagogy. She is the author of *Feminist Poetics: poesis, performance, histories* and editor of a number of significant collections on language, semiotics and poststructuralist theory and feminist theory, including *Semiotics, Ideology, Language* (with E.A. Grosz, M.A.K. Halliday and Gunther Kress) and *Feminine/ Masculine and Representation* (with Anne Cranny-Francis). She wrote the introductions to both these collections, exploring the complex terrain involved in the 'linguistic turn' in the human sciences. She has published many articles and chapters nationally and internationally.

Jan Wright teaches in the Faculty of Education at the University of Wollongong, where she is the Director of the Physical and Health Education Program. Her reseach has been substantially concerned with the discursive construction of gendered bodies, drawing on feminism, poststructuralism and systemic-functional linguistics. Major sites for her research include school sport and physical education, dance and physical therapies. She publishes in both educational and feminist/ semiotic contexts.

Notes on transcription

The segments of transcribed speech found in chapters 3, 5, 6 and 8 have been somewhat standardised. The conventions used are specified below. The purpose of the standardisation has been to make the transcriptions as readable as possible for non-specialists. Many forms of conversation analysis indicate a level of detail about the speech which is not easy to read. As well, different approaches specify different kinds of information. Ethnomethodological Conversation Analysis (CA) transcription, for example, is meticulous in indicating hesitations, repetitions, the fact and the length of pauses, and commonly numbers 'turns' in talk rather than any other kind of unit. In contrast, systemic functional linguistic transcription may be divided into either clauses or 'moves' (individual speech acts of either the same or another speaker), depending on what is to be analysed. It commonly signals both tone group boundaries and intonation contours and numbers moves rather than turns.

- *Division and numbering* of transcribed material differs in the four chapters which include transcribed speech. In three of the chapters, the transcription is continuous for each speaker's turn, so that each new speaker begins a new line. Turns are numbered. In the fourth chapter (Wright), the basis of the analysis is the individual clause so that each new clause begins a new line. The lines/clauses could be numbered (although they are not in this case).
- *Speaker identification* is by initial of either name or role—relevant information is provided at the beginning of each transcription segment.

- *Conventional orthography* is used throughout for any vocalisation that is recognisable as language. Lengthening is indicated by repetition of vowel letter (e.g. i-i-i-s).
- *Conventionalised non-language vocalisations* are represented by semi-conventionalised orthographic forms (e.g. ha-ha, ow . . .) rather than phonetic script.
- Where part or all of an utterance is *unintelligible*, this is signalled by ((unclear)).
- *Ordinary punctuation* is used, but sparingly, and usually to indicate both momentary pauses (commas) and intonation, particularly at the end of clauses (. indicating falling and ? rising intonation).
- *Longer pauses* are indicated by colons within round brackets (the more colons, the longer the pause) or by the length of the pause in seconds, again within round brackets—for example, (2.0). CA typically measures the pause.
- *Simultaneous speech* involves more than one speaker speaking at the same time. There are several kinds:
  — *simultaneous commencement* of a turn by two or more speakers but all but one speaker cede the floor, leaving a single speaker;
  — *overlaps* in which one speaker begins to speak before the previous speaker has completed their turn, slightly anticipating a change of speaker which would have taken place anyway;
  — *overlaps* in which both the original and the interrupting speaker continue to speak, neither giving way to the other;
  — *interruptions* in which a new speaker takes the floor by cutting short the previous speaker's turn before they had completed what they were going to say.

      The system employed here uses a combination of format and font, with bolding and/or underlining signalling the beginning of the overlap in both speakers. If the transcription of the beginning of the second speaker's turn is located directly under the segment it is overlapping with, not at the beginning of the line, a vertical line can be used to connect the overlapping segments, signalling the overlap very explicitly:

A   Do you think you might <u>eventually</u> get around to it?

                                      |

B   <u>All right</u>, all right, I said I would didn't I?

- *Contextual information* is enclosed in square brackets: for example, [Host's voice begins without full microphone sound, corrected half-way through the extract], [sound of girls jogging].

Transcription conventions vary not only depending on the theoretical framework of the analysis but also on the purpose for which analysis is being done. Transcriptions of material to be analysed using NUDIST, for example, would not need to include details of intonation, pausing or simultaneous speech because that particular software package cannot handle such information. This may or may not problematise such software—again, depending on the purpose of the analysis.

There is much to recommend some acquaintance with several systems of transcription before adopting any particular system for a particular project. Different approaches foreground different aspects of data, aspects that the researcher might not otherwise have attended to. There are a variety of accessible sources summarising conventions. These include Appendix 2 in Deborah Schiffrin's *Approaches to Discourse* (1994, pp. 422–33), which introduces four systems, and chapter 3, 'Data and transcription techniques', in Hutchby and Wooffitt's *Conversation Analysis: principles, practices and applications* (1998, pp. 73–92).

1 Culture & text: an introduction

Cate Poynton & Alison Lee

The 'linguistic turn' in the human sciences over the past three decades has seen increasing attention given to the significance of language and discourse in the construction of knowledge and the formation of persons or subjects. This interest has been manifested, among other things, in an array of different forms of discourse/textual analysis as important tools for social and cultural research. In the case of applied social research, in particular, such tools provide important alternatives to the positivist approaches which have dominated established 'social' fields such as sociology and psychology and which initially constituted the only kinds of 'proper' research in the new and emerging social disciplines and fields of study of the late twentieth century.

Such new fields are under substantial pressure to undertake research in order to legitimise themselves as proper academic 'disciplines' and to access essential funding. There has therefore been a broadening of the base of research and a rapid increase in the volume of social research being undertaken. In many cases, people are undertaking research for the first time in a range of institutional settings with little or no research tradition. There is therefore a considerable and increasing demand for research training and for methods of doing research appropriate to the contexts in which many researchers also work as professionals/practitioners. Much of this work has a critical inflection, as fields of professional practice in the process of forming new disciplinary fields confront and challenge existing hierarchies of knowledge. Paradigm examples of this process are the fields of nursing and health studies, critical legal studies, vocational and workplace education and training.

As well as new disciplines, new sites have opened up for new forms of critical cultural research in the twentieth century. These include sexuality, forms of popular culture, the body and the media. Such sites have initially been explored within academic fields— women's studies, cultural studies, media studies—somewhat more established within the academy than most of the new fields of social research mentioned above. The take-up of such sites in the newer fields has been rapid, however, because of their perceived relevance to pressing issues of social research. To take one example, social research in HIV/AIDS is necessarily informed by theory on sexuality, the body and the media. Because so much work in the 'new' new disciplines is applied, however, practitioners are looking to other fields not only for relevant theory but also for methods.

Contemporary 'theory disciplines' such as cultural studies hold out the promise of engagement with the ordinary everydayness of the contemporary world but, in fact, indefinitely defer any such engagement at the level of the empirical. It is as if all empirical engagement were tarnished with positivism. Bourdieu apparently experienced a very similar 'irritation' with the Frankfurt School, 'faced with the aristocratic demeanour of the totalising critique which retained all the features of grand theory, doubtless so as not to get its hands dirty in the kitchens of empirical research' (Bourdieu, 1990, p. 19, cited in Bennett 1998, pp. 30–1). Similarly, in a move of particular relevance to this book, Terry Threadgold criticises cultural studies for resisting available metalanguage concerning text, that is, for ignoring the potential usefulness of finegrained linguistic description (chapter 3; Threadgold 1997a).

In citing Bourdieu, Bennett, of course, has his own agenda concerning the need for cultural studies to connect with governmentality. His use of such terms as 'pragmatics', 'the cultural studies analyst as a technician' and 'more mundane protocols' (1998, p. 31) does suggest, however, a kind of repositioning (in part at least) of cultural studies that would be very welcome to many in the new research areas. This does not mean that cultural studies 'methods' textbooks are imminent—a substantial problem for new researchers and those in newer disciplines. The search for method is, of course, a search that can largely only be satisfied in unsatisfactory ways: ways that are technicist and decontextualised, that fetishise number and refuse interiority to human subjects. The search for method leads, at worst, to formulaic recipes—part of what the theory disciplines resist. For many in the humanities and social sciences, such critiques of conventional positivist methods will be familiar (see, for example, feminist critiques such as Harding 1987, Alcoff and Potter 1993). For those trained in 'measurement' models of education or management, however, or in 'medical science' versions of health studies, such criticisms may be less familiar but may open up new and exciting spaces for research.

The demand for more flexible approaches to frameworks for, and methods of, research has grown steadily in both the newer and the more established disciplinary fields, not only as a function of the increasing demand for applied forms of knowledge informing the emergence of the new fields but also influenced by feminist and poststructuralist insistence on the inevitably positioned nature of all knowledge. Much of the work on the 'critical' edge of psychology, for example, has been done by women and has been strongly influenced by feminist theory (see the influential work of Valerie Walkerdine (see, for example, 1985, 1988, 1990) as well as the collections edited by Sue Wilkinson and Celia Kitzinger (1995) and by Erica Burman and Ian Parker (1993)). In newer research fields, for example health (with its preponderance of women), feminist and poststructuralist perspectives have inflected the need of the field to differentiate itself from the profoundly empiricist 'medical sciences'. Hence the current interest in discourse analytic work as a further tool in 'non-empiricist' health research, following phenomenology and critical ethnography (Gray and Pratt 1991, 1995; Street 1992).

Phenomenology and ethnography (widely used in other areas of social research) operate very differently from positivist paradigms. In particular, these approaches refuse both the positivist positioning of people (ironically referred to as 'subjects') as mere objects and the Cartesian split between mind and body; both assert the significance of interiority and the already-interpreted nature of social phenomena (Thompson 1990). Postpositivist research methodologies are informed not only by different conceptions of persons but also by an abiding interest in how people become those kinds of persons, that is, by an ongoing commitment to seeing the person in the context/s in which they live. Such postpositivist research methodologies include ethnomethodology, feminist and poststructuralist approaches and certain kinds of discourse analysis—including work influenced by Michel Foucault, theorist of culture/subjectivity, and by functional linguist Michael Halliday. In all these approaches some idea of contextualisation is operative (whether or not the term 'context' is actually used). (For a useful account of a number of approaches to theorising context, see Duranti and Goodwin 1992, particularly their introduction.)

'Context' has long been used within linguistics, and elsewhere, to refer to the surrounding verbal setting of something said or written.

One of the most powerful expansions of this conception was that of anthropologist, Bronislaw Malinowski, who distinguished between 'context of situation' and 'context of culture' as frames for understanding language in use (Malinowski 1923). 'Context of situation' is what an observer needs to know about the immediate situation in order to understand a particular instance of language; 'context of culture' is what an observer needs to know about the broader culture in order to understand the meaning of what is being said or written.

The most explicit take-up of Malinowski's terms has been within systemic functional linguistics, or systemics, under the theoretical leadership of M.A.K. Halliday. The terms have been closely connected with the ongoing development of register theory—the interrelations of language and situation, using the situational/contextual categories field, tenor and mode (see Halliday and Hasan 1985/1989, for the currently most widely available version; Martin 1992, chapter 7 for a comparison between his own and Halliday's positions). Given the commitment of the systemic linguistic project to formalising the interrelations between language and situation, it is not surprising that Malinowski's 'context of culture' has taken second place to 'context of situation'. It is also not surprising (even less so in the light of Halliday's view that language is functionally organised, that is, is structured as it is because of what people use it for) that systemic functional linguistics, in effect, buys into a version of a one-way situation-to-language conception of the relation between language and context that is endemic within linguistics, while not endorsing the most realist versions of context/situation.

The broader linguistic use of 'context' has been problematic because it has tended to be reified and to involve the one-way relation between this reified 'thing' and language (more broadly, semiosis). Context is widely understood as what is 'already out there', preexisting any relevant language, rather than being in a relation of mutual constitutiveness with language. As one consequence, discourse work within such a framework is realist and empiricist, hence comfortably accommodating other empiricist assumptions and methodologies. Systemic functional linguistics does, however, take up a position which, in principle, is compatible with poststructuralist positions on knowledges/persons constituted through language. Halliday's own work has always understood the relation between language and context as being two-way: language 'determining' context and vice versa, even if such two-way determination has not always been sufficiently emphasised (Hasan and Martin 1989). Given these considerations, it is not surprising, then, to see a large number of the chapters in this book using one aspect or another of its technologies. It is also not surprising that many of those uses are anything but canonical.

In preference to 'context', we propose to use Donna Haraway's (1988) conception of 'situated knowledges'. This is elaborated below in the framing of the first of three sections into which the chapters dealing with sites and texts (chapters 4 to 10) are informally divided. 'Situated knowledges' offers a way to think about the circumstances in which texts arise, and how they are used and mean, which relate to, but are not the same as, notions such as context or intertextuality (the latter as familiar in the discipline of literary/textual studies as the former is within linguistics). Intertextuality has been extremely important, particularly as a corrective to the excesses of kinds of linguistically-based discourse analysis which have assumed that knowledges can be read direct from texts—even from single texts. Our position is one in which knowledges are distributed through assemblages of texts situated in appropriate settings, where 'text' may involve various forms of semiosis, not just language, and where 'setting' both is and is not 'context' and certainly involves 'institution'. A Foucauldian conception of the interrelations between institution, discourse and subject is what we have in mind, such that individuals come to speak as particular kinds of subjects—to speak themselves into being—through speaking the discourses that enable the particular institution.

There has been a growing appreciation, within a variety of new fields, that discourse analysis, however defined, might offer important ways of engaging with the increasing complexity of research sites and research questions. However, there is very little literature available to support researchers to develop a repertoire of techniques appropriate for their needs. At present, within the frameworks where 'discourse analysis' is practised and taught, the term means very different things. Commonly, researchers working in one tradition know little or nothing of work being undertaken in others. This is a particularly serious matter because of the limitations of any one approach used on its own.

This collection is structured around the difference between two major arms or traditions of discourse analysis, the linguistic and the poststructuralist. Chapters 2 and 3 provide critical overviews respectively of linguistic and poststructuralist approaches to discourse and most of the book's 'exemplificatory' chapters draw, in one way or another, on both. Both the overview chapters argue for the potential for relatedness of these two approaches. Such a view clearly takes up a position on the possible incommensurability of the two (Pennycook 1994a).

The two traditions of discourse analysis we focus on proceed from two distinct histories of the term 'discourse': one within European thought, within which Foucault's formulation of the term is located, and one within structuralist linguistics and semiotics. A discourse in Foucault's sense is a body of knowledge, not so much a matter of language as of discipline (McHoul and Grace 1993). For much of linguistics, on the other hand, discourse is roughly synonymous with text. In contrast with the essentially apolitical usage of 'discourse' within linguistics, the term is extensively used elsewhere as a way of attempting to capture regularities of meaning used by those positioned as members of particular institutions, regularities which serve both to make sense of, but also to continuously effect, such positionings. Discourses in this latter sense are concerned with the government of populations and the production of subjectivity. They are certainly manifested in language but not exclusively so, and they certainly do not arise from language itself, though their effectivity in continuously bringing into existence what they assert to be already the case can readily be misunderstood, especially by linguists, as an effectivity of language itself. (For further discussion of these issues, see Lee 1995; McHoul 1990; McHoul and Grace 1993, Introduction and chapter 2; Pennycook 1994a; Poynton 1993.)

We are not, however, so much concerned with discourse analysis in a purely technical way as is the kind of 'methods' textbook which stresses the technicality of the particular apparatus being proposed and pays insufficient attention to the theorisation of the situatedness of knowledge production. Such theorisation requires an account that attends to the necessary interrelatedness of theoretical, political and institutional dimensions of social/cultural phenomena and their in-evitable imbrication with the methodological.

Culture & Text addresses both these interconnections. The theoretical/methodological framework in which the whole collection is couched is broadly poststructuralist in orientation; that is, its theoretical understandings provide frameworks for exploring the re-lations between individuals, institutions and forms of knowledge and practice, including textual practice. What such frameworks commonly lack, however, is a textual analytics (or 'metalanguage') that will ground an exploration of these relationships in the specificity of what actual people actually say and do (see Threadgold 1997a; chapter 3 this book). This is the space that Culture & Text occupies. Textual analysis that is situated within the broader concerns of poststructuralist theory will, we believe, make a significant contribution to enabling researchers to understand both the complexity and multiplicity of their own positioning and that of the sites they are investigating and hence to move towards richer and more appropriate theorisations, theorisations that bring 'culture' and 'text' into new relations with each other.

In particular, we want to see 'thicker' conceptions of culture and less reified notions of text (or discourse—the terms are used relatively interchangeably at this point). The latter may seem somewhat ironic, since we also strongly assert the materiality of text and its imbrication with bodies—what Vicki Kirby (1997) calls 'corporeography'. From such a perspective, text is seen first as process—as textual practice, dynamically rather than synoptically—situated in relations between subjects within and across institutions. This does not mean that a synoptic/structuralist perspective may not be useful at times, however. Texts in this book are also very much instances of spoken and written language. We acknowledge the importance of wider perspectives—the whole world as text—but restrict ourselves here to language.

The kind of notion of culture informing our work is essentially an anthropological or cultural studies account of culture as 'way of life'. John Frow and Meaghan Morris (1993, p. x), leading Australian cultural studies scholars, introduce this conception as follows:

> . . . the 'whole way of life' of a social group as it is structured by representation and by power . . . a network of representations—texts, images, talk, codes of behaviour, and the narrative structures organising these—which shapes every aspect of social life.

This classic cultural studies account of culture clearly owes a substantial intellectual debt to Raymond Williams, the British scholar whose work was crucial in 'founding' cultural studies. Although Tony Bennett, in his acerbic insistence (1998, p. 22) that this is 'more or less ritual incantation' of Williams, suggests that such an account may need to be problematised, this does not, in fact, undermine its usefulness as a starting point for our purposes.

A number of features of this collection combine to make it a significant contribution to the emerging field of discourse analysis:

1 The Australianness of the collection offers a particular kind of guarantee of greater permeability and openness of discourse boundaries. This has been facilitated by several factors: the history of social semiotic work on discourse based in Australia, with origins in the work of Halliday (see chapter 2); the impact of feminist work within the same tradition (see Poynton 1985/1989 and Threadgold 1988); the boundary crossing between linguistics and poststructuralism of the Newtown Semiotic Circle[1]; the

multimodal work (see Kress and van Leeuwen 1990, 1996; McInnes 1998) going on now in Australia and elsewhere.

2   The collection is multiply framed by four chapters: this introductory chapter, situating the book in terms of a particular state of knowledge production in the academy and identifying problematics in the field of discourse analysis; two overview chapters (2 and 3), providing critical accounts of the two major theoretical perspectives on discourse addressed in the collection: linguistics and poststructuralism; and the final chapter (11), which problematises the relations between analyst, text and analysis (itself, of course, another text) in ways more characteristic of literary analysis than any kind of discourse analysis to date.

3   Our material draws on new scholarship, involving various kinds of boundary crossing between literary, linguistic and other approaches to discourse, where other work in the field remains, by and large, within disciplinary boundaries.

4   Our primary focus is the possibilities of imbrication of linguistics and poststructuralism, where much of our own work has been done. We wanted to include an ethnomethodological chapter, however, because we believe that ethnomethodology (and not just its 'sister', Conversation Analysis, which has been widely borrowed/appropriated, within linguistics especially) has insights which have not been widely taken up. This is demonstrably the case with the conception of culture in action used by Carolyn Baker in chapter 6.

5   The book is conceived according to two kinds of logic which are seen as complementing rather than in contention with one another. The first logic is the linguistics/poststructuralism 'divide'. The second is the set of three problematics around which the book is informally structured: situated knowledges, the body and writing.

6   The contributions are attentive to the detail of text—and have resources to do this—but do not fetishise 'analysis'.

7   The contributions likewise have a broader perspective on 'context' than the immediate situation.

8   The book is informed throughout by feminist theory but is not a 'gender and discourse' collection. Its concern with gender is a

symptomatic focus, along with other forms of difference (particularly race), in exploring how subjects take on positionalities.

The contributions to this collection have been solicited because of the particular 'take' on discourse analysis of the contributing authors. The collection addresses a rich diversity of institutional sites within which important work of analysis is currently being carried out. Chapters are variously located within the school, the law, radio, an Australian Aboriginal community, the newly restructured workplace, popular environmentalist science. They draw on disciplines and theoretical frameworks of similar diversity: sociology, anthropology, linguistics, media, cultural, educational and legal studies, literary, feminist and critical theory. There has been no attempt at representativeness of sites: it would not be possible in a book of this size, even if discourse analysis work had been done in a much wider range of sites than is currently the case. As a book about methodology, it needs to be read not simply for site specificity but also for the nature of its engagement with that site. The scrutiny of site through the lens of a particular theoretical framework in turn suggests methods which may involve new combinations of approach and/or new ways of using familiar discourse analytic technologies.

We see the diversity of the intellectual/disciplinary locations of the contributors to this collection not as an accidental benefit, let alone a problematic eclecticism. Rather, these are utterly germane to doing what we understand as discourse analysis. By this we mean in particular the need to supplement or problematise kinds of linguistic discourse analysis which appear almost to see knowledge as neutral, accessible to purely linguistic tools: an approach we call 'linguistic positivism'. At the same time, we do want to argue for the value of a variety of ways of attending to the detail of texts, both spoken and written, in carrying out discourse analysis within a broader poststructuralist framework.

In framing its particular take on discourse analysis, the book offers, in its two 'overview' chapters (2 and 3), two distinct, though interrelated, genealogies of discourse analysis, providing critical engagements with two of its major axes: linguistics and poststructuralism. The former tells a story largely of Anglo-American disciplinary formation and the emergence of a linguistic 'science'. The latter tells stories of European literary, philosophical and feminist engagements with text, reading/writing, 'subjectivity' and the body and of how these stories are constantly rewritten.

Chapters 2 and 3, together with the opening and closing chapters,

frame the book and hence situate the reader. They also suggest the
productivity, taken up in various ways in many of the following
chapters, of drawing on both traditions of discourse analysis. Both of
the overview chapters make informed reference to the terrain of the
other; both signal the necessity of engaging with central concerns of
the other in order to make good lacunae in their own project. Thus
Cate Poynton, in chapter 2, is hopeful that the rigidities of the
structuralist heritage of linguistics and its manifest inadequacies in
dealing with text in its relations with culture and subjectivity can be
made good by turning to poststructuralist and feminist theories and
their dynamic of constant theoretical reflexivity and renewal. And
Terry Threadgold, in chapter 3, maintains that poststructuralisms are
in need of a metalanguage in order to talk in detail about questions
of language and discourse and that aspects of such a metalanguage can
be usefully drawn from certain kinds of linguistics. Both look towards
further developments, of which this collection is one, in the emergence of a 'post/linguistics': the ongoing productive engagement of
linguistics and poststructuralist theories in dealing with textuality/
discourse.

Poynton's chapter explores the conditions of possibility for the
emergence of discourse analysis within linguistics, a discipline formed
within a structuralist framework relentlessly privileging grammar over
word and text. One of Michael Halliday's significant contributions to
the possibility of discourse analysis has been his emphasis on text, rather
than word or sentence, as the basic unit of language—precisely because
it is as texts that the words and sentences of language mean in
situations. Poynton notes the potential usefulness of many of the
descriptive technologies that have emerged from various kinds of
linguistic discourse analysis and from productive engagement with other
disciplines (especially philosophy and sociology). She draws attention
to current problematics, including the materiality of discourse, the
multiple modality of textuality and the problem of the widespread lack
of reflexivity within linguistics: its failure to interrogate many of the
categories (linguistic, sociological, philosophical) it uses.

Threadgold, in the parallel overview chapter, is concerned to map
the complex simultaneity of dimensions of poststructuralist analyses.
The chapter works with Saussure but, rather than treating him as
'founding father', puts him 'under erasure', that is, warns readers about
taking him at face value at the same time as acknowledging his crucial
contribution to making it possible to begin to think about issues of
signification. The chapter works through several major strands in
poststructuralist theorisation: first, the philosophical/linguistic work

which engaged with Saussure and, in many cases, turned him on his head (including the work of Roman Jakobson and of Jacques Derrida); second, Michel Foucault and his engagement with language/discourse in both the archaeological and genealogical phases of his work; third, feminist work (including Julia Kristeva, Judith Butler, Vicki Kirby and Gayatri Spivak) linking subjectivity and embodiment, moving to performativity and finally to questions of difference.

Chapters 4 to 10 offer a variety of perspectives on 'doing' discourse analysis, where part of the variety lies in the diversity of sites and part in the particular assemblage of tools for working with textual material and addressing particular questions within those sites. Each of these seven chapters elaborates a discourse-analytic problematic and the set of resources each contributor has brought to bear in addressing it. As indicated above, the chapters are grouped informally according to three important thematics. This should not be taken, however, to imply concentrations of disciplinary or analytic tradition or frame in any straightforward way. The thematics map across one another in complex ways, so that groupings are more a matter of relative emphasis.

The thematics—situated knowledges, the body, writing—represent major touchstones within contemporary theorising and serve to illustrate how discourse-analytic work can usefully elaborate ways of thinking about them. The first of these thematics concerns the implications for discourse analysis of what Donna Haraway (1988) has powerfully named 'situated knowledges'. As an important intervention into the tendency for some traditions within the broad domain of discourse analysis to continue to adopt a positivist stance towards knowledge, the chapters gathered here address in a variety of ways the necessity to acknowledge and work with 'partial perspectives', to value 'insider knowledges' and investments. These chapters, in particular, reflect the constructedness and contingency of 'truths' produced through analysis and insist on the situated specificity of their knowledge claims.

Jackie Cook's chapter on radio talk draws powerfully on her own knowledge and positionality as a radio broadcaster to explore a set of texts as specifically 'radio' texts: 'unnatural' conversations, constrained by a broader-than-usual range of positionings. The conversations at issue involve a radio talk host speaking on air and drawing attention to technical faults—and his own 'klutziness'—in ways which might be considered unprofessional. The interest of these texts lies in the light they shed on the complexities of radio speaker–addressee relations (involving variously host, studio guests, production staff, on-air callers) and on this particular host's positionings of himself within these various sets of relations. Unsurprisingly, gender issues are highly significant. The chapter works productively with attention to speaker positioning, using a combination of attention to topic and speaker alongside a more Foucauldian conception of discourse.

Gillian Fuller's chapter is on the *Wisdom of the Elders* collection, produced by environmentalist writers, Peter Knudtson and David Suzuki (1992). It can be read as an exemplary critical engagement with a 'new age' text making use of complex and contradictory rhetorical strategies. The texts of these writers are read as sites of multiple tensions and anxieties around debates of race and land. Fuller argues that the complex terrain of representations enacted in their texts cannot be adequately investigated through the overlaying of normative linguistic models, constrained particularly by their theorisation of context. The chapter presents a form of close textual analysis that draws from and constructs a dialogue between two distinct semiotic traditions: linguistics and critical literary theory, situating linguistic observations within a broader semiotic framework. It sets forth procedures by which discourse analysts can attend to both the microsemantics of cultural representations as well as the operations of larger semantic and generic tropes.

Carolyn Baker's chapter explores interactions among teachers, parents and children, together with a textual representation of teacher–pupil interaction, in her account of membership categorisation devices. This ethnomethodological approach to discourse analysis is quintessentially 'situated' in that it insists on local assemblages of meanings and practices and works with a notion of culture as being 'achieved in action'. Ethnomethodology provides a number of directions for analysing texts and talk as part of the ongoing assembling of social and moral order. Membership categorisation work is one powerful analytic device, pervasive in the doing of descriptions, the making of claims, the organisation of social relations and other aspects of the micropolitics of everyday and institutional life. Membership categorisation work can be seen as a subset of a range of social practices: in this case, practices of reasoning, describing, hearing. From this position, 'culture' does not consist of pre-given sets of norms, values, expectations and other abstractions of that kind. Rather, culture consists in social practices. By showing how membership categorisation work is done in talk and in texts, this chapter points to a critical edge that might be provided by ethnomethodological work. It shows how membership categorisation work—the reasonings and the describings and the hearings and the doings that are assembled through it —'locks culture into place'.

Chapter 7, by Hermine Scheeres and Nicky Solomon, offers a more reflexive 'take' on the 'situatedness' of knowledge and the methodological implications for discourse-analytic work. The main focus of the chapter is on the complexities of academics doing commissioned research in the context of contemporary political and economic reform. They draw on their participation in a workplace research project focusing on the new language of work as a typical site for such commissioned research. Their reflexive commentary on their work aims to bring to the surface a range of methodological, political and epistemological tensions in commissioned research in the contemporary world, with pressure on academics to produce particular kinds of knowledge. Through a reflexive commentary, they analyse the texts that were part of the research process and its final products—including those they themselves produced as training materials. Linguistic analysis is used to clarify shifts in their understanding of themselves as researchers as they struggle from a position of compliance to one of productive disruption. The insistence on the 'situatedness' of knowledge production here should not be read as a retreat to the local and the specific, however. While the commissioned project under scrutiny here is located in Australia, many of the experiences and issues are global, as most industrial and industrialising countries engage in similar restructuring and workplace training reforms.

Chapters 8 and 9, while clearly engaging in important ways with the principle of the situatedness of discourse-analytic practices and attendant knowledge claims, make a further move. This is to engage with a domain of major theoretical importance, particularly within various feminisms, one which represents a decisive theoretical challenge to dominant traditions of Western epistomology. The body, for a decade a major locus of concern for feminisms and other theorisations of difference, has been slow to arrive onto the scene of discourse analysis other than in the relatively disembodied ways in which Foucauldian discourse analysis has come to talk about inscription *of* the body but does not address the possible contribution of what is produced *by* the body. There is an irony here that, despite the heritage of idealism that characterises linguistics (see chapter 2), it may be precisely the capacity of linguistics to engage with the materiality of language (however seldom linguists may choose to do so, in the case of text) that opens up a whole new era of discourse analysis—including conceptions of inscription.

The focus in Penny Pether and Terry Threadgold's chapter is on feminist methodologies in discourse analysis in relation to legal judgements. While profoundly exemplifying the significance and productivity of cross-disciplinary collaboration, they also insist on situating their analyses within the terms of Vicki Kirby's (1997) notion of 'corporeography'. They argue that the mediating link between text and context, so central to any discussion of methodology in discourse analysis, is not 'free-floating intertextuality' but intertextuality mediated by corporeality. That is, the only way that intertextual links between texts can be made is through the specifics of 'habituated, trained, coloured and gendered bodies'. Drawing on feminist, literary and deconstructive technologies for reading the texts of 'judge-made law' in the case of an equity judgement concerning familial property rights, Pether and Threadgold demonstrate the gendered and embodied nature of the judgements that ensue from the judge's 'conscience', exposing the white, masculine, middle class liberal abstraction of what counts as 'human experience' in Australian equity law. This work, too, is profoundly 'situated'; it is knowledge that 'knows its place', in this instance, a feminist place which regards discourse analysis in this legal context as both a politics and a praxis.

Jan Wright's chapter is concerned with the textually-mediated inscription of children's bodies in contemporary schooling. Western societies have, until recently, emphasised the body as a physical and biological given, to be understood—like other 'natural' phenomena —through empirical investigation. Wright draws on other ways of thinking and writing about the body, ways which understand bodies and their meanings to be culturally produced. She is concerned with how cultural meanings of the body become recontextualised and drawn upon by teachers and students to (re)produce embodied subjectivities and relations of power in the specific context of physical education lessons. She develops a specific methodology of textual analysis informed by systemic functional linguistics, as developed by Michael Halliday, together with work on discourse and the mechanisms of power, drawing on Foucault, to understand and interpret the ways in which language and other social practices in physical education work to constitute particular notions of the body and to construct specific relations of power.

The final two chapters draw together a set of considerations around the question of writing and its relationship to analysis and methodology. Here, writing is used in its expanded sense to refer to practices of inscription and cultural production. In chapter 10, Jennifer Biddle focuses on the naming practices of Warlpiri Aborigines in an investigation into cultural inscription and identity: specifically, the ways in which mimetic modes of representation—imitation, likening, copying—are necessarily involved in the production of cultural differ-ence. Nowhere, perhaps, are the mimetic effects of replication more apparent, and simultaneously disavowed, than in the writing of a language, and the teaching of literacy, to people assumed to be 'without writing'. Biddle argues that the Warlpiri use the alphabet in terms which demonstrate not only a profound appreciation of literacy but the inadequacy ultimately of literacy, of the alphabet, to represent literate subjects. She figures Warlpiri uses of the alphabet as disrupting the 'proper' relationship between letter and sound, name and identity. Through concrete, cross-cultural analysis, a systematic reversal and displacement of the assumed relationship between not only writing and speech but coloniser and colonised is enacted. Biddle draws on deconstructive, feminist, postcolonial and queer theorising in a dem-onstration of how it is possible to 'do' discourse analysis but to refuse 'method'.

Alison Lee, in the final chapter, takes up the problem of the relation between method and writing, as she explores aspects of the relationships between discourse analysis, textual authority and writing. She points to the lack of attention, within the field of discourse analysis, to the political relations—the relations of power-knowledge —that obtain between the analyst and the object domain of analysis. Analysis is typically conceived, given the truth-revealing capacities of particular methods, as a process that strips away the 'false consciousness' of the text or object of analysis to reveal a 'better' truth. Lee teases out a further complexity in the activity of discourse analysis, one that again is insufficiently attended to. Discourse analysis is analysis of discourse, or text. Yet discourse analyses—or, at least, the results of such analyses—are themselves texts, texts which are written and read, and rewritten in discussion and debate, just as are the texts and objects they purport to write about. This final chapter presents the questions of analytic authority, textuality and writing, and the atten-dant underpinning oppositions which structure the field, as a major complex of issues which discourse analysis as an emerging scholarly field needs to address.

Locating this chapter at the end of the collection in part allows a retrospective rereading and resituating of the problematics of the earlier chapters. Its focus is on the conditions of possibility of discourse analysis and the need to call the position of the analyst into crisis, as well as the domain the analyst purports to be analysing. The chapter addresses the conditions of possibility, the politics and the aesthetics of discourse and text. And, of course, it insists that *Culture & Text* is itself a text—a writing and a rewriting of the field of discourse analysis.

CODA

We end this introductory chapter in a very practical way with a list of 'suggestions for further reading' in the emerging field of discourse analysis. The materials come from a variety of perspectives—linguistics very substantially, other fields less so—and not all are equally accessible to those not already familiar with the particular 'take' on discourse analysis involved. Nevertheless, all are accessible to a degree. There is, as yet, no general introduction to discourse analysis that adequately addresses all the major theoretical traditions, though there are some claims to comprehensiveness, usually from specific disciplinary bases.

A broadranging overview of the field would certainly be available from the following five books. Deborah Schiffrin's *Approaches to Discourse* (1994), which is based firmly (though broadly) within linguistics, does address Conversation Analysis (though not ethnomethodology more generally) but has nothing to say about other non-linguistic conceptions of discourse. Jonathan Potter's *Representing Reality* (1996) deals fairly substantially with poststructuralist approaches to discourse, as well as ethnomethodology and Conversation Analysis, but does not cover linguistic approaches. Diane Macdonell's *Theories of Discourse* (1986) is the closest yet to an introduction to poststructuralist approaches but is disappointing (though very illuminating on connections between Foucault and Althusser). McHoul and Grace's A *Foucault Primer* (1993) not only provides a very useful introduction to the work of Foucault but addresses linguistic conceptions of discourse in comparison with Foucault's approach. (See also Kendall and Wickham 1999, the first 'methods' book on Foucault.) Dorothy Smith's *Texts, Facts, and Femininity* (1990) offers an eclectic feminist account of the interrelations between textuality and femininity.

By far the largest collection of material on discourse analysis is found in linguistics. There is, however, a growing amount coming from psychology, particularly critical psychology. Valerie Walkerdine's work is some of the most exciting but some of her colleagues do not have her depth of knowledge of poststructuralist and feminist theories, tending in some cases to collapse poststructuralisms into psychological constructionism. The Walkerdine and Lucey volume cited below was chosen specifically because it is a rewriting of an earlier linguistic study.

Only a small amount of the available linguistic material is listed here—and much of that comes from the 'critical discourse analysis' tradition (see chapter 2). Much of the linguistic literature seems more concerned with reproducing the next generation of 'good linguists' than with opening up the field, especially to non-linguists. Schiffrin's book, however, is admirably organised to facilitate comparison between methods and consideration of broader (linguistic) issues. The latest van Dijk collection (1997) is designed to survey the field and, though its focus is basically linguistic, it is evident from the chapter references that many of the contributors are now beginning to reference themselves outside linguistics to 'poststructuralist' scholars—especially Foucault. Another interesting recent publication is Georgakopoulou and Goutsos (1997), which, although based in linguistics, makes substantial use of narrative theory. It draws, among others, on the work of Bakhtin/Volosinov (see chapter 3).

FURTHER READING

Burman, Erica and Parker, Ian, eds 1993 *Discourse Analytic Research: repertoires and readings of texts in action*, Routledge, London and New York

Fairclough, Norman, 1995a *Critical Discourse Analysis: the critical study of language*, Longman, London

——1995b *Media Discourse*, Edward Arnold, London

Georgakopoulou, Alexandra and Goutsos, Dionysis, 1997 *Discourse Analysis: an introduction*, Edinburgh University Press, Edinburgh

Halliday, M.A.K. and Hasan, Ruqaiya, 1985/1989 *Language, Context and Text: aspects of language in a social-semiotic perspective*, Deakin University Press, Geelong (reprinted Oxford University Press)

Hutchby, Ian and Wooffitt, Robin, 1998 *Conversation Analysis: principles, practices and applications*, Polity Press, Cambridge

Kendall, Gavin and Wickham, Gary, 1999 *Using Foucault's Methods*, Sage, London, Thousand Oaks and New Delhi

Kress, Gunther, 1985 *Linguistic Processes in Sociocultural Practice*, Deakin University Press, Melbourne (reprinted Oxford University Press 1989)

Macdonell, Diane, 1986 *Theories of Discourse: an introduction*, Blackwell, Oxford

McHoul, Alec and Grace, Wendy, 1993 *A Foucault Primer: discourse, power and the subject*, Melbourne University Press, Melbourne

Meinhof, Ulrike H. and Richardson, Kay, eds 1994 *Text, Discourse and Context: representations of poverty in Britain*, Longman, London

Potter, Jonathan, 1996 *Representing Reality: discourse, rhetoric and social construction*, Sage, London, Thousand Oaks and New Delhi

Poynton, Cate, 1985 *Language and Gender: making the difference*, Deakin University Press, Melbourne (reprinted Oxford University Press 1989)

Psathas, George, 1995 *Conversation Analysis: the study of talk-in-interaction*, Sage, Thousand Oaks, London and New Delhi

Schiffrin, Deborah, 1994 *Approaches to Discourse*, Blackwell, Oxford and Cambridge, Massachusetts

Schirato, Tony and Yell, Susan, 1996 *Communication and Cultural Literacy: an introduction*, Allen & Unwin, Sydney

Smith, Dorothy E., 1990 *Texts, Facts, and Femininity: exploring the relations of ruling*, Routledge, London and New York

Threadgold, Terry, 1997a *Feminist Poetics: poiesis, performance, histories*, Routledge, London and New York

van Dijk, Teun A., ed. 1997 *Discourse Studies: a multidisciplinary introduction: vol. 1, Discourse as Structure and Process; vol. 2, Discourse as Social Interaction*, Sage, London

Walkerdine, Valerie and Lucey, Helen, 1989 *Democracy in the Kitchen: regulating mothers and socialising daughters*, Virago, London

Weedon, Chris, 1997 *Feminist Practice and Poststructuralist Theory*, 2nd edn, Blackwell, Oxford and Cambridge, Masachusetts

Wilkinson, Sue and Kitzinger, Celia, eds 1995 *Feminism and Discourse: psychological perspectives*, Sage, London

NOTE

1   Newtown is an inner suburb of Sydney which is home to many academics. The Newtown Semiotic Circle (the name somewhat tongue-in-cheek) comprised a shifting population of academics and postgraduate students in linguistics, semiotics, media studies and poststructuralist and feminist theories. It met regularly over several years in the 1980s. Members included Gunther Kress, Terry Threadgold, J.R. Martin, Theo van Leeuwen and Allan Rumsey. Michael Halliday attended some meetings, as did Cate Poynton (then working in Adelaide).

   For those unfamiliar with systemic functional linguistics, Schirato and Yell (1996), read in conjunction with this volume, will provide introductory access to relevant linguistic technology. As well as Halliday's *Introduction to Functional Grammar* (1994), there is now a range of texts dealing with systemic functional technology. Titles listed below include material dealing explicitly with text (Eggins and Slade 1997; Halliday and Hasan 1976; Martin 1992), as well as those focused primarily on grammar.

Bloor, Thomas and Bloor, Meriel, 1995 *The Functional Analysis of English: a Hallidayan approach*, Arnold, London

Eggins, Suzanne, 1994 *An Introduction to Systemic Functional Linguistics*, Pinter, London

Eggins, Suzanne and Slade, Diana, 1997 *Analysing Casual Conversation*, Cassell, London and Washington

Halliday, M.A.K., 1994 *Introduction to Functional Grammar*, 2nd edn, Edward Arnold, London

Halliday, M.A.K. and Hasan, Ruqaiya, 1976 *Cohesion in English*, Longman, London

Lock, Graham, 1996 *Functional English Grammar: an introduction for second language teachers*, Cambridge University Press, Cambridge

Martin, J.R., 1992 *English Text: system and structure*, Benjamins, Amsterdam

Martin, J.R., Matthiessen, Christian M.I.M. and Painter, Claire, 1997 *Working with Functional Grammar*, Arnold, London

2 Linguistics and discourse analysis

Cate Poynton

The history of the term 'discourse' is complex and diverse. This introductory chapter tells one story concerning discourse—a story located within a process of Anglo-American disciplinarisation, specifically the twentieth-century invention of the discipline of linguistics. This story parallels another, set primarily within Continental Europe (especially France), told by Terry Threadgold in the companion overview chapter of this volume. The two stories have in common the foundational figure of Saussure, or at least different versions of that figure and, of course, a profound interest in language (which, likewise, may look nothing like the same object of enquiry in the two stories).

The chapter is organised in four sections. The first section attends initially to those aspects of the work of Saussure taken up within linguistics which ensured that any study of text or discourse was effectively precluded for half a century. It goes on to sketch some of the enabling conditions for the emergence of discourse analysis in the 1970s. The second section is concerned with analytic tools, both descriptive and interpretive, developed within linguistics or borrowed from outside, which have come to constitute discourse analysis as a particular kind of disciplinary enterprise. The third section gives an account of critical discourse work drawing on Hallidayan linguistics. The fourth section focuses on the multidisciplinarity claimed by the field of discourse analysis as a whole and on what might more appropriately be called the interdisciplinarity of critical discourse analysis. This section attends particularly to the relation of both traditions to the more general 'linguistic turn' in the human sciences. The chapter is intended to be read as a preliminary genealogy in the

Foucauldian sense, that is, as an account that locates discourse analysis as a significant sociocultural phenomenon in terms of its conditions of emergence and its effects.

At the beginning of the twentieth century, Saussure came to the view that the proper focus for the new kind of study of language he envisaged was *langue* (the abstract system of language that underlies actual language use) and not *parole* (language in actual use). Such a view involved a profoundly idealist conception of language study, one in which the decontextualised study of grammar (or syntax) came to be seen as the apex of scholarly achievement in the emerging discipline of linguistics. This was a world where the emergence of discourse analysis (concerned as it is with *parole*) would have to wait another fifty years, though the necessity of studying conversation was indicated well before this by the British linguist, J.R. Firth (1957, p. 32) in a paper originally published in 1935:

> Neither linguists nor psychologists have begun the study of conversation; but it is here we shall find the key to a better understanding of what language really is and how it works.

Even those linguists directly indebted to Firth were slow to take up this challenge and, through much of the twentieth century, it was not heard at all. For Noam Chomsky, that most widely-known contemporary linguist, linguistic theory could comfortably be conceived of, fifty years after the publication of Saussure's major work, as 'concerned primarily with an ideal speaker–listener, in a completely homogeneous speech community' (Chomsky 1965, p. 3).

However, it was almost inevitable that analytic tools developed under this idealist regime would be turned to social/political use in the 1960s and 1970s, given the general politicisation of that period and the emergence of socially-oriented concerns with language—the beginnings of what was to become sociolinguistics. In the United States and the United Kingdom, concerns about schooling focused linguistic attention on questions of race and class; in Germany, a concern with the situation of non-German 'guest-workers', involving a complex of questions from schooling to political rights, led to parallel investigations of the everyday language use of actual people. (See, in particular, the work of William Labov (1972a, 1972b) on race and education in the United States; Basil Bernstein (1971, 1973, 1975) on class and education in Britain; and Norbert Dittmar's 1976 critical account of the work of Bernstein and Labov from the perspective of a key participant in research into German guest-worker language in Heidelberg throughout the 1970s.) The political flavour of this period emerges very clearly from the introduction to Dittmar's book (Dittmar 1976, p. 1):

> In the last decade sociolinguistics has become a powerful factor in promoting emancipation. Attempts have been and are being made to attenuate conflicts in schools and to remove the obvious inequality of opportunity of broad sections of the working classes and peripheral social groups by systematically exposing the connection between speech forms and class structure, and by application of the insights gained to specified social contexts.

The emergence of sociolinguistics produced a new kind of linguist who moved between the academy and the classroom, shopfloor, street or therapist's office, armed with a metaphorical toolbox filled with linguistic tools in one hand and, in the other, that increasingly ubiquitous material box—the tape-recorder. Sociolinguistics was the vanguard of a new kind of *parole*-oriented linguistic work. It, and the new 'discourse analysis' which was soon to follow, were characterised by: a substantial focus on spoken language; a recognition of the need for new technical vocabularies concerning both language and the social in dealing with such material; a willingness to go outside linguistics for such vocabularies; and a failure to interrogate adequately many of the terms of those vocabularies.

THE LEGACY OF SAUSSURE: *LANGUE, PAROLE,* 'TALK' AND 'TEXT'

The eighteenth-century appearance of increasingly formalised knowledges concerning 'labour, life, language' in the emerging disciplines of economics, biology and linguistics (Foucault 1971a) marked a significant moment in the transformation of Europe from earlier forms of knowledge and social organisation to those characteristic of modernity. Labour, life and language have all been significant sites for the forms of control of populations which characterise modern systems of governance. In the case of language, control of *which* (that is, *whose*) language was to 'count' was critical to the disappearance of old regional or local identities and the building of new, national identities. The emergence of the nation-state in nineteenth-century Europe was preceded by the relentless movement of rural populations to the city, a process accelerated in the developing countries where such population movement became more and more transnational. The inevitable consequence of such movement has been the large-scale disappearance of linguistic diversity as a function of geographical location and its replacement with the contemporary diversity of urban language variation, understood in terms of hierarchies of social differentiation involving particularly class, race and ethnicity.

Closely associated with the nineteenth-century emergence of the European nation-state have been language standardisation and the provision of universal education, the latter (particularly in the form of literacy education) usually functioning as a vehicle for the spread of standard language. Speaking 'the' national language constituted a claim to a national identity and, hence, a new kind of self—an emergent, even if never completely seamless, process in the complex balancing of the imaginaries of nation against region and locality (Anderson 1983).

The twentieth-century emergence of the multilingual state, together with the spread of English as an international language, have made the relations between language, nation and identity even more ambiguous. The nation-state outside Europe, in the former colonies of Asia, Africa and the Americas (including those, such as Australia and Canada, which are dominated by Europeans and are substantially English-speaking) is typically multi-ethnic and multilingual and, if not officially English-speaking, is likely to make considerable use of English in education, government and business. The implications of such usage for identity and nation are enormous (Pennycook 1994b).

This is the contemporary scene within which the texts and meanings that speakers/listeners and readers/writers need to negotiate are increasingly produced and contested. Yet the models of language that are the currency of contemporary linguistics, including discourse analysis, are in certain key respects based in the late nineteenth and not the late twentieth century. Central to this perspective is the figure of Saussure, grounded in the nineteenth century but casting a shadow across all twentieth-century work on language and, ultimately, discourse.

The nineteenth century was a time of major intellectual work on language. This work included feats of historical reconstruction, most spectacularly of the Indo-European language, the original speakers of which inhabited what is now central and eastern Europe several millennia BC. This ancient language was the precursor of what is now known as the Indo-European language family which includes not only most of the contemporary languages of Europe but also languages extending from Europe through parts of the Middle East into northern India. Ferdinand de Saussure (1857–1913), trained in this 'comparative' tradition and an elite performer within it, subsequently reacted against both its historicism and the minutiae of its habitual data (typically, speech sounds and lexical items). He had a grander sweep in mind for his new science of 'semiology', encompassing both language and other semiotic systems.[1]

Mainstream twentieth-century linguistics has been substantially shaped by two ideas taken from Saussure. The first idea is the conviction that language should not be studied with a focus on change over time, that is, historically, but from a more synoptic perspective— what it looks like at a particular point in time (in Saussure's terms, synchronically rather than diachronically). The second idea is that what should be studied is the abstract system of language (*langue*) that underlies language use and not instances of actual use (*parole*). In particular, the view of the emerging discipline of linguistics, substantially until the 1970s, that *langue* and not *parole* was the proper concern of scholarship about language, ensured that linguistics in the first half of the twentieth century had problems even beginning to address any aspect of language above the level of the sentence. Compounding the effects of the discipline's preferred focus on grammar and phonology was the 'capture' of much Anglo-American linguistics by the psychological behaviourism of the 1940s and 1950s. This led to eschewing the possibility of any kind of 'scientific' focus on meaning, that is, what actual people are actively constructing through their language practices. Since meaning, in any conventional 'scientific' sense, could not be 'observed', it came largely to be ignored. The combined effect of these two influences, (linguistic) Saussureanism and behaviourism, produced a strong 'technicist' bias which marks linguistics to this day.

The successful linguistic challenge to behaviourism came, very early in his career, from Chomsky in a blistering review of behaviourist B.F. Skinner's 1957 book, *Verbal Behaviour* (Chomsky 1959). Chomsky's own subsequent work in linguistics, however, produced side-by-side with his influential work of social and political critique, did not take a social direction but rather was informed by philosophy and related disciplines, including cognitive psychology. This led him to a formal rather than a functional model of language, a model in which language was understood to be in some sense 'hard-wired' into the individual and only marginally 'acquired' socially: thus, speaking to young children merely gave them data to work on. Though Chomsky himself did not develop forms of social analysis within linguistics, others did, and Chomsky's fame, as a radical intellectual, no doubt contributed to linguistics coming to be seen as both intellectually challenging and an avant-garde site for bright young radicals of the 1960s and 1970s.

The conjunction of the radicalism and intellectual challenge of linguistics with the increasing availability of the tape-recorder, providing a means of 'fixing' the flux of talk, brought about a major change in the discipline, which now routinely includes discourse analysis in most programs in linguistics. The kind of non-intrusive investigation of urban language variation that began to develop in the late 1960s, however, required easily portable machines that could be battery-powered. Armed with such machines by the 1970s, graduate and even undergraduate students, and their teachers, fanned out through the urban areas of the United States, Britain, Australia and elsewhere to map how people talked. The results of their work included major publications on urban language variation such as Labov (1972a, 1972b) in the United States; Trudgill (1974) in the United Kingdom; Mitchell and Delbridge (1965) and Horvath (1985) in Australia.

It is hardly surprising, then, that, under these conditions, discourse analysis within linguistics became substantially synonymous with the analysis of spoken language (see, for example, Sinclair and Coulthard 1975; Stubbs 1983; Schiffrin 1994). This bias can be read as yet another manifestation of the 'phonocentrism' that characterises Western society, that is, its privileging of the spoken word and hence speakers in terms of such notions as 'truth', 'the real' and 'authenticity' (Derrida 1976).[2]

The field of discourse analysis now includes an increasing body of work dealing with written language. Much of this work has been carried out within the critical discourse analysis and social semiotic traditions (see below, for further detail), which tend to work across the speech/writing divide, drawing on descriptive/analytic technologies able to handle both. Areas of substantial work include news/media/advertising (Trew 1979; Vestergard and Schroder 1985; van Dijk 1987a, 1987b; Bell 1991; Fowler 1991; Cook 1992), literary stylistic work drawing on linguistics (particularly the 'East Anglia' work, overlapping with critical linguistics, for example, Fowler 1981; Aers, Hodge and Kress 1981), and student writing, especially the Australian work by Joan Rothery, J.R. Martin, Frances Christie and others. (See the two volumes of *Children Writing*, edited by Frances Christie (1984a, 1984b) and others for Deakin University and Painter and Martin 1986 for earlier work; and materials from the Sydney Disadvantaged Schools' Project (DSP) which funded much of the later work, for example Iedema, Feez and White 1994, as well as Halliday and Martin 1993.)

The opposition between spoken and written discourse, or 'talk' and 'text' (van Dijk 1997), can be read as an assertion of the validity as research object of instances of (spoken) *parole* alongside the more overtly structured and organised forms of written discourse. The status of an actual piece of writing as just as much *parole* as an instance of speech is not necessarily always transparent. This is particularly so when the stringent demands for 'correctness' in writing are couched in terms of rules directly invoking the presumed regularities of *langue*. Further, the fact that the term 'text' has come increasingly to be used for both spoken and written instances of language in use suggests that the dynamism and multidimensionality of much interactive talk (McInnes 1998) has been assimilated to the more synoptic and static understanding of writing as (completed) product (Halliday 1985), the norms for which provide the measure against which any 'text' is to be judged.

From this perspective, 'text', applied to spoken language, can be read as a structuralist claim on *parole*. This claim not only suggests an illusory completeness and finality to much speech (and, hence, to its 'analysis') but also, since the 'texts' of speech are commonly equated with their transcriptions, establishing an idealist control over *parole*, rendering it that much more *langue*-like, and hence fit for linguists.

What has been lost in this process is the materiality of speech (Poynton 1999, in prep.)—its rhythms, its tunes, its vocality, its timbres, its voice qualities—features long regarded by many linguists, conveniently, as merely 'expressive'. And with that materiality, a sense of the particularity of who is speaking is lost—a grievous loss of focus not on individuality, as such, but on positionality. For speech is necessarily embodied, not just in 'the grain of the voice' (Barthes 1977) but in the gestures, postures and movements of speakers, all of which articulate deeply cultural and social selves through their learned corporeality. The investments of speakers in what they and others say, a key aspect of positioning, is commonly much more legible from the corporeality of the speaking body than from words and sentences alone (see Wright, this volume, on the constitutive role of language in gendered embodiment).

DISCOURSE ANALYSIS AS TECHNOLOGY: TOOLS FOR DESCRIPTION AND INTERPRETATION

This section turns to a closer look at some key aspects of work both within and outside disciplinary linguistics constituting the emerging field of discourse analysis in particular ways. It indicates disciplines outside linguistics, as well as aspects of linguistics itself, that have made significant contributions to discourse analysis as 'sociolinguistic analysis' (Stubbs 1983) but excludes the various borrowings from cognitive psychology, such as schemata and scripts in discourse processing.[3] The aim is to provide a 'map' of the sociolinguistic terrain that gives salience to both its 'socio' and 'linguistic' dimensions, as constructed by the descriptive and interpretive tools mobilised by discourse analysis.

The tools of discourse analysis differ, depending on the discipline they are drawn from (see Schiffrin 1994 for an account of six approaches; Taylor and Cameron 1987 for a partially overlapping critical account). What the various approaches to discourse analysis have in common is that they are highly technical and proliferate 'analytic' tools. This technical approach makes a kind of sense when the analytic task is understood as a semiotic object. It deals better with discourse as object rather than as semiotic (meaning-making) phenomenon, however. Taylor and Cameron (1987, pp. 2–3) see Conversation Analysis as profoundly informed by structural linguistics:

> Conversation Analysis is an interdisciplinary concern: major contributions have been made by philosophers, sociologists and linguists. Yet the rules and units framework which, we claim, informs them all, is perhaps especially typical of linguistic models. Its preoccupations are with segmentation, classification and combination. Types and tokens, syntagms and paradigms—these are the classic concerns of descriptive and structural grammar, and they are present to a high degree in most currently influential approaches to conversation.

It is not entirely surprising, then, that those scholars demonstrably engaged with questions of language and discourse outside linguistics are somewhat dismissive of the empiricism and 'hardening of the categories' they see as characterising much linguistic work; including discourse analysis.

Such problems are exacerbated when 'interpretive' terms, including class, gender, race, face, power and solidarity, are 'borrowed' from various kinds of social theory in order to address relations between language and culture/society. The approach to other fields of knowledge for working vocabularies was initially an exciting development, suggesting a new openness to interdisciplinarity, particularly with respect to socially oriented fields. A degree of such openness remains an attractive feature of contemporary discourse analysis, suggesting possibilities for further productive developments. However, much of the interpretive terminology has tended to be used in reified and realist ways—analogous to the ways in which structuralist 'units' are identified and used within linguistics itself—as simply 'facts' about the world. Such usage makes sense of the disconcerting practice of linguists referencing key social terms largely within the linguistic literature itself. There may be a citation of some originary figure in sociology or social psychology, such as Goffman, Roger Brown or Bernstein, but there is no sustained engagement with social theory.

The sociological categories which continue to be used within sociolinguistics, for example, have been trenchantly critiqued by Glyn Williams (1992) (see also Joseph and Taylor 1990). Williams identifies the sociology of sociolinguistics as derived from a particular kind of theory (Parsonian functionalism) of the 1950s and 1960s, never updated—much less critiqued—within linguistics. A similar critique can be mounted in the field of language and gender, cutting across both sociolinguistics and discourse analysis. Linguistic work on gender is still largely informed by understandings based in the liberal and radical feminisms of the early 1970s (Cameron 1995, 1997; Poynton 1997) and not in the more complex theorisations of gender and the social available through recent feminist work such as that of Elizabeth Grosz, Teresa de Lauretis, bell hooks and Judith Butler, whose work on performativity (drawing on speech act theory: 1990, 1993a, 1997), might reasonably be assumed to be of particular interest to linguists.

If there are problems with sociocultural interpretive vocabularies, borrowed from outside linguistics, what has been the situation with technical vocabularies borrowed for more descriptive purposes? At first glance, the contribution of two bodies of work of major significance has been extremely positive. Speech act theory (from philosophy) and Conversation Analysis (from ethnomethodology) have made possible new kinds of attention to the interactional and social work done by utterances, and have contributed to a new respect for spoken language. The technical uptake, by linguists, however, has not always been so positive.

The critical move of speech act theory, as it was developed in the work of Austin (1962) and Searle (1969, 1979), was that utterances did not just refer—a central tenet of much theoretical work on language in both philosophy and linguistics over a long time—but could do several different kinds of 'work'. This included very literal kinds of work in the case of 'performatives' such as 'I name this ship The Golden Fleece' and 'I sentence you to be hanged by the neck until you are dead'. Such speech acts (naming, sentencing) actually produce effects: they do not simply refer, in the way that the clause 'the cat sat on the mat' is presumed to do. Paying attention to how an utterance is taken up (its illocutionary force) also makes clear that the relationship between the structure of an utterance and its meaning may not be simple and straightforward. Even though speech act theory did not work with empirically-derived data, from people speaking in 'real-life' situations, its principle of attending to the work done by utterances, not just to their structure, has been of considerable importance in a variety of forms of conversation analysis.

The take-up of speech act theory within linguistics has been various, and variously problematic. Wierzbicka (e.g. 1992), opens up the diversity of meanings of speech acts but operates with reductive conceptions of culture and the social while Martin's work on conversation (1992) closes down much of the open-ended possibility of speech act theory by developing a highly grammaticalised version of the exchange structure approach that Taylor and Cameron (1987, p. 65) criticise:

> In considering the problem of sequential ordering as it arises in models using speech act theory, we touched on the subject of quasi-grammatical rules and their role in conversation analysis. The issues and problems which rules of this kind raise assume a central importance in the 'exchange structure' model. Though in some ways it resembles the speech act approach, the exchange structure model of conversation analysis is one of the most unreconstructedly 'grammatical', and therefore exemplifies a number of pitfalls in the rules and units framework with especial clarity.

The second area outside linguistics that has been a source of techniques for the analysis of interactive talk is ethnomethodology, that branch of sociology concerned with the means by which the activities of everyday social life, including interactive talk, are achieved, originating with the work of Harold Garfinkel and continued by Harvey Sacks and others (see Garfinkel 1967, Turner 1974). The detailed attention of what became known as Conversation Analysis (CA) to the achievement of interactive talk included attention to how such talk was begun and ended and how turn-taking was managed. (Classic CA papers include Schegloff 1968; Schegloff and Sacks 1973; Sacks, Schegloff and Jefferson 1974. See also Sacks' lectures on conversation, posthumously published in 1992.) Conversation Analysis work is notable for the meticulous detail of its transcriptions with respect to pausing, overlaps, hesitations, repetitions and repairs, paying the utmost respect to *parole* by taking so much of its detail seriously (see Psathas 1995 for an introduction, and Hutchby and Wooffitt 1998 and ten Have 1999 for more comprehensive accounts).

Aspects of the technicality of CA, particularly its meticulous transcriptions, have had obvious descriptive appeal for linguists. Much less attention, and hence weight, has been given, however, to the stance of CA with respect to 'interpretive' categories. For CA practitioners, interpretive categories are not given but rather should emerge from the data itself and not be 'imposed' from the outside. The basic principle is that analysis should be 'emic' or participant-oriented rather than 'etic' or analyst-oriented. Linguists, however, are not trained to take any perspective other than that of the analyst (that is, themself) into account. This is an ongoing problem with all linguistically-informed work, an inevitable consequence of the idealised status of 'text' in even the most contextualised approach.

Discourse analysis as it has developed so far, then, can be characterised by fluidities and rigidities in both its descriptive resources and protocols and in its links with disciplines beyond linguistics. It was, after all, within linguistics itself that spaces for discourse analysis opened up, in part because of other developments within the discipline. One such development was the comparative work, arising from Chomsky's cognitive orientation, investigating possible 'language universals'. Some of this work identified phenomena—such as work on topic/focus (e.g. Li 1976)—which could just as readily be characterised in terms of 'discourse' as grammar. Work on textual cohesion also began to appear (see Halliday and Hasan 1976). Increasingly connections were made with the work of the Prague School by European linguists and by linguists working with Halliday. Such connections proved productive not only for literary stylistics but also for other kinds of textual work.

The growing legitimacy within linguistics of work on discourse also made it possible to attend to various phenomena which would not previously have been regarded as proper objects of linguistic enquiry, for example, conversational 'discourse markers' such as English *well, yeah, now, right* (Schiffrin 1987). The gradual relaxation of disciplinary 'policing' within linguistics was affected (and partially effected) by the increasing links discourse analysts were forging with practitioners doing related work in other disciplines. There were, however, limits to the legitimacy of such relationships: there was (and still is) more prestige to be found in links with philosophy and psychology than with literary stylistics and other forms of textual studies. Perhaps not a great deal has changed since Randolph Quirk, in his foreword to *Cohesion in English* (Halliday and Hasan 1976, pp. v–vi), specifically noted the relevance of the previous literary work of both authors—and the rarity of such engagement by linguists. The literary constitutes a double problem for discourse analysis, of course. It is written, while the privileged mode is spoken; and the literary belongs to the realm of the 'aesthetic' rather than to the 'scientific' fetishised by linguistics. The attachment of linguistics to a particular positivist conception of the scientific, however, not only limits the fluidity of the emerging field of discourse analysis in its links with other disciplinary enterprises concerned with language and text but legitimates ongoing rigidities in technical description. Logic and mathematics might have their fuzzy edges but linguistics prefers sharp edges and clean lines.

TEXT AS SOCIAL SEMIOTIC: STRUCTURE, REPRESENTATION AND POSITIONALITY

One of the most interesting cases of ongoing tensions between fluidities and rigidities is that of systemic-functional, or Hallidayan, linguistics and its ongoing engagement with text, context and their interrelations. This work is of particular importance because it informs, in various ways and to varying degrees, much discourse analytic work within and beyond linguistics, particularly the various forms of critical discourse analysis. The rigidities are predictable, for a linguistic model, and concern the technical apparatus of systemic linguistics, particularly in some of its more recent elaborations. The fluidities of systemically-based approaches to discourse analysis are much less predictable and concern the various kinds of interconnections with social theory that have been made in the past and that are currently being elaborated.

The emergence of systemic-functional linguistics in the 1960s as an explicitly functionally oriented form of linguistics immediately put it outside mainstream formal (that is, Chomskyan) linguistics. Its particular heresies were its view of text (not word or clause) as the basic semantic unit and its understanding of text and context as profoundly, and constitutively, interrelated. Such a move away from linguistic idealisation pushes 'text' in the direction of mode of social action rather than purely semiotic object. That is, while verbal 'text', spoken or written, is certainly a semiotic object requiring 'analysis', it is also a form of action in and on the world. This kind of view led to Michael Halliday, key systemic theorist, being viewed by conservative linguists as a kind of sociologist and not a linguist at all.

The radical nature of Halliday's proposal required two interrelated moves. The first was to see the clause (the fundamental grammatical unit) as made up not of one but of three kinds of structure, mapped onto one another, each strand realising a different kind of meaning (Halliday 1979, 1994). The three kinds of meaning (or 'metafunctions') are: ideational (with its subcomponents experiential and logical), inter-personal and textual. These are concerned respectively (leaving aside the logical metafunction) with the representation of events (experiential meaning), negotiating social relations (interpersonal meaning) and creating texture—the weaving together of the experiential and the interpersonal strands of meaning (textual meaning). The second move was to see each metafunction, and hence the particular kind of grammatical structure through which it is realised, as related in a bidirectional way with aspects of context. In other words, language constitutes context as well as simultaneously being constituted by it. The conventional systemic term for the context-to-language relation has been 'realisation', distinguishing this approach sharply from models which use 'expression'—and therefore assume that what is 'outside' language exists independently of it. Martin (1992) uses the term 'redundancy' and speaks of aspects of language and context 'redounding' with one another. The 'redundancies' hypothesised are between ex-periential meaning and field (what is 'going on' in a situation), interpersonal meaning and tenor (the relations between interactants) and textual meaning and mode (the role language is playing in the situation). (See Halliday and Hasan 1985/1989 for the basic model.)

It is this kind of linguistics which has been taken up by three groups of scholars, with overlapping membership, who have seen its potential for 'critical' analysis, that is, for political critique. In the United Kingdom in the late 1970s, Gunther Kress, Bob Hodge and others spoke explicitly of 'critical linguistics' (Fowler and Kress 1979) and addressed questions of ideology with a particular interest in media representation (see Kress and Hodge 1979 (2nd edn, with new final chapter: Hodge and Kress 1993); Trew 1979). Hodge and Kress sub-sequently became associated with a second group of scholars engaged in critical work in Australia through the 1980s and into the 1990s under the name 'social semiotics' (see Hodge and Kress, 1988; the journal *Social Semiotics* and other publications including Lemke 1995; Kress 1985/1989; Kress and van Leeuwen 1990, 1996; Poynton 1985/1989; Threadgold 1997a). During the same period, the third group of scholars, Norman Fairclough and his colleagues at Lancaster University in the United Kingdom, were developing 'critical discourse analysis' (Fairclough 1989, 1992, 1995a, 1995b). With the relocation of Kress and later van Leeuwen to the United Kingdom, and their closer working relation with Fairclough as well as European discourse analysts, the 'critical discourse analysis' label is now coming to be generalised. Thus, the subtitle of Caldas-Coulthard and Coulthard (1996), containing chapters by Fairclough and some of his former students, and by Kress, van Leeuwen, van Dijk, and various Birmingham scholars, is 'readings in critical discourse analysis'. (See also Kress 1994, 1996; Fairclough and Wodak 1997 for overview accounts of critical discourse analysis.)

What is particularly important about this body of work is its ability to move between the minutiae of a multistranded descriptive technology and some of the most productive frameworks for understanding social life as developed in broadly poststructuralist theories. Foucault has been particularly attractive—his conception of persons constituted through discourse is most congenial to linguists familiar with a model of language as social semiotic, involving the necessary bidirectionality of the constitutive relation between text and context. Bakhtin is a regular reference point, particularly his work on the multi-voicedness of text, suggesting ways of exploring the operation of discourses in text that go well beyond purely grammatical accounts. Of growing importance is a range of work in feminist and, more recently, queer theory, especially on the body/corporeality. And, returning to text, narrative theory is increasingly being drawn on. Threadgold (1997a) draws on a range of work in all these areas, for example (see also Pether and Threadgold's chapter in this volume).

From one point of view, this openness to contemporary theorisations of text, discourse and their relation to the social is quite characteristic of discourse analysis as a field. Discourse analysis, in its search for ways of understanding the cultural work carried out by (spoken) discourse, has been eclectic and much more adventurous than sociolinguistics. Discourse analysis has looked well beyond the 1960s sociology of sociolinguistics, borrowing from a range of social theory including social psychology, anthropology and various forms of sociology. Most of this work has, however, been concerned particularly with the social relations being negotiated. And once certain categories became established, there has not always been much questioning or further exploration. Thus, the categories of power and solidarity, first introduced into sociolinguistics from social psychology through the work of Roger Brown and his colleagues on terms of address (for example Brown and Gilman 1960), moved from there straight into discourse analysis with no further interrogation. And the feminist work on language and gender has done no active work to theorise power, despite its centrality to the ongoing argument about whether 'dominance', of women by men, or (cultural) 'difference' between women and men provides the better explanation of what happens linguistically. (See Thorne et al. 1975, 1983; Maltz and Borker 1982; Tannen 1994; Cameron 1995, 1997 for critique.) The lack of theoretical attention to power is even more surprising considering that work on language and gender has been carried out at a time when Foucault's theorisation of power has been immensely influential in the human sciences as well as subject to extensive feminist critique and rewriting. (See Diamond and Quinby 1988; McNay 1992; Hekman 1996.) Likewise, Brown and Levinson's now canonical work on politeness (first published 1978, republished as a monograph in 1987) uses Erving Goffman's notion of 'face', as well as power and solidarity, but includes no critical interrogation of them.

While discourse analysis as a field takes it as axiomatic that language plays a role in articulating identities and social relations, even if that role is understood to be expressive rather than constitutive, the engagement with the 'content' of texts has been more sporadic, more restricted and often quite reductive. Pragmatic work on presuppositions, for example (see Levinson 1983, chapter 4 for an introduction), focuses very narrowly on what needs to be 'known' or assumed by listeners in order to understand utterances, assuming essentially a now outmoded sender–message–receiver model of communication. In contrast, CA, through its work on membership categorisation (see Baker, this volume), offers one productive model for understanding how speakers constitute themselves as members of a particular culture through the categories they invoke and the ways in which they use them.

Critical discourse analysis, through its use of the Hallidayan technology for dealing with the clause-level constitution of representations (transitivity analysis), goes some way to attempting a more Foucauldian task—exploring the nexus of power and knowledge—as it investigates how persons engage with various ways of knowing as they participate in the social relations appropriate to specific institutions. This exploration understands persons and their relations with one another as both constituted in language, not pre-given or outside language, and understands those persons and relations as necessarily constituted in relation to knowledge. It is in their relation to the knowledges of institutions that the representations deployed by language users are of significance.

The systemic-functional linguistic account of representation is anything but unproblematic—most critically, its technologies for exploring 'knowledge' in text are crude in comparison with the sophistication of transitivity analysis in the clause. In particular, its technologies are not sensitive to momentary eruptions of non-dominant discourses, so critical to understanding the complex positionings of subjects as always multiple, never singular. Further, the continuing structuralist imperative governing all kinds of linguistics—to keep categories separate—produces serious problems in attempting to interrelate the interpersonal and the experiential (Poynton 1993). It is these aspects of the systemic-functional model which are most closely aligned with the power/knowledge nexus. Critical discourse analysis practitioners, familiar with European traditions of critical theory and discourse analysis concerned with power/knowledge, and the interrelations between representation and the positionality of speakers/writers, do seem in a strong position to offer a more integrated account of linguistic and other approaches to discourse.

It remains to be seen how far such integration might go. Pennycook (1994a), for example, explores the question of whether Foucauldian and linguistic approaches to discourse are ultimately 'incommensurable'. And Threadgold (personal communication) ultimately abandoned attempts to 'map' Foucault and Halliday onto one another, despite still teaching and writing using both—the conceptual apparatuses simply would not translate. Apart from the possibly irreconcilable difference between a Foucauldian and a structuralist 'rules and units' approach to discourse analysis (Taylor and Cameron 1987), perhaps the most intractable problem for linguists is that Foucault's notion of discourse is not restricted to language but concerns the whole gamut of cultural practices which 'speak' to persons but which they also 'speak', so bringing themselves into being as particular kinds of persons or subjects. Discourse analysts trained in linguistics, not surprisingly, have great difficulty with such a conception of discourse. The analytic practices of even those with great familiarity with European theory, and hence with a sophisticated conception of 'context', remain stubbornly 'linguocentric', despite their best efforts. This is true, for example, of Kress (1985/1989) and most notably of Fairclough's *Discourse and Social Change* (1992). Here, perhaps, lies the real value of the multimodal work currently developing within the social semiotic tradition, spearheaded by the work of Gunther Kress and Theo van Leeuwen on visual images (Kress and van Leeuwen 1990, 1996). In such work language takes its place as merely one of the multitudinous signifying practices that (in)form social life and is understood in relation to those other practices.

DISCOURSE ANALYSIS, CONTEXT AND THE SOCIAL

The inevitability of the text/context relation has been acknowledged from the beginning of discourse analysis as a field of study. (See van Dijk's 1977 study, *Text and Context*.) 'Context' has been a key term in recognising the need to look beyond language to understand the work performed by discourse. Understanding that work includes understanding that who speaks—particularly if they are a child, a woman or non-white—is commonly of greater importance in determining whether they are heard or not than is any question of content or presentation. It also involves understanding that that 'who-ness' is iteratively marked, on the body of the speaker—including the grain of their voice, foregrounding the salient identity and backgrounding the inevitable multiplicity of actual persons. It is very clear that linguistics as such has nothing to say about such issues; they will have to be approached from elsewhere, from other disciplinary frameworks.

An explicit 'multidisciplinarity' has come to characterise the field of discourse analysis (van Dijk 1997; Schiffrin 1994; Georgakopoulou and Goutsos 1997). There are several problems with the way this has been done, however. This chapter has already referred to problematic aspects of the ways in which various social categories have been 'borrowed' without being subject to further interrogation. The narrowness of the range of disciplines actively drawn upon has also been mentioned, along with some of the inevitable exclusions (particularly literary work). Beyond the particularity of such discipline-based work, there has been a growing body of European-based work on discourse and/or social theory which is barely attended to in the discourse analysis literature. Contributors to van Dijk's (1997) two-volume overview of the field cite major European theorists including Barthes, Bakhtin/Volosinov, Bourdieu, Derrida, Foucault, Habermas, Kristeva, Ricoeur—commonly involving only one citation, of the same one or two works; while another recent text (Georgakopoulou and Goutsos 1997) cites only Macdonell's 1986 introductory text on discourse. Even more rarely cited is the variety of 'textual' work done within rhetoric, composition studies and literary studies. (Georgakopoulou and Goutsos 1997 is the exception, drawing substantially on narrative theory.) In the face of the manifest incapacity of linguistics to offer any kind of adequate theorisation of context, despite various attempts, the failure to explore contemporary social/critical theory, particularly the work of Foucault, seems inexplicable.

Returning to the question of discourse analysis and those disciplines/knowledges that it does engage with, what of the relation between discourse analysis and other disciplines? Has that relationship been one where the different contributors meld into some new kind of entity or, rather, has the relation been one of coloniser to colonised: other disciplines constituted simply as 'booty' to be systematically stripped down and plundered for whatever can be appropriated that might be of use to a fundamentally technicist project?

If the multidisciplinarity of discourse analysis fails to guarantee the adequacy of the understandings of context and the social that underpin it, what of the conjunction of critical discourse analysis/ social, semiotics/critical linguistics? Can it be differentiated from other forms of discourse analysis as a more credible interdisciplinary, or even transdisciplinary, enterprise, that is, a more integrated way of knowing? Several characteristics of that nexus lend it credibility. The first is the model of technical linguistic analysis that all share. The features that distinguish this model are its functional (as distinct from formal, as exemplified by Chomsky) emphasis and its interconnection of language and context. That is, the model allows attention to what language 'does' in the world and to how particular aspects of language relate to aspects of contexts, or situations, precisely because of the 'work' they do. Of all linguistic models, the systemic view of the two-way determination of the relation between language and context comes closest to current (poststructuralist) understandings, outside linguistics, of the work done by 'language' in constituting (and not just 'expressing') knowledges and persons.

Critical discourse analysis practitioners, unlike most other linguists, demonstrate familiarity with frameworks in the 'human sciences'. Not surprisingly, many such practitioners are not located within linguistics at all but rather in English, Communications, Media and Education. This is clearly relevant to the comfortable multidisciplinarity of their work but it is also relevant to the third characteristic of this work: the balance of the 'technicist' agenda compared with other dimensions of the work done, that is, the balance of linguistic to other forms of 'analysis'. Given the extensive elaboration of the technical apparatus of systemic-functional linguistics, this is an issue of considerable import. Becoming thoroughly familiar with Hallidayan functional grammar (let alone systemic work 'above', 'below' and 'beside' the clause) is a formidable task in itself. Training in Hallidayan linguistics continues to be even more relentlessly technicist than many other forms of linguistics (but see Terry Threadgold's interview with Barbara Kamler (Kamler 1997) for the possibility of an alternative pedagogy which might somewhat redress this situation).

The most effective discourse analysis, however, involves being able to stand back sufficiently from that monolithic technical apparatus to make strategic selections of analytic focus, informed by other kinds of understandings of text, context and their possible relations. The best critical discourse analysis work is characterised precisely by an economy, even parsimony, of analytical technology informing (and informed by) wide familiarity with contemporary critical theory. It is not surprising that this body of work has profoundly informed the genesis of this book and that the marks of both critical discourse analysis and Hallidayan linguistics are to be seen on so many of its chapters.

CONCLUSION

This chapter has addressed both the successes and some of the more problematic aspects of the increasingly complex terrain of linguistically-based discourse studies. The successes lie, first, in the attention it is now possible to give to spoken language within linguistics and, second, in the progressive elaboration of text-analytic tools, drawing on vocabularies both from within linguistics and from other fields. The multidisciplinarity claimed for discourse analysis as a field, however, has in many respects promised more than it has been able to deliver. This is particularly the case when 'borrowed' vocabularies have (as they have all too often) become part of a technical apparatus used in ways which vindicate views of linguistics as a discipline utterly caught up within an empiricist scientific agenda.

The conjunction of critical discourse analysis, social semiotics and critical linguistics has been a somewhat more convincing, though not unproblematic, version of a linguistically-informed interdisciplinary discourse analysis, attempting to address the imbrication of language and the social. It is this work (especially publications such as Fairclough 1992 and Kress 1996) that is the most overtly political form of discourse analysis, offering not only critique of existing arrangements, but espousing an agenda of social transformation and change. It is difficult to see, however, how an exclusively linguistic agenda might be used proactively to imagine effectively, much less bring about, radical social change. This is in spite of the sophistication of the understandings of discourse practices and discursive formations that it has become possible to bring to bear retrospectively on the present.

The agenda of critique central to the critical discourse analysis project certainly makes available the kind of externalising 'outsider's' position from which it is possible to identify the positionings and interests of those with speaking roles in the ongoing choreography of social life. Those who actually take up such externalising positions are few, however, in comparison with the increasing number of people engaged in aspects of what Fairclough (1996) calls the 'technologisation' of discourse. By this he means the increasing use of linguistic (and other, particularly psychological) knowledge about language in the service of training in language or, more usually, 'communication' skills for workers and managers (in the workplace) and for children (in schools). The increasing availability of discourse analytic tools constitutes a critical condition of possibility for such technologisation, in those cultures where economic rationalist discourses have steadily increased the range of 'objects' of commodification, including the knowledges and skills of academics. Discourse technologisation certainly offers increasing opportunities for 'useful work' for practitioners of various kinds of discourse analysis. It may offer opportunities to better understand language use in contexts, particularly the workplace, that are crucially involved in the production of new forms of social relations (Gee et al. 1996). It certainly involves significant political and ethical problems. (See, for example, Lee 1996 and Watkins 1997 for critiques of the Australian educational linguistics project, skilling children in literacy; and Scheeres and Solomon, in this volume, for a critical reflection on a workplace language intervention.)

It remains to be seen whether all that discourse technologisation can offer to discourse analysis practitioners is the choice between co-option or some restricted kind of oppositional stance. At the end of the twentieth century, the increasing imbrication of persons and institutions within relations of power makes imagining a viable position outside such relations increasingly difficult. Possibilities for an oppositional stance—for any kind of resistance to the operations of new forms of power—are giving way to very different kinds of engagement with issues of power, government and their legitimation. Discourse remains at the heart of these issues, however, rendering critical forms of discourse analysis—current and future—of ongoing importance.

NOTES

1   Saussure's *Cours de Linguistique Générale* was published posthumously in 1916, produced by his students. The standard text is de Mauro 1972. There are two English translations, both under the title *Course in General Linguistics*, by Wade Baskin in 1959 and Roy Harris in 1983. See also Culler 1976 for an account of Saussure's work and heritage, Harris 1987 for a critical commentary on the *Cours* and Thibault 1997 for a more wide-ranging commentary on Saussure's work.

2   Derrida's claim concerning the Western privileging of speech usually simply puzzles linguists, especially discourse analysts, who have been fighting their own battle

to gain legitimacy for the study of speech within linguistics in the context of the discipline's historical privileging of decontextualised examples and written language.

3   The linguistic literature on discourse processing, as well as related literatures in psycholinguistics, cognitive psychology, artificial intelligence etc., is considerable. All need ultimately to be integrated with a sociolinguistic account but that is a task well beyond the scope of this chapter.

3 Poststructuralism and discourse analysis

Terry Threadgold

Poststructuralist modes of discourse analysis, or postlinguistics, have by their very nature denied the possibility of a 'how to do'. They have argued that the binary separation of metalanguage (or theory) and data (that which is given to be observed and analysed) is already an impossible separation. Thus, the 'how to do' of poststructuralist discourse analysis inevitably involves understanding first just why that is seen to be impossible, just what are the problems poststructuralism sees with other modes of doing discourse analysis. Then, however, comes a kind of paradox: for when we practice poststructuralist discourse analysis we inevitably need to do some of the same things that older structuralist and linguistic methodologies also do, albeit with a different understanding of why we do them. This is what I will here try to explain and also to perform as a writing.

The most important distinction between this chapter and Poynton's (chapter 2) is that Saussure's work, although it keeps reappearing here like the ghost in the machine, is not the beginning point for these postructuralist stories as it is for the linguistic stories. Poststructuralist narratives look back through Saussure (a little like his metaphor of the sign as a two-sided piece of paper) to the philosophy of Husserl, Nietszche, Hegel and Kant among others, sometimes influenced by, sometimes contesting, these earlier positions. Poststructuralist discourse analysis, then, is a multidisciplinary phenomenon found in many different disciplinary and interdisciplinary sites. This dissemination of *the idea* of discourse analysis 'within a political multiplicity' which indeed has no single mother tongue (Deleuze and Guattari 1987) or any single clearly defined approach to the subject, is what makes it so difficult for those who would use it to know where to start or even to be sure what *it* is. Mapping such a terrain requires a new kind of geography and a different sort of map—one that will allow simultaneity and difference, parallels and overlaps—a mapping of at best processual and transient moments. I will begin with some archaeological work in the field (note the change in metaphor: digging it up, imagining how it came to be as it is, searching, but never for a beginning).

The 'field' turns out of course to be a global space of migration and hybridisation. There is the ubiquitous presence of Roman Jakobson in Russia in the 1920s, in Prague in the 1930s and 1940s and then in the United States; the movement of Claude Lévi-Strauss from Czechoslovakia to the United States in 1941 and then to Paris in 1950; and there are the effects of the uncertain authorship and delayed transmission and translation of the ideas of Mikhail Bakhtin/ Voloshinov/Medvedev (Bakhtin 1981, 1984, 1986; Clark and Holquist 1984; Voloshinov 1973), whose work in Russia in the 1920s and later, known to the Prague School in the 1930s and 1940s, did not have its effect on Paris structuralism and semiotics until it was taken up by Tzvetan Todorov (1984) and Julia Kristeva (1980) in the late 1960s. And we should not forget here the oddly *poststructuralist* transmission, by way of *memory* and *translation*, of the work of Saussure himself.

It was the translation of the writings of Bakhtin/Voloshinov/ Medvedev (Kristeva 1970) in Paris in the late 1960s which in many ways marked the point at which structuralism, in the histories to come, was seen to move in the direction of *post*structuralism. Bakhtin was particularly 'readable' in a context where many of the basic tenets of earlier structuralist and semiotic paradigms, including their in-herent masculinism, were being questioned and rethought. But the work of Jakobson, like that of Saussure himself, *wanders* like a ghost in the machine of poststructuralism, constantly informing and being challenged by a tradition that is deeply philosophical and not linguistic at all. It is from this emergent paradigm of work in Paris in the 1960s and 1970s that the categories now so familiar as poststructuralist— *subjectivity, conscious/unconscious, gender, race, embodiment, intertextuality, myth, narrative, discourse, writing/ reading/re-writing, deconstruction, iterativity, performativity*—emerge as a new metalanguage (a language/ theory for talking about language) for the human sciences. In this process almost no element of the earlier Saussurean/structuralist model of communication remained intact.

SAUSSURE UNDER ERASURE: FROM SEMIOLOGY TO GRAMMATOLOGY

One possible beginning to my story is with the Russian formalists for whom *literature*, like language, was a social institution, an autonomous system governed by its own regularity. This concept of an underlying systematicity was one of the small number of theoretical concepts which formalism borrowed from Saussure. *Syntagm* (the linearity of the signifier), *paradigm* (the sets of choices provided by the system with which to make syntagms) and the *arbitrariness* of the sign, as well as the binary opposition between *synchrony* (the present system) and *diachrony* (historical states of the system) in language were the others. What is less often acknowledged, particularly by poststructuralists, is that not much of this apparatus actually survived the many years of work on it by structuralists. The focus on the literary (in a world where the literary has become suspect in cultural studies contexts) was actually crucial to the questioning of Saussure's model. Here it is the ubiquitous scholar Roman Jakobson who is important.

The starting point for his poetics of literature was the concept of the self-referential sign—the poetic function of language (as opposed to the other functions he recognised, each corresponding to an element of context: the referential, the phatic, the metalingual, the emotive and the conative) which involved a 'focus on the message for its own sake' (Jakobson 1960, p. 356). Poetry, or literary language, posed two specific problems to the Saussurean system. Driven by its incessant need for difference or 'defamiliarisation', it proved to be excessively unstable and was thus the least reliable function in terms of long-term semiotic identity. But the literature Jakobson was investigating was also *written*, a characteristic which opened the identity of the literary work to the vicissitudes of history. The question that had to be answered was how was it possible that *author* and *reader* could communicate across that gap?

Jakobson argued that 'every word of poetic language is in essence phonically and semantically deformed *vis-a-vis practical language*' and that the aesthetic/poetic function is a specific variety 'governed by its own immanent laws', yet he concluded that 'a poetic form cannot distort its material to such a degree that it loses its *linguistic* nature' (Steiner 1984, p. 231, emphasis added). Here, of course, he was recognising what Derrida (1982a) would later entrench as doxa, the understanding that *writing* goes on meaning in the radical absence of both the sender and the addressee. It was therefore phonology that Jakobson chose as the key to the identity of the literary sign, even as he argued that it was phonological parallelism and repetition that produced polysemy and heterogeneity in the literary artefact. As a mere secondary representation of sound, the written text must always be able to be read in relation to voice/sound, the primary or originary substance, institutionalised as the phonological structure of a given language.

Poetic violence, the violence of a writing that wanders (across the centuries), cannot deform this system or verbal art would lose its 'linguistic' (i.e. system-based) nature. If writing is made secondary to originary speech, merely a representation of it, then the cause of the semiotic slippage, written language, is eliminated. Thus, Saussure's contradictory and violent narrative, structured around the speech/writing binarism, of the violence done to speech by writing (Saussure 1959, chapter 6) and Jakobson's parallel theory of poetry's violent *deformation* of the system (*la langue*).

Enter Derrida (1976) to chastise them both for *phonocentrism* and *ethnocentrism*. But Derrida's move is more complex than merely to chastise. His *deconstructive* argument involves the rhetorical play and metaphor of *intertextual* analysis. Derrida (1976, p. 39) begins with the unworkable binary opposition speech/writing which constitutes a specific hierarchy of values in which speech is seen as innocent and primary and writing as violent and secondary:

> Declaration of principle, pious wish and historical violence of a speech dreaming its full self-presence, living itself as its own resumption; self-proclaimed language, auto-production of a speech declared alive, capable, Socrates said, of helping itself, a logos which believes itself to be its own father, being lifted thus above written discourse . . . Self-proclaimed language but actually speech, deluded into believing itself completely alive, and violent, for it is not 'capable of protect[ing] or defend[ing] itself' . . . except through expelling the other, and especially *its own* other, throwing it *outside* and *below*, under the name of writing.

This is a significant *re-narrativisation* of several elements of Saussure's argument and a reversal of the binary opposition. It is now speech which is violent because it cannot insist on its own autonomy without expelling writing, but speech is also deluded, believing *itself* to be language. Morever, Derrida argues, the binary speech/writing (with its implications of nature/culture, irrational/rational etc.) is unworkable, because writing cannot both be a *representation*, an *image* (*icon*) of speech and in an *arbitrary* relation with it and, of course, Saussure argues both things. Moreover, to be *arbitrary* the sign must be institutionalised; but institution is dependent on writing (Derrida 1976, pp. 44, 45):

The very idea of institution—hence of the arbitrariness of the sign—is unthinkable before the possibility of writing and outside of its horizon . . .

The thesis of the arbitrariness of the sign thus indirectly but irrevocably contests Saussure's declared proposition when he chases writing to the outer darkness of language. This thesis successfully accounts for a conventional relationship between the phoneme and the grapheme (in phonetic writing, between the phoneme, signifier–signified, and the grapheme, pure signifier), but by the same token it forbids that the latter be an 'image' of the former. Now it was indispensable to the exclusion of writing as 'external system', that it come to impose an 'image', a 'representation', or a 'figuration', an exterior reflection of the reality of language.

One must therefore challenge, in the very name of the arbitrariness of the sign, the Saussurean definition of writing as 'image' . . .

Derrida (1976, p. 53) then locates another inconsistency in Saussure's argument:

. . . it is impossible for sound alone, a material element, to belong to language. It is only a secondary thing, substance to be put to use . . . [T]he linguistic signifier . . . is not [in essence] phonic but incorporeal—constituted not by its material substance but by the differences that separate its sound-image from all others.

Here Saussure contradicts the argument for the *naturally* phonic character of language, allowing Derrida to query on other terms the relationship between speech and writing on which Saussure founds linguistics. Derrida now rewrites *writing* as an *instituted trace*, the *arche-trace* and *arche-writing* (Derrida 1976, pp. 42, 47, 60). Speech, he argues, is a version of this *instituted trace*, his new term for *writing*. At this point he has moved beyond the reversal of the binary opposition to a deconstruction which will not permit the opposition speech/writing to stand. Speech is a form of what he is calling writing. Because he needs a new metalanguage which does not bring with it the baggage of linguistics, he uses philosophical terms. But they too have baggage. A *trace* generally represents a present mark of an absent (present). The terms *instituted trace* and *arche-trace* still carry the connotation of presence/absence, as well as nature/culture and origin.

The arche-trace, on the contrary, is the movement which produces the difference of absence and presence constitutive of the colloquial sense of trace as well as the difference of nature and culture constitutive of the idea of institution . . .

The arche-trace is the origin of all relation to an Other . . .

It opens up the possibility of all relation to an Other, of all relation to an exteriority, in short, the structure of reference in general. (Gasche 1995, p. 45)

The arche-trace, then, is not specifically linguistic. It is any mark capable of referring to (by excluding) what is Other. The arche-trace, the instituted trace is rewritten by Derrida as in fact always both the mark of an absence and the mark of the presence of 'the completely other' within all structures of reference (Gasche 1995, p. 45). The terms then serve to deconstruct the opposition between inside and outside, between signifier and signified, signification and reality. One of Derrida's most famous pronouncements is that there is no 'outside the text' (1976, p. 158). Derrida is using these new terms to think with, to 'make strange' the linguistic metalanguage by hybridising it with philosophy, using the term which relates to the *origin*, the *referent*, the *other* (*arche*) in order to deconstruct it. He uses it *sous rature (under erasure)*, another strategic deployment, but one which must be made because, in a slightly different sense, there actually is *no outside the text*. We are stuck with the tools and the concepts that we have to work with and there is therefore no way of making visible, transparent, what is at stake here.

Derrida then goes on an intertextual walk, seeking other metaphors and narratives in the texts of the sciences of structuralist linguistics and semiotics. He finds parts of what he needs in C.S. Peirce and in Hjelmslev. Peirce, he says, goes a long way towards the deconstruction of 'the transcendental signified', his theory of the *interpretant* denying the possibility that 'the thing signified may be allowed to glow finally in the luminosity of its presence' (Derrida 1976, p. 49). In Peirce's work, signs refer only to other signs. The represented is always already an interpretant for another sign (see Eco 1979). Peirce also understood that this process could work across semiotic systems. His theory was about semiotics, not about language or verbal signs, so that a visual sign might refer to an object (corporeal) which would become an interpretant for another object (an idea) which would become an interpretant for another object (verbal) and so on. This, if you are Derrida wanting to show that linguistic (and philosophical) imperialisms had not got right the processes by which meanings are made, is very useful. Hjelmslev (1961), on the other hand, was helpful to Derrida because he criticised the idea that 'language was *naturally* bound to the substance of phonic expression', arguing that there was no reason why the 'substance-expression of a spoken language should consist of "sounds"'(Derrida 1976, p. 58). It might well consist of visual images, gestures or movements of any of the 'striate musculature', not just those associated with the so-called organs of speech—the throat, nose and mouth (Hjelmslev in Derrida 1976, p. 58).

Having put 'under erasure' both *arche-writing* and *arche-trace*, we now arrive at a rewriting of the *trace* as *différance, as always difference and deferral* (Derrida 1976, p. 62). The trace is according to Derrida 'by rights anterior to all that one calls sign' (1976, p. 62). He goes on to say that this '. . . *différance* is therefore not more sensible than intelligible and it permits the articulation of signs among themselves within the same abstract order—a phonic or graphic text for example—or between two orders of expression' (1976, p. 63). Writing as *différance* is not confined to a single semiotic system. Unlike the sign, such writing may be material or sensible: the world is articulate and it writes.

Thus Derrida substitutes grammatology, the science of the gram (writing) for Saussure's science of the seme (semiology). It is the linguistic dominance and repression of other sign systems that is at stake here, along with the imperialism of the linguistic sign which cannot imagine meaning happening differently. Grammatology as the science of writing, of the iterable mark (Derrida 1982), is a deconstruction of the usual understanding of signification as produced in language through a relationship between signifier and signified within the same semiotic system. *Différance* in Derrida functions as a *hinge* or *brisure*, the deconstructive term referring to the folding of the sides of a binary into one another, refusing the construction of the one based on the exclusion of the other. Perhaps it is helpful here to use a metaphor and a narrative from two other poststructuralist scholars (Deleuze and Guattari 1987, p. 11) to articulate what it was that Derrida was struggling to say in this text:

> On the contrary, not every trait in a rhizome is necessarily linked to a linguistic feature: semiotic chains of every nature are connected to very diverse modes of coding (biological, political, economic, etc.) that bring into play not only different regimes of signs but also states of things of differing status . . . it is not possible to make a radical break between regimes of signs and their objects.

THE MATERIALITY OF DISCOURSE: BODILY INSCRIPTION

Foucault, who taught Derrida, also struggled to articulate this difference, to rewrite discourse as material practice, to contest the hegemony of linguistics. 'Orders of Discourse' is the text of Foucault's inaugural lecture at the Collège de France, delivered on 1 December 1970. It is the text in which Foucault acknowledges his intellectual debt to his teachers Jean Hyppolite, Dumezil and Canguilhem. His hypothesis in this lecture is that:

> [I]n every society the production of discourse is at once controlled, selected, organised and redistributed according to a certain number of procedures, whose role is to avert its powers and its dangers, to cope with chance events, to evade its ponderous, awesome materiality. (Foucault 1971b, p. 8)

It is his arguments at the end of this lecture which bring us closest to understanding the difference between what Foucault means by *discourse* and what linguists and philosophers do. Foucault lists a number of philosophical themes which, he argues, contribute to the limitations, the exclusions and the constraints on understandings of discourse which he mentions in the quotation above. The philosophical principles which 'deny the truth of discourse' as he sees it are:

- proposing an ideal truth as a law of discourse;
- proposing an imminent rationality as the principle of philosophical behaviour;
- assuming an ethic of knowledge which sees it as sufficient to desire truth to have the power to think it. (Foucault 1971b, p. 20)

He sees these principles as accompanied by the following further deeply ingrained philosophical understandings:

- To discourse: a verb seen to relate speaking and thinking, it implies thought rendered visible, and involves the representation of thought in the world.
- The concept of the founding subject: understood as involving someone who puts thought into words and can take meanings out of them.
- Originating experience: the idea that things are simply out there in a pure originary form to be named/represented in language. Meaning, in other words, is seen to be already there, fully made. All the *cogito* has to do is to reflect, to represent.
- Universal mediation: the idea that logos (language/logic) enables consciousness to recover the rationality that both orders and is intrinsic to the world.

In this context, then, *discourse* is only an activity, of writing, of reading, of exchange. 'It never involves anything but signs' (Foucault 1971b, pp. 20–1). All of this constitutes a form of control, Foucault suggests, and involves a profound logophobia:

> . . . a sort of dumb fear of these events, of this mass of spoken things, of everything that could possibly be violent, discontinuous, querulous,

disordered even and perilous in it, of the incessant, disorderly buzzing of discourse. (Foucault 1971b, p. 21)

To overcome this fear, endemic in philosophical thinking about discourse, Foucault argues that three things are needed: 'to question our will to truth, to restore to discourse its character as an event, and to abolish the sovereignty of the signifier' (Foucault 1971b, pp. 21–2). He then articulates four principles of action—reversal, discontinuity, specificity and exteriority—which would permit us to do these things.

1   The principle of reversal. The terms *author, discipline, will to truth* have always been seen as positive, creative things. Let us, says Foucault, see them instead as the negative activities of *constraint, control, rarefaction*, where the last term implies the imposition of exclusions and limits.

2   The principle of discontinuity. It is important, he says, to understand that the system of rarefaction which sets limits to what can be known as true within the disciplines does not imply that there is a 'great vista' of 'unsaid things' that has 'been driven back by them'. Discourse is, on the contrary, everywhere, transgressing institutional and disciplinary boundaries. Its different manifestations are often unaware of one another, often exclude each other, but this does not mean that they do not exist. The non-discursive, in the sense of what is not legitimised, institutionalised and disciplined, occurs in a discontinuous series with the discursive. This is the sense of *discourse* as sets of statements about an object, event, as discursive practices, which circulate without authorship and without discursive and disciplinary controls, that has become the stock understanding of *discourse* in poststructuralist contexts in the humanities and social sciences. To speak of discourses of race, gender and class, for example, is to use discourse in this sense.

3   The principle of specificity. In a complete reversal of the normal understanding of the relationship of discourse to signification, Foucault argues that no prior system of signification will enable us to simply decipher/decode discourse. Discourse is, says Foucault, a *practice* we impose on things. 'It does not work hand in glove with what we already know', rather it produces the things of which it speaks. The principle of specificity is the located practice which produces the regularity of discourse, the functions for a subject, the positions for a subject, the possible technologies, the objects

and the behaviours that the term discourse encompasses for Foucault. *Discourse* here, then, has become a set of material practices of which language is only one.

4   The principle of exteriority. We should not 'burrow' into discourse looking for meanings. We should instead look for the external conditions of its existence, its appearance and its regularity. We should explore the conditions of its possibility. Just how is it possible to know that, to think that, to say that—these are the questions we should be asking.

Corresponding to these four injunctions there are four principles of analysis: *event, series, regularity* and *the possible conditions of existence.* These terms are to replace, in order, the terms: *creation, unity, originality, signification.* These latter are the notions, Foucault argues, which have dominated the history of ideas. What is needed is a 'theory of discontinuous systematisation' (Foucault 1971b, p. 22). Series of events have discontinuous kinds of regularity across the materiality of institutions, genres, texts, oeuvres, subjects. The subjects these discontinuities position, then, must be seen to be dispersed across a multiplicity of possible positions and functions. There can be no causal links between these events and subject positions, no linear narrative of progress from one to another, and we must accept 'the introduction of chance as a category in the production of events' (Foucault 1971b, p. 24). Discourse fractures the unities of *subject, author, text, instance,* crossing and transgressing these categories. In this respect, Foucault's conception of discourse is not unlike Bakhtin's (1981) much earlier notions of dialogism and heteroglossia, or Barthes' intertextuality, the murmur of things and the voices that circulate through and from the farthest corners of the culture.

Such then is Foucault's understanding of discourse in the earlier (sometimes called archaeological) texts. He offers in this list of 'things to be done' something like a list of instructions for doing discourse analysis in his way. In the later (genealogical) texts, Foucault is much more influenced by Nietzsche, from whom he borrows the term *genealogy.* The object of this work is power as it functions within institutions and in the creation of knowledges and truths. He is interested here in the constitution of the subject and in the way in which the body is formed, shaped and branded in disciplinary practices. *Discipline and Punish* (1979) is a study of the discursive formation of the prison (see Threadgold 1997a) and of the making of a disciplined and criminal population. *I, Pierre Riviere . . .* (1975) is a companion piece to this book which includes a dossier of archival materials, including a confession and medical, legal, psychiatric and media texts which demonstrate how disciplined subjects are produced in relations of power and how the criminal subject is made subject to and by disciplinary and discursive knowledges. The book demonstrates, incidentally, how a Foucauldian discourse analysis, focusing on *event*, *series*, *regularity* and *possible conditions of existence*, is actually put into practice. In 1980 Foucault argued that:

> The body is the inscribed surface of events (traced by language and dissolved by ideas), the locus of dissociated Self (adopting the illusion of a substantial unity), and a volume in perpetual disintegration. Genealogy, as an analysis of descent, is thus situated within the articulation of the body and history. Its task is to expose a body totally imprinted by history and the process of history's destruction of the body. (Foucault 1980, p. 148)

In these contexts, the body replaces the mind as the mark of the subject, so that to effect social change ceases to be a question of ideology, of changing the way people think, and becomes a question of finding ways of inscribing bodies differently. Since bodies are produced discursively, through the violent practice of discourse and discipline, this remains a discursive question, much as it was in Althusser's (1971) understanding of the material nature of ideology and the interpellation of the subject. The difference is that discourse here is not just language, but practices, behaviours, objects, technologies and concepts, all of which shape and form the disciplined body.

Feminist theory has made much use of Foucault, of his theory of discourse (Weedon 1997), of his understandings of the body (Grosz 1994), but feminists have also had questions to ask about Foucault's unreflective comments on rape and child sexual abuse (Alcoff 1996). More recently, Stoler (1997) has reread and rewritten Foucault's *History of Sexuality*, querying some of its uses for the analysis of postcolonial questions, pointing to the absence in Foucault's work of 'the object of knowledge' against which, and in relation to which, his four 'objects of knowledge'—the masturbating child of the bourgeois family, the 'hysterical woman', the Malthusian couple and the perverse adult—were inevitably produced. That absence is, of course, 'the libidinal energies of the savage, the primitive, the colonized', an absence, she argues, which enabled Foucault to ignore the fact that the 'sexual discourse of empire and of the biopolitical state in Europe were mutually constitutive' (Stoler 1997, p. 7).

THE BODY AS MARK OF THE SUBJECT: GENDERED SUBJECTIVITY, CORPOREOGRAPHY, PERFORMATIVITY

The earliest attempts to think the subject of humanism differently, as difference and as *différance*, as decentred, were also connected to structuralisms and linguistics. In Jakobson's work, the split reference of the double-voiced poetic message, the metaphor/metonymy nexus derived from Freud, finds its correspondance in a split addresser and a split addressee (1981, p. 42). The linguist Benveniste (1966) took these questions further when he theorised the difference between the 'I' of the enunciation and the 'I' of the enounced, that is, the I who writes/speaks and the I who is represented in writing or speech (see Threadgold 1997a).

The first theorist to develop a theory of gendered subjectivity, whatever its problems as a theory, was Julia Kristeva (1984). Her theory of language and semiosis, and of the literary, is strongly mediated by various linguistic paradigms, by a Marxist and later Bakhtinian structuralist semiotic and materialist focus, and by psychoanalysis. For Kristeva, the speaking subject is always in process, never fixed or finished. She understood that the analysis of discourse could not be done without reference to the body and to the speaking subject. She also understood the relationship between writing and revolution (social change), first in avant-garde literature, later in relation to the analysand as a subject in process/on trial: 'In the best of cases, analysis is an invitation to become a narrator, the "novelist" of one's life . . . memory put into words and the involvement of the drive in these words' (1998, p. 28). Kristeva's term 'analysis' envisages a different kind of 'making visible' which *writing* might accomplish for and through the speaking subject.

Kristeva's focus on writing *as analysis* is similar to Barthes' (1974) work on subjectivity and intertextuality, where *analysis* became a very productive reading process in which reading always involved rewriting. Barthes' *S/Z* (1974) was in some ways one of the first embodied *performances* of what it was to *rewrite* a story *intertextually* and tell it differently as a form of literary and cultural criticism. These theoretical understandings of writing as intervention, as research, as analysis, are not to be kept too separate from Derrida's writing as grammatology, and they anticipate later feminist work on writing and the body.

Vicki Kirby (1997), in a radical use of Derridean deconstruction for feminist intervention, rewrites Judith Butler's work to question metaphors (derived from Foucault, psychoanalysis and feminism) of the inscription or the rewriting of the body. Kirby points out that Derrida's deconstruction of the inside/outside binary with respect to

language (the 'there is no outside the text' argument), actually acknowledges the 'articulateness' of the outside, 'a knowing outside that,
in as much as it does not lack language, must be articulate' (1997,
p. 90). Taking Derrida seriously, she argues, means understanding that
everything that is normally excluded (as radical alterity) from the
written, the rational, the cultured spaces of patriarchal knowledges—
the spoken, the irrational, the primitive, woman, child, the racialised
other—all is already articulate.

Kirby's argument is that linguistics, unlike Saussure (whose work
she also submits to a radical rewriting), always assumes a non-language,
a 'reassuring world to which language ultimately refers' and thus fails
to see what Saussure understood: that 'within the particularity of the
language textile' there is always to be found the 'incontrovertible trace
of what is purportedly an extralinguistic reality' (1997, p. 45). How,
Kirby asks, are we to think the 'corporeal place', 'the envelope of
immanence', the body that our textual agendas keep wanting to make
'other', to reduce to anatomy, to biology, to put outside the text? How,
in other words, do we write the

> . . . textual adventure of the peristaltic movements of the viscera, the
> mitosis of cells, the electrical activity that plays across a synapse, the itin-
> erary of a virus and so on? . . . the oozings and pulsings that literally
> and figuratively make up the differential stuff of the body's extra-ordinary
> circuitry? (Kirby 1997, p. 76)

Biology, Kirby argues (1997, p. 78) is a

> . . . volatile, mutual intertexture, the stuff that informs our interven-
> tions. And such is the implication of biology, the intelligence of its
> performativity, that Irigaray's *poetique de corps* might also be thought as
> biology rewriting itself.

It is thus biology, ourselves as bodies, that write. This, for Kirby,
is the beginning of a definition of *corporeography*: the body *at* the scene
of writing, the body *as* the scene of writing. In this work, the subject,
the embodied, sexed and raced biology of the subject, the material
world, and language, are enfolded, folded into one another. It is
impossible to rewrite one without the other. Radical alterity is always
folded into the writing (Grosz 1995). There is no outside the text.

OR IS THERE?

In *Bodies that Matter* (1993a), Judith Butler records the way in which
she has been criticised for interrogating the limits of the body, for not

accepting that the body is simply there, in all its physical reality, to set limits on human existence—there 'outside the text'. These criticisms were in response to her 1990 argument that gender, and thus the gendered body, is a compulsory performance of heterosexuality that could be rewritten or performed differently. Butler explores the nature/culture interface through the question of corporeality, bringing together the understanding of the interpellation of the subject into relations of power (from Althusser) with Foucault's notion of bodily inscription, Austin's of performativity (1962) and Derrida's understandings of iterativity.

Almost her first enterprise is one that connects with Kirby's (1997) and Grosz' (1995) questions about the complex folding of reality and language into one another. It concerns the question of the cultural construction of the body and the ways in which what Kirby calls the 'topography' or 'scenography' of this construction might be said to matter. Butler (1993a, p. 9) sets herself the task of showing that, despite the fact that we cannot access an 'outside of language', nevertheless the 'material' cannot be left outside consideration. We must analyse the 'process of materialization that stabilizes over time to produce the effect of boundary, fixity, and surface we call matter'. This is important to her because of the link between matter and bodies. We must, she says, challenge the hegemony which banishes certain ('lacking'/deficient) bodies to an abject and excluded realm, a realm that is aligned with the natural, the brutish and the animal—the realm of the material, of matter. We must challenge this in order to force 'a radical rearticulation of what qualifies as bodies that matter' (1993a, p. 16). Kirby (1997) agrees with and supports Butler thus far, but she points to the foreclosure of matter in Butler's own work, suggesting that it is Butler's *linguisticism* which is the problem, that she has not understood the way in which Saussure radically problematises the relationship between the sign and matter.

I would argue that it is not so much foreclosure of matter as the reinstatement of the metaphor of inscription that is at stake here. The body is always posited as prior to signification in psychoanalysis, but Butler argues that the body that is imagined as prior to signification is in fact 'an effect of signification' (1993a, p. 30). This is so because it is the speech act as performative (for example, psychoanalysis as speech act) which both *materialises* (produces) and *makes bodies matter* (makes signify as matter). Thus, Butler argues, the psychoanalytic body is always already inscribed. In Butler's use of Austin's term *performative* as rewritten by Derrida (1982), however, there is a different reading possible. She also argues that language *performatively* 'delimits and contours the body' (1990, p. 30), shapes the matter of the body (as I read it). Here, I think, there is a confusion between (or a conflation of) performance and performativity: the former term would imply practice, a doing involving language perhaps; the latter involves the practical/material effect of a speech act. Read this way, Butler's inter-textually derived metaphors—inscription/discipline (Foucault), enunciation/performativity (Benveniste and Austin), interpellation (Althusser), habitus (Bourdieu), and so on—produce a body which is materially crafted in and through practice *and* inscribed in and by discourse. Butler overworks the term performative. The result is cer-tainly not the same as Kirby's corporeography, but nor is it as different as Kirby thinks when she argues that: 'What I am trying to conjure here is some "sense" that word and flesh are utterly implicated' (1997, p. 127).

In a sense both are arguing that the question of the matter of bodies and of how it is that some, and not other, bodies matter, must be central to feminist agendas. Kirby is concerned that bodies are foregrounded so that the 'proper' subject cannot continue to imagine itself as mind, not made of matter at all—separate from the radical alterity of otherness. This conceptual legacy, she argues, is what produces homophobia, sexism and racism. This is why she is so insistent on the need to examine matter/substance itself, through scientifc discourses and understandings, if that helps, to 'make strange' our own commonsense understandings because these issues are 'wrought with/in flesh' and can only be changed when the conceptual universe makes it *impossible* to other them, to put them outside the universe of signification where, in effect, they are beyond our concerns.

BUTLER, ITERATIVITY AND INTERVENTION

The issue of performativity, and the associated question of iterativity, which are discussed only in passing in Kirby, remain issues for those engaging in feminist postlinguistics. Butler uses the *iteration of the perfomative* to explain how bodies are gendered, crafted and inscribed with sexuality—a compulsory heterosexuality—but she is also using the notion of *iterability* to theorise the possibility of change. Iterative prohibition as performative speech act, she argues, produces what it names, the very things it seeks to prohibit. She derives this idea from the fact that the very structural stuff of the iterable performative, a mark which exerts a force, which 'operates' (Derrida 1982, p. 321), ensures that it will 'engender infinitely new contexts' (Derrida 1982, p. 320). Now I have a problem here, even if we add to this the fact that Butler is also conflating iterability with Foucault's concept of productive power.

My problem locates itself around the question of intervention. Butler clearly wants to intervene but there is no indication that she actually succeeds, except textually. She does 'make visible' the gender hierarchy and its mode of production via the constructivism of the performative. But there is no real reason why that construction should have functioned to produce *just that* form of compulsory heterosexuality if, in fact, power is productive and iteration will bring change.

According to Butler, 'culture' already excludes that which it cannot normatively contain; so are we to suppose that this exclusion is the *productive* result of iterable performativity?

> Gender is the repeated stylization of the body, a set of repeated acts within a highly rigid regulatory frame that congeals over time to produce the appearance of substance of a natural sort of being. (Butler 1990, p. 33)

We still need to understand this, however, against the argument that the very complexity of the 'discursive map that constructs gender' holds out the possibility of 'a disruption of [its] univocal posturing' (Butler 1990, p. 32; see also Threadgold 1997a). The difficulty here is one that Butler acknowledged in Gender Trouble (1990, pp. 240–1), the problem of what constitutes a politically useful ('affirmative') resignification (notice how we are back in the realm of the signifer, not in the space of the materiality of bodies) and how to ensure that it happens.

So the question we have to ask is whether 'making visible' what iteration does and then allowing iteration to do its work is actually enough to effect a change, to radically alter the system of gender hierarchy and compulsory heterosexuality. Like Kirby, I do not think this is enough and I do think Butler's account in the end is limited to a linguistic rewriting which fails to understand the way oppression may actually craft and shape the materiality of the body through, for example, starvation, torture, long hours of lowly paid and exploited labour and so on. As Pheng Cheah (1994, pp. 138–9) has argued, the materiality of the body, its physical substance, in many contexts (some perilously close to home) 'bears the instituted trace of the spacing and timing of imperialism' but this body of 'the (other) woman' cannot be accommodated within an academic feminism informed by the 'whiteness' and the privilege of the psychoanalytical and poststructuralist narrative. Even if we return to what might constitute a successful *textual* intervention (a process of resignification), we find that Derrida, the theorist who 'invented' iteration, was never satisfied that *iteration* itself was enough.

Returning to what Derrida had to say about Austin, Derrida argued that Austin saw the *conventionality* of the contexts in which statements were made but failed to understand the 'intrinsic conventionality of locution itself' (1982, p. 323). This was the circumstance which impelled Derrida to theorise *iterativity*, to place the focus firmly back on the structure and form of the utterance, which must be iterable to be comprehensible. Iteration was a term which recognised this but which also deconstructed the opposition between repetition and change, understanding that repetition always involves a certain instability. But Derrida certainly did not stop there. He was, and always has been, concerned primarily with disrupting citationality, the iteration of deeply embedded understandings.

The structure which maintains itself despite the changing context, the 'huge stabilities' of discourse, 'a very profound and very solid zone of implicit "conventions" or "contracts"' which 'require analysis' (he is speaking here (1988, p. 144) of Rousseau's texts), 'stratifications that are already differential and of a very great stability with regard to the relations of forces and all the hierarchies of hegemonies they suppose or put into practice' (1988, p. 144)—these are what he is interested in deconstructing. He can only do this, however, he can only perform the 'doubling commentary', the reading/writing which is deconstruction, the paraphrase, the interpretive reading, if: (a) he can count on 'a very strong probability of consensus regarding the intelligibility of the text'; and (b) he is able to 'analyze the play or relative indetermination' that opens a space for his interpretation. And that requires a knowledge, he says, of the French language, 'its grammar and vocabulary', 'the rhetorical uses of this language in society and in the literary code of the epoch etc.' (1988, p. 144). Barbara Johnson, in her introduction to Derrida's *Dissemination* (1981), demonstrates very effectively how it is possible to outline the methodology of Derrida's texts and how many of these methods are in fact based on linguistics or rhetoric, even if he uses these tools to deconstruct their very premises.

It seems, then, that there is absolutely no reason why, on the assumption that we are being poststructuralist, we should simply wait for iterativity to do its work. We may indeed find it very useful, if the task is to understand how the iteration of performative speech acts affects and shapes the stuff of bodies, and if we want to change that, to use other kinds of discourse analysis which help us to focus on the materiality of texts (Threadgold 1997a; Fairclough 1989) and other kinds of theories which help us to understand how texts and bodies fold into one another (Grosz 1995; Bourdieu 1990; Smith 1990). As Derrida says, there are many different kinds of iteration. Processes of resignification (Butler's term, to be compared with 'making visible' in critical discourse analysis) may work in some contexts (if, as he also says, we rely on a consensus as to interpretation to make space for radical change) where we are literate and privileged. But, in the end, doesn't Derrida too, suffer from a certain linguisticism? The idea that, in rewriting textual significations, however deeply sedimented, however profoundly embodied, however the writing carries its others within itself, you will radically change the world, is and can be only a partial answer to social change.

Writing is a performance of the body. It may also have performative effects, but not always. The metaphor of performance (Parker and Sedgewick 1995; Threadgold 1997a) is more useful than that of performativity alone because it will not allow the elisions of the body that performativity permits. To perform is to struggle with the substance of the body. Writing/performance involves the electrical currents of brain activity, memory and forgetting (Wilson 1998), the active use of the musculature, the weeping of tears, bodily sensations, connections with other bodies, seepings and reactions (Kirby 1997). In a sense, writing always forces us to engage with the other that is in ourselves—the body, nature, race, woman and so on—but it is very easy to forget, to deny this and too easy to believe that matter, the matter of difference, is beyond the limits of our activities.

SPIVAK AND CORPOREOGRAPHY

It is interesting to consider here Spivak's reading of the chapter from Derrida's *Of Grammatology* which I read earlier. She reads it in the context of arguing that Foucault's work has led to the kind of positioning just described: the first world intellectual, having decided that the other is forever other, 'letting the oppressed speak for themselves' (Spivak 1988, p. 292). Derrida, she thinks, is less dangerous than Foucault. He is less dangerous because he does not argue that 'deconstruction' leads to 'ideological demystification'. He understands that it cannot escape empiricism (Derrida 1988, p. 292) and he knows that the political question is whether deconstruction can stop the 'ethnocentric Subject from establishing itself by selectively defining an Other'.

For Spivak, Derrida's warning is precisely against 'too great a claim for transparency' (the claim of 'making visible') because of 'an awareness of the discourse of presence in one's *own* critique'. Derrida, unlike Foucault, is aware of the 'complicity between writing, the opening of domestic and civil society, and the structures of desire, power and capitalization' (Spivak 1988, p. 293). Her conclusions are interesting (1988, p. 294):

> [W]hat I find useful [in Derrida's work] is the sustained and developing work on the *mechanics* of the constitution of the Other; we can use it to much greater analytic and interventionist advantage than invocations of the *authenticity* of the Other. On this level, what remains useful in Foucault is the mechanics of disciplinarization and institutionalization, the constitution, as it were, of the colonizer.

The politics of writing, writing the body, corporeography at the scene of writing, discourse analysis using poststructuralist methods and metalanguages, all of these are different to politics which intervene in corporeal and 'Othered' spaces, but as Spivak's reading/writing shows, as Butler's struggles with language demonstrate and as Kirby's intervention argues, they can never be entirely separate: they are enfolded and we can never, even if we would, work on one without intervening in the other. Perhaps one of the most interesting developments in recent years has been the growing use of poststructuralist methodologies by postmodernist and feminist geographers (Gibson-Graham 1996; Nast and Pile 1998) who understand, because of their own disciplinary trainings in reading the writings of space, just how closely imbricated bodies and writing, bodies writing, writing bodies, are, in the making of the material spaces we inhabit. Pheng (1994) argues that the metaphor of inscription would have to be rethought as *habitation*. Perhaps this is what is happening in this work which makes space matter to understand the matter of bodies but knows that matter and discourse are also enfolded. The unpredictabilities of that, the dangers of believing we can know and do, and the constant need to know and do more, remain then the most immediate and challenging aspects of work in feminist discourse analysis and in postlinguistics as we approach the millenium.

4 Dangerously radioactive:[1] the plural vocalities of radio talk

Jackie Cook

In this chapter I suggest, along with Bell and van Leeuwen (1994), that contemporary Australian talk radio is producing diverse, complex, heterogeneous and multilayered texts. Yet both radio as a medium and radio talk as a site of discursive social formation are regarded within the limited research literature on talk radio as monolithic and unitary institutional sites, producing transparent conversational texts, continuous with other examples of everyday casual talk. My work thus seeks to problematise 'radio talk', by setting it back inside its institutional contexts, to examine how these influence and constrain the talk in which we participate as both listeners and students of radio.

Non-critical understandings of radio as a talk site perhaps indicate the extent to which radio is a victim of its own success at naturalising itself within multiple layers of social and cultural activity. In its heyday—the 1930s and 1940s—radio's developing production techniques rapidly became buried beneath the exigencies of wartime censorship. The subsequent emergent dominance of television saw to it that radio in Australia, as elsewhere, became the poor relation in media studies. Its dramatic transformation into an interactive talk site, through the developing prevalence of interview over commentary genres, remained largely unnoticed in media studies, as did the development of new formats with the arrival of talkback technologies. Radio's latter-day flexibility, its use of modern outside broadcast techniques and cellular phone links, and the pluralism of vocalities produced by the enduring success of the community broadcasting movement, have each been under-recognised and rarely discussed within media scholarship.

One result of this inattention to contemporary developments has

59

been the inadequate critique of the persistent construction around radio of a myth of spontaneity and free participatory access, in turn giving rise to the sense that radio talk is initially identical with unmediated everyday social conversation. This perception has proven at once a strength and a peril. While at one level it has opened radio—as a source of powerful and very often disputational social 'talk' texts—to research, it has too often failed to deal with that talk as 'text', specifically situated within complex layers of radio production and listener reception, as well as socially and culturally embedded within established discourses. Analysis of radio talk too often fails to take into account those other conversations with which it is always intertwined. Those studies which have been undertaken, for instance Higgins and Moss (1982) and Scannell (1991), either submerge the medium of delivery in the analysis of ensuing social relations and power differentials or, conversely, limit the social analysis, in detailing the talk of specific format genres.

Since radio is the only mass communication medium limited to a single sensory output, perhaps it is the seeming purity of its exclusive basis in talk which has led to its being critically conceived as particularly close to the broader discourse practices of its social setting (see, for instance, Hilmes 1997, chapter 7). But, while radio talk is undeniably a powerful agent of discursive social formation, it is not and can never be an entirely 'natural' site. At a point when its powers are demonstrably accelerating in a period of re-emergence (Miller 1993), its new formats are showing its capacity once again to 'vanish' perceptually into an intensified hyper-naturalising whose progress we can trace as it occurs around us. The re-technologisation of new layers of ubiquitous siting, such as radio rediffusion in shopping malls, elevators and workplaces, or during telephone call-waiting, demonstrates how contemporary radio as a medium should call for more, rather than less, critical attention. And, as part of this rendering aware of the existence of an increasingly omnipresent radio voice within everyday existence, there needs to be a technique which can estrange that radio voice, to divide it from the talk of everyday conversation, and reveal the complex layers of its own particular selectivity. My work seeks out and stresses what the production practices of 'talk radio' bring to what is increasingly under scrutiny as 'radio talk'.

RADIO AS A DISCOURSE

While my own study shares Fairclough's (1992) view that radio talk, like all media text, has much to reveal about the transformations currently occurring inside and alongside dominant discourses, my contribution to this field is a focus on how radio as a set of institutional practices, in regard to both its station-based production (Miller, Lucy and Turner 1993) and its listener reception (Hilmes 1997), continues to elaborate distinctive discursive forms and power relations. While these are continuous with, and even overtly promote, those broader social discursive patterns which Fairclough identifies as contributing to the establishment and maintenance of specific orders of discourse (1992, pp. 68–71), their effectivity is not only intensified by the processes of mediation which the broadcast spoken word still carries, but is formed into peculiarly multilayered structures by the processes of broadcasting 'production'.

Radio is more than simply a technology of delivery or a representational text. It has developed strategies which can simultaneously familiarise and defamiliarise talk in ways immediately perceptible to any individual who is interviewed or who phones in to a talkback program and subsequently hears themself on-air. Radio has its own distinctive techniques for selection, regulation, and transformation of talk, all the time constructing myths about itself— representing itself as immediate, spontaneous, low-tech, accessible, democratising and 'real'. So successfully has it developed and deployed these techniques for the production of particular forms of radio talk, and the simultaneous suppression of its own formative and regulatory practices, that it has become a site where a powerful, top-rating station such as Sydney's talkback specialist, 2UE, can insist on your right as a listener-caller to their programs to 'have your say', without arousing any consciousness of the ironies of the invitation.

Analysis of radio talk, and especially of that which, like the discourses within and around talkback, represents itself as openly 'interactive' with (misnamed) 'listeners', must take into account those elements of radio practice occurring during the professional production of that talk, as well as in the highly active 'reception' of listener 'talkback'. Here I accept Fairclough's schematisation, admitting into the analysis the complex meshing of what he calls his 'three-dimensional conception of discourse' (1992, p. 72). This positions the 'discursive practice' of production, distribution and consumption of texts as always and everywhere carried out within, and on behalf of, broader social practices—at the same time admitting, as in Hall's formulation (1980, p. 1996), the existence of negotiative and resistive responses as well as consensual reception. Where my analysis differs from Fairclough's (other than in its focus on radio, a rare sectoral choice in Fairclough's work) is in its consideration of those parts of the resultant radio 'text' not produced by interactive talk with the community of listener-callers. I accentuate instead those aspects of the talk which result from the in-studio broadcast practices of program presenters, acting as 'talk hosts.' The talk as it goes to air with its invitations to respond is already simultaneously caught up in other dialogues: those covert or even disruptive exchanges with in-studio production team colleagues, which manage the flows of broadcast talk. In other words, my analysis recognises that a part of the elaboration of the 'relational' aspects of radio discourse practice is initiated before what Hall would see as distribution of this mediated talk-text. It is this processing which then models discursive relations for those other talk relations which ensue, first as listener-callers 'talk back' to the program hosts on air and, subsequently, as they talk through 'reception' within their own social networks. Perhaps most significantly, I problematise this extended relational processing in the conversations which ensue with listener-callers, not by accounting for the differences between officially 'on-air' texts and in-studio talk, but by uncovering marked continuities.

Talkback radio claims that it centres around the potential for participant callers freely to 'air their point of view', yet it simultaneously constrains that participation within a range of control techniques. The in-studio communication behaviours shown in the off-air talk of production teams have much to reveal about the processing of this particular illusion of free access. Those audio channels which do not usually go to air, on which frenetic instructions, interpersonal banter, time-control cues and even frustration-release comments constantly occur, have a powerful influence on the structuring of on-air talk. The 'at home' situatedness of the listener-caller is equally formative. The interventions of partners, mates, party guests, kids and even pets 'get into' what is said, not as irrelevancies or interruptions but as significant elements in the formation of the talk. The now classic insistence of talk hosts to callers that they 'turn down their radio' to prevent distorting feedback through the telephone, acts as an important element of the transformation from listener to listener-caller: a re-channelling of the voice and an implicit assent to the many regulatory processes which going on-air entails. Each process involves elements contributing to the social positioning of radio talk within the broader contexts of power-within-discourse. Talk radio is never the intensely focused two-way interaction it represents itself to be. Instead it is 'opened' at each end simultaneously into the broader social, with all that that entails.

It is these dimensions of radio as a consistent and coherent 'practice' which this chapter attempts to reintroduce. I do not, however, undertake this through observational study of the in-studio behaviours of production staff or those of listener reception—although each might profitably be undertaken, and full observation study of radio reception in particular is markedly overdue. I work instead to foreground the ways in which what can be called the radio texts, the conversations which result from the interaction of talk show hosts and their callers, can themselves reveal in-studio, regulatory practices at work. I seek out the textual moments in a given broadcast where the smooth linearity of production to reception is disrupted; where there are what Fairclough calls 'cruces and crises' in the discourse—and especially in the relational work of that discourse. Nor are disruptions difficult to detect. Indeed, so prevalent are the breaches in the techniques and behaviours that radio discourse seeks to establish, that they dominate transactions between hosts and callers. They can be seen to have a major influence on the production of a dominant relation of (conversational) exchange. If, as many commentators have observed, talk radio discourses do go on to modify broader social discourses in their turn, I contend that it is at the moment of active co-production between broadcast team, on-air host, and 'caller-on-behalf-of-all-listeners', that meaning is most forcefully made, and power relations forged.

RADIO TALK'S UNIQUE DISCURSIVE SPACE

In the first instance, the discourses established within radio talk are a product of their connection at one end of the continuum that is broadcast talk, to the 'in-studio' locatedness of the talk show host and his production team (in Australia, most hosts are male; most production teams are female). It is at this point that they engage with the institutional discourses of a professional media organisation: language policies, advertising or sponsorship roles, and so on, and beyond the organisation's ideological positioning within the public service, commercial or community. Whether A, B or C-licensed,[2] a given Australian radio station maintains watchful limits on the talk which constitutes its program delivery. It directly controls on-air talk through the broad generic restraints of program formatting (see Miller 1993; Stewart 1990) to the narrower constraints involved in the regular feedback on presentation behaviours from program managers to on-air staff and production teams. Indirectly, a radio station's controls are extended through its response to ratings, licensing and other policy regulation, and the flow of advertising or sponsorship revenues.

Operating even more implicitly are specific sets of what Bourdieu (1995) would recognise as 'dispositions', manifested in the attitudes and practices of broadcasters. Particular forms of vocality, acquired registers, expertise within formats and favoured speech genres, together comprise a broadcast performance which listeners are encouraged to regard as indicating the existence of a distinctive individual 'personality', but which the radio industry's hiring-and-firing procedures and selection of personnel to work particular shifts demonstrate are acquired skills.

These preferred behaviours, rendered and read back as 'personality', do not operate only in constructing that flow of conversation with interviewees and callers. In commercial talkback in particular they are also demonstrated on a daily basis in the negotiations and contestations occurring in-studio, enmeshed in the talk of production teams. Intersecting the broadcast comments of the presenter are the unheard organising conversations of technical and program producers; researchers and news journalists; and receptionists and call-screeners, who prearrange and pace the flow of talk. The increased seepage of such in-house talk into what is actually broadcast says much of the powers of contemporary radio talk's myths of its own spontaneity and 'interpersonal' immediacy. Conventionally suppressed on the advice of training procedures and station manuals as 'unprofessional', such half-joking collusion with breaches of good conduct and 'correct' public discourse practices, shows how far institutional radio talk's familiarity and friendliness is building a private into a public voice.

The tendency is conterminous with Tolson's (1991) isolation of 'populism' as a major transformation in the order of public media discourse: a blending of earlier and more formal 'public service' informational styles with a drive towards entertainment (Scannell 1992). At the same time, it engages a long-established tradition inside radio's own programming practices which Hilmes describes as a simultaneous marking out of the 'sacralised', or not-to-be-mentioned-on-air, and its selective violation. The success of many of America's early radio shows she attributes to this tendency: 'it may be the very balancing acts performed by these programs that made them so popular' (1997, p. 185). In talkback radio it is the rehearsal of combative semi-insult and apparent professional ineptitude which licenses participation from listeners; a kind of highly-skilled and carefully produced amateurism which works as an anti-glossiness in the on-air presentation, and so invites 'the everyday' voice of the caller onto the air. The process is most consistently modelled in those violations of formality and consensual, seamless, professional radio flow allowed to go to air on commercial talkback.

Such comment and banter should, however, not be seen as a disruption to the flow of broadcast talk. On the contrary, it is continuous with its broader ideological positionings. It both speeds up the pace of exchanges by adding to their mass, and adds to the characterisation of the talk as combative, argumentative and competitive. As Fairclough would have it (1995b, p. 60), this is a moment where the 'communicative event'—in this case, spontaneous criticism, personal or social, directly voiced—intersects with and endorses the 'order of discourse'. Talkback radio conversation, a genre whose greatest successes occur within the free-market 'enterprise discourse' of commercial stations, thrives on competitive argument.

In this chapter I follow the programming presentation 'talk' behaviours most consistently engaged in in a night-time talkback program: 'The Stan Zemanek Show'. Here the host's persona is built around an untrammelled and aggressive masculinity, developed over familiar patriarchal notions of unassailable authority and a perverse yet concomitant larrikin disruptiveness and resistance to regulation— all played out as argument. Broadcasting on top-rating Sydney talkback station 2UE, home to John Laws and Alan Jones (nationally top-ranking talk hosts), host Stan Zemanek, with over twenty years experience in radio (*Sydney Morning Herald*, 'The Guide', 18–24 August 1997, pp. 4–5), and a staggering weekly programming output of between fifteen and twenty-five hours of talkback, regularly breaches the flow of listener-directed talk to give priority to those in-studio staff and broadcasting procedures usually unheard. He becomes, in Goffman's (1981) terms, both 'author' and 'animator' of the discourses at play in his programming. He is attending to talk which produces and gives priority to his own power as it places him at the centre of a production team, and at the same time allowing it to be 'overheard' by what is effectively, at that moment, a secondary audience of at-home listeners. Zemanek's behaviour within the conventionally unheard exchanges of in-studio talk demonstrates the continuity, and thus doubled power, of his position.

At one level many of his spontaneous comments on his own broadcasting practice appear as very much the sort of errors that Goffman analysed in his 1981 study. Zemanek reveals, however, a far more cavalier attitude towards the preservation of an aura of expertise than was the case for the 'announcers' of the earlier, more formal radio formats that Goffman analysed, or even for the strongly performative stylings used in DJ programs on music radio from the 1950s on (see Montgomery 1986). Zemanek actively reveals the often chaotic technical processes at work around him as he broadcasts.

The following texts are extracts from 'The Stan Zemanek Show', Radio 2UE, recorded 1–4 April 1996.

Extract 1

[Host's voice begins without full microphone sound, corrected half-way through the extract.]

> Z: Aaaand . . . a very good evening: YES! I suppose it would help if we turned the microphone on properly! Good evening and welcome . . .

The extract breaches the immediacy of the broadcast relation between host and listener in two ways: first, by indicating the presence of the technology and, second, by the recognition of a multiple presence within the studio, where 'we', and not 'I', turn on microphones. The immediate swing into listener address, 'good evening and welcome', does nothing to mitigate the heavy criticism of the 'aside', in which the host addresses in-studio staff. Both breaches show openly the split focus of talk-program address.

Extract 2

[The host comes out of a pre-recorded segment without engaging the seven-second delay required for phone-in security.]

> Z: It was 14 after the hour: this i-i-is, Stan Zemanek; and what am I gonna do now? I suppose . . . go into . . . delay.

While the host now accepts it is his own responsibility to correct the microphone delay, again he has no hesitation in talking the problem through on air, actually displaying those elements of broadcast practice designed to protect hosts from abusive callers, and so supposed to remain concealed. In a later exchange with a young caller who has Internet expertise, the host works to rebuild exactly this illusion of a non-technically-mediated immediacy of relation to his listener-callers yet, at the same time, cannot resist the technology's efficacy in 'magically' endorsing his own powers. The following exchange with caller 'Michael' reveals the centrality of the host's technical control over listener-caller voices and so enhances the importance of the destabilisation allowed in moments of banter or criticism with staffers —especially those which involve technical matters. They are, as Hilmes (1997) has suggested, instabilities set up and rehearsed to reassert rather than to release control.

Extract 3

[The caller, 'Michael', tells the host about the existence of a Stan Zemanek 'hate' page on the Internet. The caller has altered the 'hate' page to a 'like' page, and hopes to impress the host.]

 1 M: Hi how are ya Stan?
   Z: Yes Michael.
   M: (uhh, uhh) Yeah uum (uhh) you know how that person rang up said he was gonna do a hate page on the Internet?
   Z: (:::) Yeeess?
   M: A long time ago?
   Z: Yes . . .
   M: Well um he actually, did it,
10 Z: Did he really?
   M: Yep
   Z: He did a whole hate page on me!
   M: Yeah! (uhh) but, um, I did a favour for you Stan:
   Z: Yes . . .
   M: I changed it. I wrote: 'The best things about Stan'.
   Z: Oh this'll be good!
   M: An' um, I've had some, ah, someone sent me five letters? And they said, um, he doesn't like, how you cut off people?
20 Z: Yes—
   M: But he likes um the show.

[section deleted]

34 M: Can you like on the show tell them about the, show? I mean about the Internet? Um, the hate, er, like page?
   Z: Well I mean, I don't know anything about it—how about you send me in all the information?
   M: Send you all the information?
40 Z: Yeah, send me all the, er send me all the information by mail.
   M: By mail but I'm—
   Z: See we don't have the Internet here at 2UE we're not that up to date.
   M: Eh? What about your house, do you have the Internet?
   Z: No we don't.
   M: You don't! (haha)
   Z: No we don't. I can't even work a computer.
   M: Oh ha ha ha!

50 Z: I have about a dozen computers but I don't know how to
        work either one of them.
    M: Oh Stan I was wondering
    Z: Yes—
    M: —how do you cut off people?
    Z: Very easily:

[music sting]

The extract is particularly interesting given the arrival at 2UE in
the following month of their own Internet website, preparations for
which must have been well under way when Zemanek received this call.
The final rejection of this caller is of course specifically motivated by a
question (lines 51 and 53) about concealed radio practice: the host's
capacity to cut off a call with the flick of a switch. This question has
the potential to unearth some of the host's own professional abuses of a
still powerful, if outdated, technology—but at the same time the host's
reticence in approaching new technologies (and especially somebody
else's 'new') is there throughout the discussion. It is at one level an
extraordinary position from a commercial talkback host so strongly
directed towards the constant renewal of consumer desires for the new.
Yet the position is consistent with his awareness of the conservatism of
his mostly ageing audience, and of the degree to which the intensified
access to opinion formation represented by Internet use threatens his
own dominance via radio. His slip in grammatical control over the
number of computers he has ('I have about a *dozen* computers but I can't
work *either one* of them', line 49) and his apparent openness in admitting
a lack of expertise in the new technology, are immediately compensated
by his refusal to explain his control over the old, and by his demon-
stration of the power he thus retains, cutting off the caller who has dared
to question him. Nor is this preservation of power to himself, and
attribution of weakness or error to others, an isolated moment.

Extract 4

[The host comes out of a cart-taped promo-sting, and has trouble with
his headphone sound levels.]

    Z: Why are my headphones sooo . . . (::) so, ah, top? (::)
        Why are they . . . I don't know why (uhhh). This studio
        just seems to change, from day to day to day (hh) (:::)
        One of these days, somebody's going to wake up and say
        (uhh) (::) 'Let's get it fixed . . .' (Public voice resumes) 13
        13 32, aand, what have we got here: Terry hello!

Extract 5

[Coming out of a live-cross sports report, the host has failed to consult with the call-screener over an incoming VIP call: he goes off-air to do so. When he returns, his microphone is still engaged to the call-screener's—so he picks up and transmits the next call in both 'real time' and 'delay time'.]

Z: [music sting] YEes! 13 13 32 is-our-tele-phone-nu-mber
     . . . And, um—just excuse me folks I've just gotta tell
     Natasha something. [5 seconds of dead air] OK. Thank you
     very much for that; sorry, folks, I just have to (er-er)
     take—those little breaks—every now and then: Hello!
     Hello—Wayne! (::) [2 second delay-sound feeding back through the
     host's microphone, off broadcast output: thank you much for that: sorry
     fo -'] Way-ne! [delay sound: 'take those little breaks every now and
     then'] I see-ee . . . (ahem) [mic. lead noise] Are you there
     Wayne? [mic. lead noise, phone beep] Hello! [phone hangs up:
     engaged beeps] See! [engaged beeps as host speaks] Fantastic, isn't
     it. [beeps] Absolutely wonderful. [beeps] The apprentice
     Labor people [beeps] they haven't yet quite worked out
     [beeps] how to work a phone [beeps] They don't have the
     brains [beeps] to be able to sort of converse on the
     telephone and [beeps] to er communicate with their fellow
     human beings

The host is already working here to recover the breaches in those barricades of powerful speech behaviours and technical devices behind which he constructs his unassailable position of authority. It is arguable, given the range of such moments across shows, extending even to examples which capture staffers' voices on the host's microphone as they respond to his off-air demands, that such comment from the host operates less as a revelatory breach in control than as yet another opportunistic incursion into a new area of social space: the usually unheard form of in-studio communication. This, in effect, adds to the pervasiveness, and so the power, of the Zemanek position. After all, inside this newly revealed social space, the host is still dominant, making open demands on a group of very much subordinate, and universally female, production staff, who thus come to occupy, in technology analyst Sadie Plant's (1995) terms, 'the inside of the machine':

> In a sense, women have always been the machine parts for a very much male culture. Women have been the means of reproducing the species,

reproducing communications—secretaries etc.—which is obviously similar to the role of machines and tools.

Ultimately then, this interior world, in which every aspect of the
host's demands for the authoritative information and technical
enhancement that sustain his power must be met and where lapses
are just as instantly exposed and criticised, is also reproductive of
male power. Certainly, whenever there is error or inadequacy in the
technologically-armoured carapace of the host's voice as powerful
persona, the host's self-representation of inviolable authority, it is
attributed at once to women staff.

Extract 6

[Music: *Johnny-be-good*—host begins to speak before the end of the
track.]

  Z: Yes [music] Oh! [music] oh! [Music] Yes—that is *Johnny-
       be-good* and that is Doug Parkinson and let me tell you
       they're gonna be all over the joint: ah, so you, better get
       along, to see the Doug Parkinson Buddy Holly Show, ah,
       because it is fantastic (uhh) Apparently they're, aaahh,
       they're . . . still travelling around: they're gonna be at the
       Parra—Riverside Theatre at Parramatta on the 20th of
       April, and ah, Yalla Wool Shed, ah that's down near
       Wollongong, on the 26th and 27th of April, ah, and ah
       Belmont Sailing Club up there in ah Port Macquarie on
       on as they head off on their northern New South Wales
       tour, (::) What is it I say? (:::) Did I say La—(::) I said
       PORT Macquarie did I? OK it's LAKE Macquarie, thank
       you Shirley—well you are from that way aren't you. You're
       just a Newcastle girl at heart aren't you. (:::) Hunter
       Valley. (::) Muswellbrook. I see. OK. (Uhh) well now that
       we've found out where Shirley ah comes from, ah anyway,
       ah up there at uh Lake Macquarie on ah Belmont there
       Belmont Sailing Club on the 4th of May . . .

Extract 7

[Caller 'Rocky' in a reasonably friendly, bantering tone, accuses the
host of behaving badly to an earlier female caller.]

  R: . . . but I agree with that last lady mate (ha) you are a
       pig, there's no question about that.

Z: I am a pig! Shirley: this man just called me a pig! can you
   believe that?

[section deleted]

Z: Now, listen, my producer's here, and, um, she's the reason
   why this show's the way it is
R: (indecipherable)—my heart's bleeding for you
Z: Well I mean she's the one that tells me what to do, I
   ju—I don't—I just sit here and I'm just a mouth piece for
   Shirley.
R: . . . well that's true.

[section deleted]

Z: Shirley do you think I'm a pig?
S: [voice off] No . . .
Z: I'm—there's—there was (hahaha) a little bit of hesitation
   in that (hahaha) Shirley! Hahahaha! There was a bit of
   hesitation in that! Ohohohohoho! Oooh, Shirley! (:) Can
   I have another cuppa tea please?

Extract 8

[Host moves into a new call sequence: uncertain of the next technical
change; he is presumably taking off-air instruction from producer
Shirley through his headphones.]

Z: Yeees, OK, what have I got here, what do I have to do
   now? I'm just taking directions from the lovely Shirley, an'
   I think I'll press this button:

[an ad plays]

In each of these examples women staffers, attempting to remedy
the host's technical incompetence or factual error, are submitted to a
kind of direct or indirect teasing mockery which is not far removed
from manipulative violence. Producer Shirley, in Extract 6, making
an important correction to the locale of an advertised performance—
a sponsor's product, and so an element central to the show—is first
of all bunted hard with reference to her obscure country origins, then
manoeuvred into appearing to be wasting program time with trivia,
and finally slapped firmly into place as 'tea maker' to the star. She is
rendered first as local, rather than having the globalising powers to
rove at will across sectors which the host preserves for himself; then
she is demoted to the merely domestic. When, in the subsequent call,

Extract 7, 'Rocky' rebukes the host over just such a contemptuous and violent treatment of an earlier female caller, the host retaliates by claiming, in a surprising mock-anti-heroic ploy, to be 'Shirley's mouth-piece'—at her beck and call—so effectively shifting all blame for program misdemeanours onto her. It is however a timely reminder of the one element of accuracy in his portrayal of the power relations in play in-studio: the producer's capacity to be speaking off-air to the presenter throughout his on-air conversations, and so to be, in effect, inside his head.

What is centred here—by the hurt the host's persona has sustained, once outside an arena of his own control—is the degree to which his vocal presentation, his radio style, constitute a powerful masculinity, built against any hint of female authority or autonomy. This is beyond the representations of patriarchal authority detailed in earlier studies of radio talkback (Potts 1989; Higgins and Moss 1982; Hobson 1980) in which paternalistic male authority directly asserts itself and seeks to control female opinion and behaviour. While 'The Stan Zemanek Show' overtly revisits this aspect of patriarchal authority, what is under scrutiny here is the role that radio can play in the constitution of masculinity, rather than simply its rehearsal in relational talk with women callers. The spread of that constitutive masculinity across all layers of social space, the private as much as the public; its equation with dominant social values; and the apparent fixing of those values in the construction of a coherent, stable and powerful 'King Stanley' as the ultimate embodiment of a dynamic 1990s entrepreneurial masculinity, work together in a continuous line from in-studio spats to every other form of on-air interaction.

RADIO'S DISCURSIVE GENDERING OF SOCIAL SPACE

The beliefs expounded in 'The Stan Zemanek Show' are thus founded on the daily elaboration of a myth of outwardly-directed male agency over the reality of in-studio female control. The myth is then extended outwards from its base in bullying control of female staffers, to a rehearsal of its powers in combative exchanges with aggressive male callers. Setting up a relation of dispute and argumentation through his construction of an unassailable masculine authority, extended to his male callers as a challenge to try out their power against his own, Zemanek produces a rarely-countered gender divide in his callers. Female callers respond with collusive strategies which operate as a form of fan adulation—and even as direct financial gain for the host, as regular women callers set up social groups to track his cabaret performances across metropolitan Sydney's Rugby League Club venues and to sell tickets to their friends. The collusive nature of these calls is displayed in their endorsement of every opinion the host voices, and in their personal response to criticism of the host from other callers. The collusive relation is capped by an extensive program of gift exchanges (most often sponsors' promotional give-aways in return for home-baked treats) which epitomises the classically patriarchal role played out with women callers.

Male callers are positioned in a more complex relation. In accepting the invitation to verbal combat, which the technological inequality of their bandwidth-suppressed voices and the host's powers to override their opinions never allow them to win, aggressive male callers still reproduce the host's authority. He is consistently the 'winner' in each debate, however, and the ratings victor in the red-hot and no-holds-barred verbal sparring which results.

There is on-air undeniably what Hutchby (1996) has identified as an 'asymmetry' in Zemanek's social relations. It runs all the way from the host's power to represent even his own errors in studio as the mistakes of his colleagues, through his persistent use of a range of other abuses of conversational power relations. When he disrupts conventions of conversational and disputational turntaking by over-riding responses with the 'ducker' device (an automatic control on the microphone which runs the host's voice over the caller's), by cutting callers off to ensure that the host has the last word, or even by summarising a call after it has been cut off, the technically-enhanced powers to control conversational exchanges help to produce what is subsequently read as a powerful masculinity within the talk of this form of contentious talkback. As with the commercial exchanges which such talk shows promote, and the intensely competitive marketing ethics they both espouse and deploy, all the talk texts admitted to air—and especially those selected for replay as promotional clips or for marketing as CD compilations—demonstrate submission to the powerful talk strategies of the host. The more aggressive the contention and argumentation, the more dramatic the conflict—the greater the power exercised by the host, and the higher the ratings.

Turntaking, Fairclough reminds us, 'depends on (and is a part of) power relationships between participants' (1989, p. 134). Hutchby (1996) analyses its regulatory systems to isolate asymmetrical power relations in argumentation, demonstrating in great detail the strategies used both to prolong and control debate—and to end it at moments of peak advantage. His analysis does much to identify techniques that Zemanek can be shown to use to assert his own persona as one of unassailable authority. But beyond the systems of interaction, both Zemanek and his callers explicitly equate this combative structuring of talk with the sorts of physical and aggressive masculinity once identified with Australian larrikinism. Caller 'Henry', angry with Zemanek for both his racism and his scorn for the older forms of physical power displayed, for instance, in the heroic manual labour of wharfies, reads the host's talk performance as the explicit invitation to combat that such talk actually enacts. Henry's response to the host's aggressive banter presumes an already articulated masculine discourse of insult and challenge to combat and, in so doing, creates a new context for their actual articulation, by challenging the host to abandon the unlocatability of his mediated, virtual radio self, safely within its studio and protective technologies, in favour of a direct hand-to-hand stoush in a Brisbane boxing ring.

Extract 9

[Caller Henry and Zemanek.]

H: So whatta ya got against us wharfies?
Z: Against you wharfies?
15 H: Yeah (..) (and a) blackfella
Z: I don't have anything against blackfellas as well
H: You DO ya has a go all the time
Z: Well no I don't I don't have a go all a the time, I call a spade a spade
H: What, you calling me a spade now?
20 Z: Aw . . . you idiot. I mean, what did . . . what did you do for brains?
H: What are you doin' when you come up 'ere?
Z: When I come up . . .
H: (gonna come up 'ere?)
Z: When I come up where?
25 H: To Brisbane.
Z: When I come up to Brisbane?
H: Yeah.
Z: What about it?
H: When ya come up.
30 Z: Yes, when I come up . . .
H: . . . you're always pickin' on people
Z: No I don't

H: You do

Z: I give people a serve who are . . . who're not doing the right thing

35 H: (indecipherable) call 'em out

Z: You what?

H: You wanna call 'em out all the time.

Z: (. . .) Mate, you really have an inferiority complex.

H: You wanna call us out.

40 Z: Call—call you out for what?

H: I'll fight every time.

Z: Who're you?

H: (. . .) I could beat you.

Z: You probably could.

45 H: (. . .) Well 'ow come you always back down?

Z: Back down for what?

H: From a fight. When somebody calls you out.

Z: Really? Are you calling me out?

H: Yeah.

50 Z: OK, well, where do you live—where are you tonight?

H: In Brisbane!

Z: In Brisbane! Alright, well you wanna meet me on the, aah, the, the, the steps of the Town Hall in Brisbane tonight?

H: You're not up 'ere . . .

55 Z: That's ve-ry clev-er of you: boy, what a bright spark YOU are!

H: When you come up in a coupla weeks eh?

Z: Oh, look, yeah—when I come up in a coupla weeks how about I meet you on the steps of the Town Hall?

H: OK

60 Z: Will you be there?

H: I'll be there.

The degree to which the host himself recognises the accuracy of this reading of his insults as a game of calling out, enjoys the exchange and works to prolong it, is marked in the degree to which his usual abuse of turntaking slowly evolves into a far more equal exchange. By the later stages of this exchange (actually more than twice the length of the extract given above, and an unusually lengthy exchange with a single caller), Zemanek is offering conversational gambits, rather than fielding them or cutting them off. Within this particular genre of aggressive and combative talk, which Zemanek has made his own, an initial asymmetry in power relations can shift significantly—even perversely to a kind of consensus.

To examine what has produced this shift within the exchange between Zemanek and Henry, it is first necessary to move beyond the careful structuring of the turntaking displayed, and into a broader vision of where each party places the other socially. Hutchby's awareness of the mixing of social spheres and associated genres sets up his study of talk-radio argument as asymmetrical power. For him, 'utterances are not produced as isolated actions but as actions embedded in an ongoing context of interaction' (1996, p. 10). This is a context which can alter, can achieve better definition, as each party gains a better sense of who they are dealing with. So Zemanek, initially intent (line 20) on dismissing Henry as an inarticulate 'idiot'—a common base strategy for closing down comment he cannot control—is forced by the strength of the denials which confront him to fight through the exchange on Henry's terms. The quickness—and wit—of the wordplay at line 19, 'What, you calling me a spade now?', forces the host back to his base strategy, and contributes to the decision to maintain the call, for the host cannot cut a call while he is losing both the interaction and the race politics.

This conversational exchange is enmeshed within two simultaneous processes. The first consists of the in-studio processes which act upon the structuring of the broadcast talk and which, proceeding unheard throughout it, keep 'good', that is, contentious debate going. The second is the drive within the broadcast talk towards the construction and maintenance of a social relation which will advantage the host. While Conversation Analysis (CA), the form of analysis used by Hutchby, can work to isolate the techniques at play in each, it is less useful in revealing the interplay between them.

Conversation Analysis is a finely honed tool for reading relational power at a micro level—but it needs to be reset within its contexts, to pick up its engagement with orders of discourse which are not always easily aligned. Hutchby's isolation of an asymmetry of power relations needs to be enhanced and extended, by recognition of its release of an impulse towards, and repeated rehearsal of, a resistant and combative response, which has contradictory consequences within the original relations of power. As Butler discovers, working with what seems an example of asymmetry within the discourses of racism, repeated experience of derogation framed as insult—a favoured 'direct assault' diversion strategy with talkback hosts as they seek to regain turn-taking primacy—can evoke an equal or more powerful resistance:

One is not simply fixed by the name that one is called. In being called an injurious name, one is derogated and demeaned. But the name holds out another possibility as well: by being called a name, one is also, paradoxically, given a certain possibility for social existence, initiated into a temporal life of language that exceeds the prior purposes that animate that call. Thus the injurious address may appear to fix or paralyse the one it hails, but it may also produce an unexpected and enabling response. If to be addressed is to be interpellated, then the offensive call runs the risk of inaugurating a subject in speech who comes to use language to counter the offensive call. (Butler 1997, p. 2)

By moving from the micro-analysis of conversational power relations to its politicisation at an ideological level, Butler has shown the degree to which a discursive continuum is in operation, along which reversals and inversions can be and are achieved. Her perspective can even alert us to the possible dangers of too homogeneous a discursive positioning along that continuum, from relations of talk to orders of discourse: ways of knowing, believing, acting and being. Within his apparently unassailable 'King Stanley' Zemanek persona, the radio host of my own data corpus can be seen to be becoming increasingly stranded behind the barricades of an unreconstructed masculinity, itself rapidly becoming outmoded. During another caller discussion, this time with 'Cameron', a young footballer new to the city, the host's characterisation of his own capacity to sustain antagonistic exchanges (referred to as 'baggin'') reveals his attachment to the images of potent superiority and invulnerability he likes to project through his talk.

Extract 10

C: Yeah whattya think a those people, I listen to you a few times, every time I, listen to yer, yer get people baggin' ya all the time, I was jist wonderin' why's, what, why's, is, yer got people jist sorta drunk alla time or . . .

Z: Well, like, look, it's a good laugh, I mean, I have a good laugh at all these people, I mean and other people listening to the program have a bit of a laugh as well because they think that ah, yeah those people that are listening to us think well their life isn't so bad after all after they hear some of these half wits . . .

C: Yeah . . .

Z: But no mate I—look it just—it's—water off a duck's back for me.

C: = 'eah . . .

Z: = couldn'—couldn't care less . . .

In fact, despite the insouciant stance of invulnerability, Stan Zemanek can be seen to care a great deal. He does everything to elicit and to escalate—even to promote—his regular 'baggin'', seemingly safe in his projection of traditional virtues of physical prowess, linked to a particularly Australian convention of association between male public status and an heroic sporting past. He is always, for instance, quick to remind listeners of his own earlier, but still occasionally practised, yachting expertise, in the requisite terms of masochistic pleasure to indicate his toughness.

Extract 11

> Z: Yeah a lot of people have been talking about the ah surf carnival in Queensland where the young man lost his life and, was a tragedy. And, um, (.) but, you know, people have been saying oh look, you know they should have called it off

[section deleted]

> Uum, but you don't call off sporting events I suppose, ah, because conditions are a little inclement. I . . . these people are professional life-savers, as we were professional sailors out there to do a job an', um, you know, if you ever come down Sydney Harbour in a 18 footer with a spinnaker up, screaming down the harbour with a bloody southerly buster up yer backside you'll know what fear and intrepidation is all about I can tell you . . .

Discussing visual representations of contemporary masculine formations in popular texts, Easthope (1986, p. 53) comments on hegemonic Western versions of masculine identity: 'the most important meanings that can attach to the idea of the masculine body are unity and permanence'. Thus, the Zemanek vision of powerful masculinity is one which prevails against the worst of all intrusive forces, to the extent that dangers are deliberately sought. Physically and discursively, his risk strategy actively courts the dangers of disruption— only to reassert his own dominance, and that of the order he represents. His radio conversation (re)produces social structuring not just within its on-air interactions, but within those interactions which begin in the production practices of in-studio talk. From here, the host licenses his own disruptive access into otherwise independent commentaries, extending through every genre: narrative, argument, processing talk, advertising copy, even intruding into news bulletins,

sports reports and phone-in promotions. The accessibility and participation that such 'radio-activity' promises proves dangerous, even when
it appears strongly resistant, for it can provoke equally powerful
responses. Nor is the strategy limited to this one show, or even to
talkback radio, or commercial broadcasting.

Bell and van Leeuwen (1994), in isolating within the high-status
public service broadcasting sector of the ABC (Australian Broadcasting Corporation) the favoured genre of the interview, and
demonstrating its ideological positioning within a particular bourgeois
disciplinarity of self-scrutiny and critique, show clearly the intensity
of the ideological operation of one strand of current radio discursive
practice. My own work shows the degree to which Stan Zemanek's
elaboration of a highly gendered discourse of power, one which underpins the authority of his own social and political views, is built over
and continuous with the in-studio practices of his relations with his
production team. It is this discursive position which is reproduced all
the way to his ratings success, providing for his commercial station
managers and their small business sponsors exactly the same forms of
irresistible, active, self-starting tough-guy authority he acts out across
his in-studio and his broadcast talk—a persona managers and sponsors
endorse as the official discourses of what Norman Fairclough calls
'enterprise culture'. As Fairclough himself suggests (1995b, p. 55):

> Language use—any text—is always simultaneously constitutive of 1)
> social identities, 2) social relations, and 3) systems of knowledge and
> belief [. . .] That is, any text makes its own small contribution to shaping
> these aspects of society and culture. In particular cases, one of the three
> might appear to be more important than the others, but it is a sensible
> working assumption that all three are going on to some degree.

Within talkback radio, the social identities which are under
constitution and the systems of knowledge and belief they engage are
always partially connected already into existing structures of social
relations. Both presenters and callers bring to the conversations in
which they engage on air those other conversations which are simultaneously occurring, to recreate and endorse talkback radio's myths of
its own immediate engagement with 'social reality'. It is precisely this
sense of the 'real' which has built around contemporary talkback its
new power as a claimant for political opinion representation: a power
which political institutions around the world simultaneously fear and
yet cannot resist, and which commentators appear unable to critique
without lapsing back into Frankfurt School views of irresistible media
and passive and vulnerable mass audiences (Roberts 1991, Groppe

1994). My own work suggests that micro-analysis of the 'talk' of talkback, showing a particular relational politics always under construction in the complex multiple spaces of its conversational exchanges, is a useful way not only to display which social and political choices are being made in talkback, but how to reveal how they can be contested.

NOTES

1   'Radioactive' is a promotional term used in the advertising of talkback programming on Radio 2UE, Sydney, Australia.
2   There are three types of radio licence in Australia. A licence stations are public broadcasters, run by the Australian Broadcasting Corporation under its own charter. B licence stations are commercial broadcasters, run for profit. C licences are granted for non-commercial broadcasters, including universities and community groups.

5 The textual politics of good intentions: critical theory and semiotics

Gillian Fuller

The discursive terrain of popular science is sustained by certain symptomatic representations about the role of science and the benefits it offers to 'society'. *Wisdom of the Elders* (Knudtson and Suzuki 1992) occupies a somewhat ambivalent position within the rhetorical tradition of popular science. It does not exhort the environmental benefits of Western technology but rather seeks to heighten awareness of indigenous epistemologies of the natural world as part of its project to save the planet. While *Wisdom of the Elders* proceeds in its project with the best of liberal intentions, this chapter will argue that it is nevertheless a highly problematic text that is fundamentally complicit with many of the discursive traditions that it attempts to write against.

The 'sign work' of popular science extends beyond the instance of the single text under consideration. Its meanings must be considered in relation to those of other social texts as well as the meanings these texts may have for different social groups. As Bakhtin 1981 (p. 291) notes:

> Thus at any given moment of its historical existence, language is heteroglot from top to bottom: it represents the co-existence of socio-ideological contradictions between the present and the past, between differing epochs of the past, between different socio-ideological groups in the present, between tendencies, schools, circles and so forth, all given a bodily form. These 'languages' of heteroglossia intersect each other in a variety of ways, forming new socially typifying 'languages'.

In other words, issues of textual history and power, both individual and institutional, are crucial to any form of text analysis. They are particularly compelling in the case of popular science, because science has had such a controversial history with respect to the many social groupings who have been constituted as the object of scientific inquiry. For instance women, 'Natives', gay men and lesbians have often found themselves on the nature side of the nature/culture divide (Haraway 1992).

Using the inherently historical and thus theoretically partial formulations of Bakhtin, I want to present some ways in which the analytical technologies of linguistics, in particular functional linguistics (Halliday 1994), can be used to read the complex social histories and present day social functions in the new evolving discourses of 'popular science' and environmentalism. However, issues of positionality are also of primary importance to the investigation undertaken here. In this respect I draw upon what is often called 'critical theory' to examine issues of cultural difference and power as they are manifested in the discursive practices of *Wisdom of the Elders*. The term 'critical theory' has been used to allude to a diverse range of theoretical positions and disciplinary approaches to text analysis. In this chapter, however, feminist and critical scholarship around the complexity of notions of 'race' and 'gender' (for instance, Gates 1986; Spivak 1987; Trinh 1989; Mohanty 1992; Gallop 1988; Gunew and Yeatman 1993; Gatens 1992; Grosz 1989; Haraway 1981, 1992) will serve as the major points of interdisciplinary interface.

The history of interdisciplinary relations between linguistics and critical theory is complex and has often been construed as antagonistic (Derrida 1976; Volosinov 1986; Threadgold 1986). This chapter however argues that there is much that is complementary—particularly in some of the critical approaches from disciplines such as philosophy, literary theory and feminist and cultural studies. The use of critical theory in this chapter does not merely supplement linguistic analysis but motivates a kind of linguistic analysis that is explicitly 'designed' to explore issues raised from other disciplines.

The approach, therefore, does not attempt to incorporate the distinctly motivated theories of critical theory and linguistics into a comprehensive and unified semiotic theory. Rather, these disciplinarily distinct modes of text analysis have been brought together in a semiotic space where they can mutually inform one another. The methodology pursued in this chapter is therefore as follows:

- *Describe the site* in terms of the discourses that it draws upon (i.e. discourses of science, race and environmentalism) and the rhetorical force these discourses carry in terms of time and place.

- *Build an intertextual history* by discussing the history of these discourses in relation to one another (i.e. the history of race in environmentalist debates, the connections and disjunction between 'science' and 'environmentalism').
- *Analyse the text linguistically* by selecting an area of textual focus. that will illuminate the grammaticalising effect of discourse in the text. In this instance, analysis will focus on the grammatical resources of voicing (Fuller 1995) to explore the inequities and complicities of cross-cultural representation in *Wisdom of the Elders*.

THE SITE—*WISDOM OF THE ELDERS*

Knudtson and Suzuki's *Wisdom of the Elders* (WoE, 1992) pushes at the borders of what is normally considered science popularisation. Influenced by Lévi-Strauss' *The Savage Mind* (1972) and the more recent writings of Native American anthropologists such as Pam Colorado (1988), WoE draws comparisons between Native and Western theorisations of the natural world in an attempt to raise the profile of Native sciences. This is done in an attempt to lay the foundations of a universal environmental ethic in which the often competing claims of science and environmentalism are resolved in the 'sacred ecologies' (Knudtson and Suzuki 1992, p. 15) of Native metaphysics.

Knudtson and Suzuki (1992, p. 4) explain their title thus:

> *Wisdom of the Elders* is an exploration of the often striking parallels between traditional Native ecological perspectives and Western scientific ones, particularly in modern biology. As biologists, one specialising in animal behaviour and the other in genetics, we have found ourselves increasingly intrigued in recent years by the shared truths, as well as the undeniable differences, in these two distinct, yet often strikingly complementary ways of knowing about the natural world.

> One of these ways of knowing might be called the world of the shaman— the ancient, ecstatic healer and holy person of many traditional indigenous societies who serves as a primary repository of Native nature-wisdom. The other might be called the world of the scientist— particularly, for our purposes, as interpreted by some of the most articulate, compassionate, and wise 'elder statesmen' of science, whom we see as science's true 'elders'. We refer to these shared ecological truths collectively, as the book's title suggests, as the nature 'wisdom of the elders'.

Wisdom of the Elders is a continuation of the themes laid out in Suzuki's *Inventing the Future* (1990), in which the final chapter is devoted to the Aboriginal world view. Here, Suzuki argues that '[i]f we paid attention to [the Aboriginal world view], we could restructure our priorities and return to a balance with the environment' (1990, p. 229). This notion of the 'return' is most problematic in *WoE*'s representations of the Native knowledges that are set forth as an ecosocial model. Hatzimanolis (1993, p. 128) has claimed that 'timing' others as the embodiment of the past is a 'way of keeping "them" out while simultaneously suggesting that "we" gain access to "our" past through "them"'. She quotes Parekh, who states that:

> Liberalism has always remained assimilationist: others must become like us, my present is your future. (Cited in Hatzimanolis 1993, p. 128)

Wisdom of the Elders is a seeming reversal of this: here, 'we' must become like 'them'. Our future lies in their present. In *WoE*, despite countless disclaimers, 'they' are shown to be like 'us' and yet not like 'us' at all. Natives are consistently represented as childlike, pure and most importantly intrinsically connected to the land. By forwarding the 'sacred ecologies' of Natives as the path through which the alienated West can, in the words of E.O. Wilson, '*rediscover* [emphasis added] our *kin* [emphasis in original] the other animals and plants with whom we share this planet'(cited in Knudtson and Suzuki 1992, p. xxiv), *WoE* construes a genealogy of 'scientific' thought that posits Natives on an evolutionary timeline that precedes the West. Thus, the difference between 'us' and 'them' is a matter of timing rather than culture. In this way, *WoE* is a well-intentioned appropriation of Native knowledges, but an appropriation nevertheless: 'we' must become like 'we' were, 'our' future lies in 'our' past.

In its attempts to broaden the parameters of what 'we' consider science to be, *WoE* evokes the rhetoric of scientific clarity and detachment to upturn racist commonplaces and to clear away the cultural misconceptions that it locates in the realm of commonsense. It does this by assuming the authorial voice of the wise elder, of the expert on the high moral ground. In this way *WoE* rhetorically affiliates the social authority of science with neo-colonial environmentalist desires to reconcile with Natives, not only by presuming a shared ecological perspective, but also by assuming the mantle of 'elder'.

The reconciliation that this book seeks to effect between Native and Western sciences is complicated not only by the hegemony of racism against which the authors attempt to write, but also by the ambivalent status of science in environmental discourses. First, *WoE*'s promotion of Native knowledges can be seen, within the context of historic developments in environmentalist discourses, as an attempt to recuperate a place for science in environmentalism—where science has traditionally been aligned to industry–technology. Second, the use of Native epistemologies as the model for the West's 'return' to ecological harmony has a problematic intertextual history. Implicated in this is WoE's use of anthropological texts and translations as the media through which it negotiates with Native texts.

Before analysis can proceed, the intertextual history of the rhetoric employed in WoE needs elaborating. This is necessary because, despite Knudtson and Suzuki's awareness of a long colonialist history of representing Natives in 'sentimental, romantic, or culturally subordinate terms' (Knudtson and Suzuki 1992, p. 3), the success of WoE depends on the endurance of such tropes. In WoE, difference is consumed for moral edification, rather than racial vilification, but it will be argued that the discursive effects of this new negotiation between 'us' and 'them' are remarkably similar. Before moving on, I should like to state that I do not doubt that 'we' have much to learn from 'them'. This is not my quarrel with WoE. Rather, I am concerned that the formulation of relations across colonised and colonising cultures in ways that present 'us' as dichotomised entities whose cultures await abridgment, normalises and homogenises difference in ways that often ignore the material and social context in which such relations are produced and negotiated.

DISCURSIVE HISTORIES

Science and the eco-agenda

Science occupies an ambivalent but important position in environmental debates. Samuel Hays' 1987 historical study on public environmental movements between 1955 and 1985 discusses the shift from a managerial approach to conservation to the more recent environmentalism. Hays states that the conservation movement has been 'an effort on the part of leaders in science, technology, and government to bring about more efficient development of physical resources', whereas the environmental movement 'was far more widespread and popular, involving public values that stressed the quality of human experience and hence of the human environment' (Hays 1987, p. 13).

In earlier conservation movements, science was considered the tool by which Nature could be sustainably managed. More recently, however, there has been an increasing reluctance among some eco-activists to align themselves with a science which is seen to be emulating techno-capitalist relations of manipulation and prediction with Nature (Killingsworth and Palmer 1992, p. 46). Similar misgivings are present in *WoE* (p. xxiii):

> But we are waking to the dangers of clinging to a faith that science and technology can forever resolve the problems they helped to create in the first place.

This scepticism concerning the ability of science to resolve environmental dilemmas has much in common with deep ecology.[1] Deep ecologists argue that political reform must be accompanied by widespread attitudinal and behavioural change as well as extensive social reorganisation. These ideas are echoed by scientists Paul Ehrlich and E.O. Wilson, according to Knudtson and Suzuki (p. xxiv):

> Both of these eminent scientists are suggesting that science alone is not enough to solve the planetary environmental crisis and that we must recreate for ourselves a sense of place within the biosphere that is steeped in humility and reverence . . .

Killingsworth and Palmer (1992, p. 15) claim that:

> . . . for science to form a hegemonic link with deep ecology or social ecology . . . it would have to be a transformed science that formed the model for scientific management and that provided the impetus for large scale technological development.

Wisdom of the Elders makes an effort toward renegotiating a place for science in eco-debates by presenting a reformed model of scientific management based upon the Native's 'traditional skills in sustainably managing very complex ecological systems' (Knudtson and Suzuki 1992, p. 18). In *WoE*, the Native's 'sacred ecology' is foregrounded as an alternative to the 'scientifically restricted' (Knudtson and Suzuki 1992, p. 15) term 'ecology'. Thus, in *WoE*, the managerial ethos of liberal science is recast through the ethos of indigenous politics, deep ecology and sociobiology.

Natives and representations of race

The rhetorical mode of *WoE* is to reconcile the technical authority of science with the moral authority of deep ecology. Thus, the authors must convince the reader that Native science is the appropriate site for this reconciliation. The path to reconciliation in *WoE* is achieved through essentialising discourses that position Natives as a natural complement to their environment and whose 'sacred ecologies' provide a path to salvation for the eco-alienation of Western cultures. In a discussion of environmentalist visions of Australian Aboriginal people, Andrew Lattas (1990) suggests that environmentalists fully draw upon colonialist construals of Natives in terms of both 'otherness' and 'origin'. This ambivalence is made clear in the *WoE's* introductory chapter which continues to present Natives within the confines of a primitivised and essentialist colonialist template:

> Historians suggest that Native peoples too have, on occasion, committed environmental 'sins'—through wasteful hunting and trapping practices, for example, or through the gradual depletion of agricultural soils. But the worst of these excesses were generally of relatively recent vintage and occurred under the influence of powerful, imposed non-Native economic incentives and value systems. (Knudtson and Suzuki 1992, p. 17)

Implicit here is a notion that Natives form a preconstituted spatialised culture rather than an historically constituted other. In the schema in which Natives constitute this pregiven other, they are construed as locked into stasis with their environment, manifesting a passive harmonious melding with the ecosystem as opposed to the violence and agency of 'our' Western relationships with the environment.

Wisdom of the Elders construes cultural difference as the correlate of a world of 'peoples' whose separate histories wait to be bridged by anthropologists and concerned citizens. Gupta and Ferguson (1992, p. 16) suggest that such humanist perspectives need to be shifted towards seeing difference 'as a product of a shared historical process that differentiates the world as it connects it'. Much of the problem with *WoE* is that it constructs similarities between differences which are assumed to be pregiven and natural rather than exploring how difference is produced within a common and connected space.

This is evident in the universalisation of the concept of the 'elder' and the way in which Native texts are used to represent 'timeless beliefs' (Knudtson and Suzuki 1992, p. 51). Biddle (1991) and Rumsey (1994), however, both note that Native stories are always told to particular someone/s in a particular context. In the foreword of *WoE*, current strategic voices of Natives, who discuss the role that conservationists, anthropologists and government bureaucrats have had on their political/social situations, can be heard. Yet the contingency of Native stories is subsumed by the 'unadulterated' voice of the wholly other tribal wisdom when the rhetorical points of 'sacred ecology' need to be made. In *WoE*, often the story of one nameless Native informant is adduced to speak for the culture as a whole. Of the forty-eight Native 'vignettes' presented in the book, the Native informant is named only five times (Knudtson and Suzuki 1992, pp. 31, 118, 136,

162, 171). This is indicative of an assumed universalisation of myths and knowledges that cuts across social organisation within 'tribes'.

The conundrum of *WoE*'s particular cross-cultural dialogue is exemplified in an anecdote that Knudtson and Suzuki present in the introduction to their book, which is used to testify to the authors' sincerity in addressing anthropology's problematic history. Knudtson and Suzuki (1992, p. xiv) distance themselves from the racist reductionism of many anthropological texts by claiming to have used 'the most respected and culturally sensitive material available'. However, their description of a meeting between Knudtson and 'a shy, elfin, Chewong elder named Beng' (Knudtson and Suzuki 1992, p. xix), ostensibly to confirm the reliability of an anthropological book, has many disturbing resonances of the very tradition they claim to be attempting to undermine:

> He [Knudtson] showed Beng a copy of Howell's book and, with the help of a government interpreter, asked him to comment on the accuracy of its different depictions of the traditional Chewong cosmos. Beng's reply was quick and unequivocal. Yes, he assured us, the book was indeed a trustworthy account of Chewong beliefs about the natural world.
>
> How did he know? Because, he said with a toothless grin, he himself had been one of Howell's principal informants during her prolonged stay with the Chewong . . .
>
> In fact, he added with a smile, he happened to have his own personal copy of the book, which he kept near his handcrafted blowgun and poison-tipped darts in his nearby hut.

Mindful of a discursive tradition in which Natives are consistently represented as supplicating (but ultimately uncontrollable) children in relation to Western adults, the information that Beng is 'shy', 'elfin', 'smiling' and the possessor of a blow gun is not extraneous or merely interesting but is fundamental to the *WoE* project. In a project that has as its major political agenda the construction of an environmental ethic for a Western audience, this book constructs the authenticity of the Native by engaging in a discourse of othering practices in which notions of essentialised difference make sense. If the Native is not timeless, eternal, identified with space rather than time, traditional and untouched by the corruptions of Western culture, then this book has no rhetorical foundation.

Wisdom of the Elders reproduces many of the racist discourses that it anticipates from its readers and that it supposedly works against. The ambivalence of this eco-desire—of a corrupted 'Western' self yearning for a pristine other (manifest in the life of a 'Native')—

resonates uncomfortably with colonialist and ethnocentric desires that have stereotyped 'raced' others as extensions of the environment. Within the biophilic value system of deep ecology, such representations may seem ideal; however, viewed from the context of colonialist history, such restrictive and non-reciprocal representations of the West's others have a long destructive history in which the effects of such ambivalence 'fix identity as the fantasy of difference' (Bhabha 1986, p. 169). The privileging of Native science anchored in the construction of the Native as a natural complement to their environment is thus a compounding of, rather than a resolution of, problematic discourses.

The rhetoric of authority in the WoE genre

The generic purpose of the WoE texts is to assert the worth of Native knowledges as repositories of scientific knowledge that are more ecologically sensitive than Western modes of scientific knowing. Thus, each text has certain tasks: first, it asserts the 'naturalness' of the Native; second, it provides details of Native knowledges (generally through an anthropologist); third, it compares the Native knowledge to Western scientific knowledge; and last, it reiterates the worth of Native science as a model of 'sacred ecology'.

The rhetorical task of WoE is to convince the reader that Native knowledges of the natural world and enlightened Western sciences are natural allies. Within this project, the technical authority of Western science is generally positioned as uncontentious, even if its moral authority is questioned. Thus, the major rhetorical effort is directed towards affirming the scientific and ecological worth of Native knowledges. Concomitant with the validating of Native science is the related discrediting of certain forms of Western knowledge. These 'fragmented', 'disconnected' and 'reductive' forms of Western science (Knudtson and Suzuki 1992, pp. xxii–iv) are the problem to which Native and enlightened forms of Western science offer an antidote.

The general sweep of the WoE genre will now be elaborated through analysis of a typical text, 'In praise of the red ant ally' (henceforth known as 'Red ant'). The starting point of each essay is a quote from an 'elder'. These elders are generally, but not always, Western scientists.[2] These quotations from acknowledged sources of expertise form an uncontroversial orientation to the text. The full title and provenance (Amazonia: Kayapó) of 'Red ant' is prefaced (p. 51) by the following quote from E.O. Wilson, 'entomologist and evolutionary biologist':

> A few of the species [in the tropical forests of Surinam] were locked together in forms of symbiosis so intricate that to pull out one would bring others spiralling to extinction. Such is the consequence of adaptation by coevolution, the reciprocal genetic changes of species that interact with each other through many life cycles.

This text projects a proposition or propositions from a prestigious source of authority that will be shown to be manifest also in the Native world view. Thus in 'Red ant' the principle of coevolution discussed by E.O. Wilson is shown to be recognised also by the Kayapó. The validity of these orientational propositions is not argued for; the status of their 'sayers' is deemed to obviate the need for justification. In *WoE*, the initial scientific quote sanctions what follows in a way that is inimical to reader involvement. Presented above the title of the essay, the quote speaks for itself and forms an implicit triumvirate of support between the cited author, the writer of the text and its propositional content, without any structural point of arguability between the three. (See Figure 5.1.)

Figure 5.1   Effects of *WoE*'s textual juxtaposition of Wilson and the Kayapó

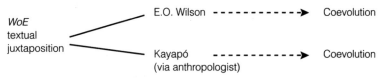

After the initial proposition by the Western elder, the Kayapó are introduced in terms which locate them spatially in the rainforests of the Amazon and make mention of their political struggles to maintain control over their lands. The initial foregrounding of Native spatial location is a marked feature of *WoE* texts, indicated in the following examples by italicised circumstantial elements. It occurs in the opening sentence of 'Red ant' (p. 51):

> The Kayapó Indians are a people who, against great political and economic odds, continue to inhabit and lay claim to *vast tracts of tropical rain forest [in the Amazonian heartlands of Brazil]*

and in the openings of other *WoE* texts, where location may be literal or more abstract—even mythical (emphasis added):

1   The Inuit live *upon the vast expanse of windswept, treeless tundra* . . . (p. 41)
2   *Through the dense, humid, equatorial rain forests of eastern* Colombia . . . (p. 23)

3 *In traditional Gitksan society*, a newborn baby emerges . . . (p. 127)
4 *Since their mythical beginnings*, the Chewong people of Malaysia
   . . . (p. 89)

Each of the examples above locates the Native participant in relation to their spatial environment in some way: either through directly saying where they live ('Red ant', examples 1, 2 and 4 above) or through collocating them with aspects of a 'traditional life' (examples 3, 2 and 4 above). Even when the location referred to is not literal, the idea of locative space—within which the Native belongs—is realised abstractly. Note in the final example (4) that this is mythical non-historical time. Thus where scientific qualifications authorise the Westerner, spatial credentials authorise the Native.

This use of Native spatiality as a point of departure for the text is wholly consistent with colonialist representations of Natives as existing in a dimension other than history. Niranjana (1992, p. 75) discusses the problems of the discursive repression of history in representations of Natives:

> Refusing the name of 'history' to the pre-colonial past implies that the anthropologist bestows on it the name of 'nature'. Even an ethnologist like Lévi-Strauss who professes to be anti-colonial and anti-ethnocentric repeats the dehistoricising gesture, inherited from Rousseau, that marks non-Western man as 'natural'.

Tropes of the natural Native exert great rhetorical weight in those eco-discourses that articulate a wish to effect a return to 'the ancient bonds of kinship between human beings and other species' (Knudtson and Suzuki 1992, p. 3). At the beginning of *WoE*, its authors express their dismay that Native sciences are often represented as a 'poetic and endearing' yet 'inferior' stage in human cultural 'progress' (Knudtson and Suzuki 1992, p. 6). But by foregrounding the spatial credentials of Natives, and then conflating these with their cognitive processes, this type of liberal racism is reinscribed as the text's point of departure.

The next move in 'Red ant' is to justify why Native myth should warrant reader attention. This is simply achieved by the authorial assertion that such 'tales glow with enduring ecological meaning'. The Native text and the anthropologist who translated the tale are then introduced. Importantly, Posey, the anthropologist adduced in 'Red ant', is claimed to have 'exceptional rapport' with the Kayapó. It should be noted that the initial teller of the tale, 'an unnamed Kayapó woman' requires no such authorial assurance of expertise. Her membership of the Kayapó ensures this, thus further reducing the specificity and hierarchicalisation of Native knowledges. The myth is then retold, after which authorial and anthropological commentary evaluate what the myth means. During this phase of the text, the Native myth is read as science.

Following this period of exegesis, the text adduces the work of biologists who 'in recent decades' have studied coevolution. Thus, the concept of coevolution which was prefigured in the initial orien- tational quote is shown to be implicitly recognised in the 'red ant myth' of the Kapayó. This point is the rhetorical linchpin of the text. It is here that WoE justifies its project by asserting that Natives have known for a long time that which Western science is only beginning to study. The moral point of this is brought home at the end of 'Red ant' when Posey laments 'that Native myth has not seriously been studied as a transmitter of encoded ecological knowledge', indicating the knowledge that has been lost because of Western racism.

The question of voices: assimilation and semantics

The universalising rhetoric in WoE, in which all enlightened people (namely 'good' scientists and Natives) are of one mind environmen- tally, authorises a particular type of structural dynamic in the text: WoE speaks for everyone. It does this initially by quoting other people, so a reader can track who is saying what, but eventually the text moves to a point where everyone's ideas (those of the authors, the readers, the 'Native' informants, the anthropologists) are structurally merged to project the one proposition. This is achieved through the resources that English grammar deploys for representing the voices of others (Fuller 1995). The most widespread of these resources are quoting and paraphrase, but these do not exhaust the grammar of representing what other people say and think.

By exploring the grammar of 'voicing', we can get a clearer picture of how WoE manages through a grammatical 'sleight of hand' to ventriloquise Native voices while appearing to allow people to speak for themselves. We can think about the grammar of voicing as moving along a cline from 'representing' to 'assimilating' (see Figure 5.2). Where the texts of others are 'represented' (through resources such as direct and indirect speech), there is a structural differentiation in the grammar whereby the other text is sourced to someone and projected as content. As we move down the cline, the 'content' of someone else's text becomes merged onto the same order of 'reality' and becomes a form of unsourced textual variation; that is, 'The land is a mother'. Figure 5.2 maps the major trends of these resources for incorporating the sayings and ideas of others into text.

Figure 5.2 Regions of other text sourcing: cline of representation to assimilation (Fuller 1995)

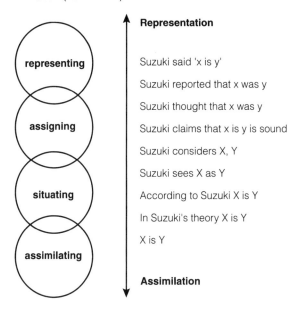

Representation

Suzuki said 'x is y'

Suzuki reported that x was y

Suzuki thought that x was y

Suzuki claims that x is y is sound

Suzuki considers X, Y

Suzuki sees X as Y

According to Suzuki X is Y

In Suzuki's theory X is Y

X is Y

Assimilation

The region of *representation* covers discourse that is represented as semiotic content. It runs on a cline from most differentiated, such as direct speech quoting, into a more indeterminate space where the status of the 'other text' is less clear.

The region of *assigning* deals with those instances where text produced by others is no longer 'projected' as semiotic content but is recontextualised as elements of the text that bounds it (the bounding discourse). In the assigning region, the saying or idea is grammatically moved further away from its original context and structurally merged into the text that contains the saying or idea. In this region the source of meaning does not 'project'; rather it 'assigns' meaning. Thus:

1   They refer to the brain *as kai.*
2   They speak of *the bonds of kinship.*

In these examples, the 'other text' is assigned a place within the grammar of the bounding discourse. This is achieved by attaching concepts (usually through circumstantial clausal elements denoting 'role' (example 1) or 'matter' (example 2) to verbal processes that convey a sense of saying, thinking or referring. These sayings or thoughts still connote the idea that the proposition derives from another source, yet what was actually said has become significantly recontextualised.

The region of *situating* covers the space where meaning is rendered as deriving from elsewhere, but it is not represented or assigned. Its source is located grammatically as a clausal element of circumstance, usually by a prepositional phrase. Thus the 'other text' moves from being realised as deriving from symbolic and sensing processes (someone's sayings or ideas) to being more incorporated into the experiential domain of the bounding discourse, for example: 'In the Waswanipi world, relations are not mechanical' (p. 56).

The region of *assimilating* covers the region where distinct discourses are negotiated through relations of restatement and reformulation. Thus the original context through which the meaning was derived is fully assimilated into the bounding discourse as semiotic variation rather than difference. Thus the original situation of someone saying the land is a mother becomes recontextualised as a statement about the world: The land is a mother.

The following examples deploy the resources of *assignment*, which is the dominant form of realising Native ideas in *WoE*:

1   . . . their culture . . . spiritually cherishes them *as manifestations of a sacred, richly interconnected natural world of which humans are an integral part* ('Red ant', p. 55)

2   In essence, they see the environment itself *as their storehouse.* ('An observational biology', p. 68)

3   The diverse inhabitants of the natural world are seen *as intimately* bound together by virtue *not only of their common mythic origins* . . . ('The nature of things', p. 57)

4   . . . the Desana shaman refers to its . . . paired . . . hemispheres *as the other house or the other dimension.* ('The architecture of the human brain' p. 72)

5   He tends to look upon these two halves *as structurally symmetrical* ('The architecture of the human brain', p. 72)

The use of structurally merged rather than representationally distinct forms of voicing points to a different relationship being enacted between the authors and textual participants motivated by the overarching rhetoric of *WoE*. The transcendent nature of the scientific field is enabled by the transcendent authority of its authors, who speak *for* everyone.

This speaking for everyone also includes the structural merging of anthropological texts into *WoE*'s bounding discourse. Yet these texts retain the sense of their 'original' authenticity by being rendered in the original in italics. Thus graphology allows *WoE* to suggest a closeness to its sources while fully recontextualising the source quotes within the bounds of its grammar. This enables *WoE* to put the words of anthropologists into the minds of Natives in an insidiously seamless way. Consider this example from 'Red ant': '. . . clearly, their culture recognizes certain coevolutionary complexes . . .' (p. 55). Here 'our' implicit intersubjectivised thoughts and anthropologist Posey's observations are more indistinctly rendered in terms of structure but retain their sense of coming from somewhere else (namely, the Native culture). This is enabled through graphology (in the case of Posey's italicised text, as cited in *WoE)* and through the interpersonal comment *clearly.* (See Figure 5.3.)

Figure 5.3   Natives think what antropologists say

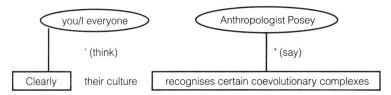

However, when the texts of Western experts are adduced, certain complementarities emerge in the resources of voicing. Below are some characteristic examples of how Western experts' texts are realised in *WoE.* In 'The architecture of the human brain', brain biologist Roger Sperry states his factual locution 'succinctly':

> In the human head, Sperry states succinctly, there are forces within forces, as in no other cubic half-foot in the universe. (p. 75)

Likewise in 'The nature of things', anthropologist Feit's credentials are adduced alongside with a reflective interpretation:

> Canadian anthropologist Harvey Feit, in his perceptive studies on Waswanipi Cree society, suggests that modern Western ecology and traditional Waswanipi Cree thought may have much in common. (p. 57)

On the occasions when Native speech (as translated by the anthropologist) is realised, their sayings are not interpretive; instead they form the object of 'Western interpretation'—that is, they tell myths and stories, like the red ant tale in 'Red ant':

> The story was told by an unnamed Kayapó woman . . . 'The trails of the fire ant (mrum-kamrek-ti) are long. They are ferocious (akrê) like men . . .' (p. 52)

Unlike Westerners who succinctly state or perceptively observe, Natives express humble ignorance. The example below is from 'The architecture of the human brain':

> [T]he Desana can do no more than murmur softly: '*It contains colors that we don't even know the names of.*' (p. 75)

Or Natives may ask questions, as in this example from 'The nature of things':

> [H]e or she might understandably be more inclined to address the natural world by asking, '*Who did this?*' and '*Why?*' rather than '*How does that work?*' (p. 57)

In this example, the 'quoted text' is actually flagged as being hypothetical. Indeed reference to the Feit source text reveals that it is the anthropologist who asks, 'Who did this?' not the Cree 'informants' (Feit 1973, p. 116).[3] Similarly in 'An observational biology', the representation of a Native text is hypothetical:

> *After all*, he is likely to say, *the ultimate source of such knowledge resides not in him but in the wisest and most experienced elders of his community.* (p. 69)

This ability of the authors to know what a Native would say is guaranteed not only by their asserted sensitivity to and authority over Native cultures but is also informed by notions of stasis that surround Native knowledges and mythologies of homogeneity that make all Natives the same. The function of Native quotes is crucial in WoE, as they connote a closer connection to the Native source than any other type of discourse representation. However, despite these stories having been told many times in many contexts by many people, in WoE they are left to stand as forms of static wisdom, as perpetual originals.

The tendency of WoE to merge all its sources—Natives, Western scientists and anthropologists—onto the one content plane of text enables it to succeed in its task of construing a unified but multi-sourced field of 'sacred ecology', a 'quiltlike whole' (Knudtson and Suzuki 1992, p. xiii). However, it also simultaneously subverts its liberal desires for 'cross-cultural dialogue' (Knudtson and Suzuki 1992, p. xviii).

CONCLUSION

In a critique of *The Absence of the Sacred: the failure of technology and the survival of Indian nations* (Mander 1992), another text championing 'indigenous world views' as the path to 're-establishing global ecological equilibrium', Native American scholar Ward Churchill claims:

> No matter how well intentioned or insightful, regardless of how critical of the dominant conceptual paradigm and 'sensitive' to non-Western perspectives, the theoretical writing of EuroAmerican men—and most white women as well—seems destined with a sort of sad inevitability to become yet another exercise in intellectual appropriation, a reinforcement of the very hegemony they purport to oppose. (1993, pp. 139–40)

While Churchill's reading of Mander may seem applicable also to Knudtson and Suzuki, his reading needs to be made more complex and contradictory. Knudtson and Suzuki are not just simply like 'all white men'. Such homogeneity reproduces a singularity of subjectivity that cannot be supported by the semiotic approach adopted here. (Indeed Suzuki's own complex body could itself occupy another chapter.) The problems of *WoE* are amplified by its failure to address the complex of contradictions and ambivalences between science and environmentalism, Natives and nature, technical and hortatory rhetoric to name just a few. *Wisdom of the Elders* is a problematic text. It attempts to construct a new seamless field of pan-cultural rationality without any attempt at deconstructing the existing discursive practices that would prevent the achievement of the transcendent field so longed for.

Wisdom of the Elders ruptures the monologic authority of science and negotiates with other discursive cultures while still reaffirming the primacy and transcendence of a scientific clarity that knows what is best for its subjects. Thus, its well-intentioned pluralist discourse ultimately effects a reaffirmation of the culturally reductive and totalising practices that it seeks to contest.

> Pluralism is precisely a discursive practice demanding the analysis of power/knowledge that Foucault calls for when he asserts the need to think power *without* the king. (Rooney 1986, p. 560)

Rooney's formulation of the problematic of pluralism is relevant not only to the texts analysed but to the mode of analysis. The discourse analysis conducted in this chapter is acknowledged as being partial. Its selective positioning between linguistics and more literary forms of text analysis has been motivated by questions that are ultimately political in their formulation and functional in approach. The methodology adopted in this chapter is therefore both enabling and constraining: it highlights certain textual problematics while overshadowing others. It is here that the notion of critical discourse analysis as a situated and strategic discursive practice is crucial. Any form of interdisciplinary text analysis needs to know its place: disciplinary interests require acknowledgment, along with the recognition that exclusions are inevitable. In this way, critical discourse analysis situates its own practices knowingly and strategically within the hierarchy of social discourses.

NOTES

1   This movement is largely associated with Arne Naess who is cited as a Western Scientific Elder in *WoE* (p. 114).

2   There are three instances in *WoE*, where a 'Native' is granted the western elder position: Paiaikan (p. 111) (contemporary Kayapó activist), Vine Deloria (p. 196) (academic/activist) Black Elk (pp. 187–8) (late Sioux leader). The poet ecologist, Thoreau (p. 174) and the literary critic, Northrop Frye (p. 154) are also adduced as 'elders'.

3   This is the source text: 'Causality, therefore, is personal, not mechanical or biological, and it is in our experience, always appropriate to ask "who did it?" and "why?" rather than "how does that work?"' (Feit 1973, p. 116).

6 Locating culture in action: membership categorisation in texts and talk

Carolyn D. Baker

Ethnomethodology provides a number of directions for analysing texts and talk as part of the ongoing assembling of social and moral order, and for analysing 'culture in action'. This chapter introduces one powerful analytic approach, membership categorisation, and shows its use by writers, readers, speakers and hearers in educational settings. Membership categorisation work is pervasive in the doing of descriptions, the making of claims, the organisation of social relations, and other aspects of the micropolitics of everyday and institutional life. This chapter contributes an approach to analysis that puts culture inside action, rather than action inside culture, already preconstituted.

By showing how membership categorisation is done in talk and texts, this chapter points to a 'critical edge' that can be provided by ethnomethodological and conversation-analytic work on texts and transcripts of talk in institutions and elsewhere. While Button (1991) provides detailed papers on how ethnomethodology offers a 'foundational respecification of the human sciences', this chapter's scope is limited to briefly describing some main concepts in membership categorisation analysis and applying them to some sections of text and transcribed talk. A second purpose, then, is to substantiate the view that categorisation work, in addition to its descriptive and explicative character already well documented in the literature, is powerful in the organisation of discourses. Specifically, I work with the idea that categories and categorisation work lock discourses into place, and are therefore ready for opening to critical examination.

MEMBERSHIP CATEGORISATION ANALYSIS

Membership categorisation analysis, as a subfield of ethnomethodology, arose in the early lectures of Sacks (1992). Sacks explored how actual instances of talk-in-interaction constituted, in their own right, materials for sociological analysis. In his lectures on conversation, he showed how some classical problems of sociology—social order and social structure—could be addressed by studying the organisation of talk-in-interaction. In addition, his studies have contributed very different takes on how 'culture' can be understood and studied.

The notion of membership categorisation addresses how people 'do' descriptions and how they recognise descriptions: matters of cultural knowledge and relevance (Sacks 1974, p. 216). This interest is exemplified in his analysis of a story told by a child: 'The baby cried. The mommy picked it up'. Sacks made the point that we all 'hear' the mommy who did the picking up as the mommy of the baby who cried, not some other mommy. People accomplish this hearing routinely and economically by using the resources of what Sacks called the 'membership categorisation device':

> . . . any collection of membership categories, containing at least a category, which may be applied to some population containing at least a member, so as to provide, by the use of some rules of application, for the pairing of at least a population member and a categorisation device member. A device is then a collection plus rules of application. (Sacks 1992, p. 219)

Applied to the baby–mommy example above (elaborated in much more detail by Sacks), we connect the two persons by calling on the membership categorisation device 'family' which collects them both. This hearing is both adequate and economical. On other occasions the term 'baby' can be found to be part of other devices such as 'stage of life' (baby–child–adult).

Following the early work of Sacks, literature studying the membership categorisation activities that occur in a variety of settings has been published, including work on reading newspaper headlines, classroom interaction and police–suspect interrogations, among other topics (for an overview, see Hester and Eglin 1997, pp. 7–11). Such studies have been concerned with the descriptive and explicative work that is done in the course of talk-in-interaction, and have refined a number of the original notions proposed by Sacks.

CATEGORISATION AND CULTURE

Within ethnomethodology, a membership categorisation device is understood, not as a pre-existing structure of category-organised knowledge (a decontextualised notion, a reified entity like a schema, or a machinery, such as might be found in cognitive anthropology or linguistics), but as an always locally assembled corpus: a corpus that is occasioned and produced in a given moment of use (Hester and Eglin 1997, pp. 12–18). An implication of such local embeddedness and practical accomplishment of membership categorisation devices (for this occasion, this time) is:

> . . . not just that members use culture to do things, but that culture is constituted in, and only exists in, action. For membership categorization analysis, this means that the orderliness of cultural resources (categories, devices and the rest) is constituted in their use rather than pre-existing. Our central point is that it is in the use of categories that culture is constituted this time through . . . (Hester and Eglin 1997, p. 20)

What such a view offers is a radically different take on 'culture'. It has situated culture in action (which is a reversal of normative theories of culture) and suggests that we look at membership categorisation activities as 'culture-in-action'; or, put another way, that 'culture is internal to action' (Hester and Eglin 1997, p. 153). So, to find culture, we look differently, and in different places, from those ways and places that more conventional theoretical approaches would direct us to look (and listen).

This approach to culture is a release and a relief from conventional formulations of culture—as the way of life of a group, including norms, values, artefacts etc.—that are prevalent at least in the field of education. It is a relief from the weight of a notion of culture where people 'share' and things connect and ideas relate, and a release from a unitary notion of culture as a single thing that a group has (a notion that is not undone by theorising subcultures within cultures and so on). Situating culture inside action opens the possibility of seeing the different, competing ways in which culture might be done. Studying membership categorisation work—looking at how people occasion and hear descriptions, connections, claims and other activities—is one way of addressing matters of text, discourse and power. That is the direction in which I take this chapter.

MEMBERSHIP CATEGORISATION: OUTLINE OF TERMS

Membership categories are categories of person, place or activity. The ubiquitous matter of reference to persons is a place to begin to appreciate how consequential categorisation is, socially, politically and morally. Any one person can be referred to through a range of possible descriptors: frequent flier, mother, stranger, daughter, Catholic, wife, taxpayer, teacher, Australian, witness, client, and so on. For any given person, all could be correct—some for some of the time, some for all of the time. But, when is one made a 'daughter'? When is one relevantly a 'taxpayer'? The selection of descriptor is occasioned by the circumstance in which the description is done, but is not predicted by it. People can be surprised by who they are (made to be) this time, just now, right here.

A number of the categories above imply a second term to a standard relational pair, such as wife–husband or daughter–mother. Others have second terms which are strongly suggested, such as client–professional (a client is always somebody's client). Some categories in particular contexts will routinely, relevantly invoke a second term (Catholic–Protestant, but not necessarily, or everywhere), while other categories used in particular contexts can hint at silent but still relevant second terms (single–married–divorced). The hearing of the second term implied or suggested by the first is the joint activity of the speaker and a listener both using the resources of membership categorisation.

Membership categorisation devices are collections of categories plus 'rules' of application. Rules of application are not external rules or mandates, but summations of how members will ordinarily hear second and even third and fourth pair parts. Some examples follow of commonly used membership categorisation devices which can 'collect' (imply, invoke) a number of individual categories within them:

'family'	(mother, father, children . . .)
'stage of life'	(infants, children, adolescents, adults . . .)
'school'	(principal, teacher, children, students . . .)

These membership categorisation devices show that the category 'children' might belong to any of a number of membership categorisation devices and it is a local matter for members to determine which device is in play this time, often by hearing a next item and locating the relevant list that way. Similarly, a description of a person as, say, a 'taxpayer', does not settle which categorisation device might be pertinent until some other terms are produced (taxpayer–government, taxpayer–politician, taxpayer–unions, or other locally occasioned contrasts).

There may be various degrees of association made in interaction between categories and particular activities or qualities. These have been termed 'category-bound activities', 'category-tied activities', and 'predicates'. This category-boundness is heard in the baby–cry example given above. Babies cry and mommies pick them up. Crying is something that babies in particular do. Crying is a strong activity descriptor that can occasion the search for a baby doing that crying. This reasoning is all routine. People equally do work with membership categorisation devices in putting together unexpected combinations of categories and activities, in headlines such as 'Killer Sheep' (category-predicate anomaly) or in descriptions such as 'The mommy cried, the baby picked it up'.

Membership categorisation work is arguably central to all description. It is also in different places and times socially, morally, legally and politically implicative (Jayyusi 1984) and materially consequential. By selecting and hearing descriptions in particular ways, (i.e. by doing membership categorisation analysis) people propose specific courses of cultural action—often, how to reason and how to account for things. Membership categorisation analysis is not just what the formal analyst does. It is done in all sites of reading, writing, hearing and speaking.

Drawing on the outline given above, I proceed to show how membership categorisation analysis is used in various sites of reading, writing, hearing and speaking. I will add to the analysis commentary on the critical edge that can be brought alongside membership categorisation analysis to show how categorisation works in the organisation of social relations, including the organisation of discourses and power.

EXAMPLE 1: 'THE BIG DAY CAME'

An analysis of this text from a beginning school reading book shows how anyone reading the text needs to draw on their membership categorisation knowledge to get the story right. This is a segment from an old basal reader series (see also Baker and Freebody 1987).

Here We Go
The big day came.
Miss Brown and the children were ready
for the bus ride.
Some mothers had come to help.
'Will there be room for everyone?'
asked Susan.

'Yes, Susan,' said Miss Brown.
'There will be room for all of us.
It is a big bus.'
'When will our bus be here?'
asked one of the girls.
'Very soon,' said Miss Brown.
'Now, is everyone here?'

On the surface, this is a very simple text that most people have no difficulty following. However, it is possible to identify the quite considerable categorisation work that goes into an apparently straightforward reading of an apparently simple text. We are introduced to a cast of characters, but their relations with one another are not explicitly given. We derive these relations by looking at what the characters do, that is, we look at their activities. First, whose children are the children? Are they Miss Brown's children? Who is Miss Brown? What is the relation between Miss Brown and the children? Who are the mothers who came to help? Are they just a random collection of mothers? Or, are they the mothers of some of the children? Who is Susan? How do we read her as one of the children and not one of the mothers? Whose big day is it? Who goes with whom here? The text does not spell out any of this.

The resource for reading this text 'correctly' is our use of membership categorisation devices, including the 'activities' that are assigned to categories of characters in this text (category-bound or category-associated activities: predicates). For example, the question asked by Susan is heard as an excited child's question: the big day is the big day for the children—bus trips are big days for children, not mothers or even Miss Brown. It is 'mothers' who come to help. Everyone can be tucked away into their correct place in the story by importing this knowledge about what kinds of activities/predicates go with what categories. Seeing the activities/predicates helps us to decide, for example, that Susan is a child and not a mother (though it is not the only way anyone can decide this). The texture of relationships in this example has to be assembled out of the surface clues in relation to knowledge of culture.

The resources for reading the text are the same as the resources for writing it; in this case, membership categorisation resources. Eglin and Hester (1992, p. 250) identify

. . . two sides to the study of sense-making, namely the production 'problem' and the recognition 'problem'. The former speaks to the practical interactional uses to which persons may put the formal structures of action for the accomplishment of recognizable actions and activities. The latter refers to the hearer's or reader's work of using the same structures to make out what actions and activities are being produced. Members are conceptualised as having at their disposal their knowledge of the interconnectedness of language, action and world for 'solving' these problems. This knowledge is conceptualized as procedural. The study, then, becomes that of discovering the methods or practices members use to produce and recognise those connections that thereby render the world of actions, events, persons and settings analyzably transparent. Spoken and written texts . . . become rich sites for discovering these practices-in-use.

THE TEXT READ IN SCHOOL: LOCKING CULTURE INTO PLACE

Any texts which reiterate categories and their associated activities are assembling a version of social and moral order. In practice, this assembling amounts to more than merely an invitation to read the texts this way. Not any reading will do. A student who heard Susan as one of the mothers would not be deemed to be reading competently. In schools at least, some form of collusion with the text's basic categories and their related activities is part of competent reading. It is possible to illustrate this claim by examining what occurred in a reading lesson using this text (transcript courtesy J. Heap, simplified from original).

Teacher, Students

1   T: Who can tell me what happened [on] that first page
2   Ss: ((calls of Oh, I know))
3   S: Three mothers came to help and they ( )
4   T: OK three mothers came to help. Why did three mothers
         come to help?
5   S: To help the children?
6   T: Why?
7   T: Why did—why were the three mothers there though? ( )
         Where were the children going?
8   S: To the woods
9   T: They were going to the woods. They were going on what?
10 S: On a bus
11 T: They were using the bus to go where?
12 S: To the woods
13 T: They were going on a ?

14 S: ((inaudible))
15 T: Good for you.

As the transcript shows, the category of 'mothers' receives considerable attention regarding its place in the membership categorisation device (the school class in that story that day, comprised teacher–children–three mothers). The teacher's questioning arose from one student's observation that three mothers had come, and her questioning seems to pursue a reason for the mothers being there. The activity of 'helping' is bound to the category 'mothers' in the text, and also in the reading of the text. It is accepted by the teacher that the mothers had come to help, but that does not seem to be her puzzle for the students, 'why were the mothers there though?—where were the children going?'. It seems that the solution resides in something about that particular trip on a bus to the woods—what the children were going to do—rather than in the qualities of (these three) mothers. There is no questioning of why mothers are there at all (rather than fathers, say), no questioning of the category selection or of its predicate, that mothers help. Later in the story 'Miss Brown and the mothers got into the bus too' and that is the last that is heard of the mothers in the story.

We can connect this text and its classroom reading with Smith's (1987, pp. 134–40, 167–75) commentary on the dependence of classroom work on mothering work, and the professional and institutional discourses and practices that secure mothers' work within extended organisational relations. While the students in the class, and probably the teacher as well, have not read Smith, they have read and reflected back the ideological order that the text both presupposes and, in this naturalised reading, itself achieves. Such complicity with the presence and later disappearance of mothers in the story line, and the representation of mothers' work as 'helping' the class in the text—though no specific things done are mentioned—is one brief course of contact with the mothers-as-general-helpers discourse. Other points of contact would presumably be encountered repeatedly. For these reasons, 'critical' reading practices need to address the categories and predicates that underpin the natural logic of texts. These categories and predicates are the quiet centres of power and persuasion that naturalise texts.

EXAMPLE 2: A PARENT–TEACHER INTERVIEW

The next example of membership categorisation analysis comes from a study of parent–teacher talk (Baker and Keogh 1995). In this example, a teacher and two parents of a secondary school student meet to discuss the student's progress in the year so far. There are clear indications here of proposals about the relation between the work of the home and the work of the school.

The analysis shows how the teacher and parents' category memberships are central to the organisation of the talk, how they attach particular 'activities' to the categories they speak from, or as, or to, and how they disattach others being assigned to them. The analysis also shows that the work of category-elaboration is synonymous with the assembling of institutional relations and that the categorisation work involves the production of sometimes competing (moral) descriptions of persons. The talk in this interview can be examined for the speakers' competing claims to competence and the pragmatics of their describing activities. I will focus here primarily on categories and activities.

The interview took place as one in a series that the teacher conducted at a parents' evening in a secondary school in Queensland. The analysis will proceed in stages through the opening part of the interview, showing how the categorisation work proceeds sequentially.

Teacher: Ellen
Student: Donna
Parent(s):   Mother and Father
1   T: Ok all right we'll just forget it I should cover it up or
            something I hate tape recorders! (hh) Right um Donna
            um I just took over Mister Jay's class um four weeks ago
            so, I don't really know a lot about Donna's work I've had
            a quick look at her work in her folder, and from her marks
            she um, you seem to have, passed in the first part of the
            year and then really gone down in last two um, pieces of
            work which was a poetry oral? and a um a novel (2.0) a
            novel in another form that was putting part of the novel
            into another style of writing. Now um (2.0) in class (1.0)
            Donna's a little bit distracted? often? down the back there,
            with um the girls that she sits with, though she does give
            in class when she's asked to, she does do all her work, um
            I'm (1.0) would you like to—do you work with Donna at
            home with her schoolwork at all? do you see it at all or?

This opening statement by the teacher is replete with categorisation work. It can be treated as an initial sketch, a proposal, for who the participants relevantly are in this interactional event (their categorical incumbencies), what they do and should do (activities that attach to these categories), and how these categories and activities (should) connect. It is an initial map of the social and moral terrain in which representative of the school meets representatives of the home as idealised courses of action. Through re-categorisation work, some features of this map will be open to redrawing as the talk and its implications unfold.

The teacher first identifies Donna as the incumbent of the category 'students whose parents I am meeting tonight': 'Right um Donna um I just took over Mister Jay's class'. But her comment does more than this: it lines up herself as 'the teacher of Donna', and as 'a successor to Mister Jay', presumably the teacher she has replaced. This double categorisation is central in the teacher's characterisation of her own work. Simultaneously these words line up the parents as 'Donna's parents' and as people who might not know that she is now acting in Mister Jay's place. The further comment, 'so, I don't really know a lot about Donna's work I've had a quick look', additionally characterises the parents as 'interested in Donna's work' and wanting information from this teacher about it. 'I've had a quick look' also self-attributes the quality of being busy, perhaps, but certainly warns that she will not be completely informed about what she has attributed them with wanting to know.

There is then a sketch of her observations of Donna both from the markbook and from her first-hand knowledge ('seemed to have passed and then really gone down', 'often a little bit distracted . . . down the back with the girls that she sits with', 'though she does give in class . . . does do all her work'). These are produced, and hearable as, relevancies for parents as well as teachers. After a short pause the teacher issues questions to the parents which are themselves descriptions of activities which are attachable to the category of parents:

1   T: would you like to—do you work with Donna at home
          with her schoolwork at all? do you see it at all or?

This attribution of activities by a teacher to parents is a clear move in the description of home-school relationships, and particularly the work of the home, but equally the preceding desorption of 'Donna in class' casts these parents as needing or wanting to know all this about Donna, and it is for this reason they have come to the school this evening. With this handful of categories, and interactional work with them, the teacher has sketched a complex set of relations, knowledges and motivations. The parents are handed the floor at this point.

2   F: Not really no=
3   M: =(We very rarely) see her schoolwork
4   F: they generally disappear off to their bedrooms with their
         homework and um=
5   T: =Ye:es (2.0) Well um
6   F: We don't see much of (it)

The parents, led by father, have responded to the final questions, not to the preceding descriptions. 'Not really no' is a mitigated response, acknowledging that parents could be held accountable for doing these kinds of things: working with Donna, or even seeing her homework. The parents have accepted their accountability for not seeing (much) of Donna's homework but have done other than and more than confess: they have furnished a reason that could re-characterise Donna as a student who is keen to get on with her homework. This possible Donna could be one of the unspecified 'they' who 'disappear off to their bedrooms' so fast that their parents have not got a chance to see the homework. These same parents might well wish to see the homework but cannot. At this point, the parents have disattached from themselves any irresponsibility—for not working with Donna at home.

The teacher proceeds with more apologies about not knowing enough about Donna, and the parents begin to ask some questions themselves. These questions return the accountability to the teacher and the school. In (12) below, the teacher turns the talk back to what she does know first-hand about Donna.

7   T: Let me see yes I didn't mark this this was all Mister Jay's
         (1.0) This is a summary, they had to summarise um this
         (1.0) um let's see where her, mistakes seem to lie. (3.0)
         Oh it seems all right. (3.0) Why did she only get four and
         a half for that Hmmm. It's awful when you're when you're
         talking about, something another teacher's (hh) done!
         (5.0) Only seems to have limited English grammatical
         mistakes, um (4.0) oh it seems fine it's not covered all in
         red,
8   F: mm no
9   M: ( )what's the problem with it then ( )?
10 T: I don't know. Obviously maybe it's the the standard or the
         um (4.0) the ideas I'll see what Mr Jay's written here let's
         have a look. (2.0 Good more impact in conclusion is
         possible. That doesn't really say a lot does it.
11 M: Not really, no ( )
12 T: No. (3.0) Uh this is, I'm sorry about this because I haven't,

been with Donna's class so I'm not sure, I've only just
come back from leave. I know, the piece of work that I've
done with the class was a, radio play which we've just
done. And (2.0) we spent a couple of weeks in class
learning about it and then we did um had some time to
prepare it, and the girls the group of girls really didn't do
a lot of work on it I wasn't really happy with the work
that was done, and the work that did come out was um,
read from Dolly magazine or Cleo just onto the tape? So
I found that um, that wasn't not just Donna the three of
them together working together really didn't put a lot of
work into it an' [I

In (12) the teacher turns to what she does know about: the radio play,
and generates through this description a Donna who didn't do much
work. Previously the teacher had said 'She does do all her work'. The
classification of Donna as a particular kind of student is not a
straightforward matter. Any of the descriptive detail produced earlier
in the talk can be reworked in further pursuit of the apparent problem.
In (13) the mother asks a question that could be heard as informational (who was she working with) or as accountable (if Donna is
distracted, maybe she should sit with someone else).

13 M: [Who was she working with?
14 T: Umm (2.0) Joanne someone and Vicki(3.0), Joanne
        Williams
15 M: ( )
16 T: an' Vicki (2.0) Hawkins
17 M: ( )?

The parents appear to have gained some ground through getting
these names. The teacher attempts a topic switch back to her own
limits of knowledge about Donna. The parents then present another
Donna, who hates oral. The force of this is to make oral hateable.
Perhaps it is not Donna who is at fault but the character of the work
she is asked to do. The teacher issues only some agreement tokens
before changing the topic once again.

18 T: No. So on on the whole, um that's the only work I have
        real experience from, from (2.0) Donna. Um,
19 F: She said she wasn't keen on this oral
20 M: No she hates oral, she hates getting up an' [(standing up
        in front)
21 T: [Speaking, right

22 M: ['N if she ever has to stand up in front of the class, or anything like that she's not that
23 T: Yeah, [well
24 M: [( ) you know I suppose that a lot of kids are the same
25 T: Well this is um (1.0) this is where she's got a very low mark here. Wonder if her oral, oral paper's here. Oh it hasn't been put into her folder. [turn continues]

In what we can take to be carefully designed talk, teacher and parents are producing category-descriptions: of themselves as teacher or parent, of the other as parent or teacher, and of Donna in the classroom and at home. Donna is silent in all this talk about her. However, the talk is not only about Donna: it can be heard as self-description of competent category-incumbency as teacher or parent. The talk is about what activities could, should and do attach to a (competent) teacher or parent and to a (good) student. In this sense the talk is about possible ways of describing extended institutional relations as much as it is about Donna's academic work. In this instance, the categories themselves are quiet (and uncontested) but the predicates are not.

CONCLUSION: CATEGORIES AND CULTURE

We can ask of all varieties of critical discourse analysis: Just what is it that is the target of the critique? How are you critical of it? Where does this criticism lead in terms of social practice? I have proposed that by studying membership categorisation work as done in the course of speaking, hearing, reading and writing, we are able to observe uniquely how categories and associated categorisation practices permeate and organise texts and talk. The more natural, taken-for-granted and therefore invisible the categorisation work, the more powerful it is. Like the foundations of a building, categorisation practices go deep underneath the surface of words, ideas, and images that are produced in conversations, texts, and dialogues. They provide for the shape and contours of the surface configurations. They are powerful also because they are double-sided resources for speaking and hearing, writing and reading: there is collusion in their deployment.

By extension, I have argued, we can identify the categories and the categorisation work that lock cross-situational discourses and practices into place. Rearranging categories and associated activities is difficult excavation work because one encounters a history of sedimentation of usage and, therefore, of commonsense and 'logic'. This has been encountered in feminist work which has attempted to dislodge persistent and pervasive connections between gender categories and associated activities such as forms of work and rights.

By showing the pervasiveness and tenacity of the largely unnoticed and taken-for-granted work that all members do with membership categories, I have implied that a first step in challenging discourses and practices is to recognise the force of categorisation practices in social and institutional life. This chapter has sketched some initial procedures for doing the recognition work in the analysis of a text or transcript. First, identify the categories in use, especially those that are otherwise taken for granted as points in a matrix of some social institution or encounter. Second, show how various attributes, activities, qualities are attached to categories and, if relevant, how they are contested or disattached. Monologic texts and dialogic texts may well differ in the arrays of candidate activities proposed for different categories. Show how categories are related, and how they are related through descriptions of activities. Look especially for tenacious category-bound activities such as babies cry or need help, mothers help. These are the categories that lock the discourse into place, and possibly the practices that flow from them.

The specification of how discourses are secured through membership categorisation work assists the identification of how discourses are called on and how they are invoked in the mundane activities of talking, hearing, reading and writing. The use of membership categorisation analysis is always local, and always occasioned: done on an occasion of talk or writing, reading or hearing. Culture is internal to action, and can be found in the course of membership categorisation work as well as in an array of other social practices.

Membership categorisation device analysis offers a socially critical perspective on text and culture by showing a different order of phenomena in texts and in talk than is retrievable through other critical discourse analysis approaches, and by locating 'culture' in social practices. The social practices to which membership categorisation work is central include describing, accounting, and reasoning. Recall in the first example the teacher's attempts to have students find a reason for mothers to be helping at school that day in the story. For the teacher at least, there seems to have been one real reason why the mothers were there that day. That mothers were there, and that they were there to help, was treated as obvious. The students were encouraged to think about the surface of the story (the plot, the events) and not the category-predicate connections that underpin the 'reality' of the story.

While I have proposed that membership categorisation work can be studied as a means of locking texts, talk and discourses into place, and therefore 'excavating' their foundations, it needs to be recognised that this does not provide directly for the characterisation of texts, talk and discourses as conservative or not. The judgement about that matter comes from observations of how they work *in situ* or in general to arrange relations of power, privilege and advantage. That is, the political valency of a categorisation analysis is found in its material, social, symbolic applications and consequences, rather than in its contents or form per se.

7 Whose text? Methodological dilemmas in collaborative research practice

Hermine Scheeres & Nicky Solomon

This chapter focuses on the complexities of academics 'doing' collaborative research. We draw on our participation in a specific commissioned workplace research project, focusing on the new language of work, as a typical site of such collaboration. Our reflexive commentary on our work aims to bring to the surface a range of methodological, political and epistemological tensions in commissioned research in the contemporary world that puts pressure on academics to produce particular kinds of knowledge (Stronach and MacLure 1997, p. 101). We anticipate that through this reflexive process we can explore ways of developing methodological practices that open up, challenge, incite and disrupt what might be regarded as inevitable non-negotiables or closures. Collaborative research has been thought to involve compliance on the part of the academic but we argue that academics can be strategically optimistic about collaborative research, when working with notions of hybridity.

The chapter begins by positioning our commentary within the inevitable tensions of the current economic, political and social context. This is followed by a reflexive commentary on the project itself; here we analyse the texts produced both as part of and as end-products of the research process. The analysis reveals a shift in our understanding of ourselves as researchers as we struggle from a position of compliance to one of productive disruption. We present this new position as a site for further exploration of the methodological possibilities of collaborative research.

The experiences and issues addressed are both specifically Australian and also global, since most industrial and industrialising countries are also engaging in similar restructuring and workplace training reforms. Globalisation and the accompanying dismantling of borders and boundaries (be they national, commercial, or disciplinary), together with the foregrounding of vocational and workplace education and training as keys to national competitiveness and success in the global economy, are familiar themes in 'global' economic discourse. The Australian National Training Authority, for example, sees vocational education and training as 'now well-positioned to contribute significantly to a socially progressive and economically powerful Australia in the 21st century' (Australian National Training Authority 1994, Foreword).

Collaborative partnerships between government, industry and the university have been hailed by politicians as a significant cornerstone in recent workplace training reforms. The collaboration of these three partners is seen as a critical part of the technology for increasing the knowledge and skills of Australia's workforce. The alliance of government, industry and education has allowed for 'collaborative' policy construction and implementation heavily supported by commissioned research and curriculum development funding. However, such partnerships are not unproblematic.

Fuelled by the dominance of economic goals that tie together production, performativity and the master discourse of economic rationalism, workplaces are the common site of interest of all the partners. But with such partnerships, a number of dilemmas surface at local levels. These relate to tensions around the different histories and positions of the participants who, in the contemporary moment, are located within the dominant discourse of economic rationalism—with which they engage with varying degrees of resistance and compliance.

These tensions were particularly evident in the Commonwealth government commissioned project in which we were involved. The project had two stages. First, a research stage examined changing work culture and practices in enterprises that were undergoing restructuring in the context of post-Fordism. The second stage developed training programs on spoken and written language competencies relevant to communicating in these 'new' workplaces.

Before moving to details it is important to discuss the significance of this particular project in terms of the contemporary moment. This collaborative project exemplifies the intersection of a number of social changes. The first is to do with the nature of the 'new' workplace and 'new' work practices. Post-Fordist workplaces are characterised by the introduction of new technologies, ongoing job training and increased consultative and participatory processes at all levels of the workplace.

Many enterprises are currently implementing flattened hierarchies in which work roles are becoming less differentiated and where the notion of teamwork or working in teams underpins the new relationships (with team members ranging from operator level workers to managers). The contemporary privileging of social relationships at work and the construction of workers as social subjects have foregrounded the role of language at work. Spoken and written language were once invisible at work, only noticed if there was a communication breakdown, particularly in the case of non-English speaking background employees. Yet now, with the textualisation of the new workplace and the accompanying privileging of the relational, 'communication' has a central place in workplace and training discourses. Communication in the workplace not only encompasses a range of spoken and written language practices, but is now regarded as the key to 'effective' work practices and thus to productivity increases.

This new interest in communication in workplaces is accompanied by what has become known in contemporary cultural analysis as the 'linguistic turn', where theorists from a variety of disciplines:

> . . . have declared language to bring facts into being and not simply to report on them . . . Meaning of any object resides not within that object itself but is a product of how that object is socially constructed through language and representation. (du Gay 1996, p. 42)

The interdisciplinary interest in the relationship of language to social and cultural process, and thus to the production of knowledge, has opened up interest in language and discourse analysis as methods for studying social change.

The project was possible not only because of the increasing recognition of the importance of language in the changing contemporary workplace but also because of the growth of significant academic expertise in discourse analysis. Our own location, in such a climate and given our own particular academic training in applied linguistics, positioned us as particular kinds of researchers. In Fairclough's (1992) terms our research could be seen as part of the 'technologization of discourse' where, as institutional agents, we consciously intervened in discursive practices in order to bring about change. The research focused on describing and developing efficient, effective practices of the new workplace and our task was to influence the practices of workplace trainers.

This contingent coalition of interests is highlighted in the recent book, *The New Work Order: behind the language of the new capitalism*

(Gee, Hull and Lankshear 1996), whose authors lay out their project as follows:

> Framed within a socio-cultural studies perspective, we want to determine what particular social identities workers are expected to construct and display, and what related social practices they are expected to learn, demonstrate and value. What ways of talking, listening, reading, writing, acting, interacting, believing and valuing are expected in newly organised and reconstructed workplaces, and how close or far are these from an egalitarian ideal of empowerment? (p. 75)

Governments, industry and educational institutions are all emphasising the importance of language, literacy and numeracy skills. One Commonwealth government department commissioned report (Courtenay and Mawer 1995, p. 14), for example, states that:

> . . . economic and industrial imperatives, access and equity considerations, and current thinking in the fields of adult learning and language and literacy development, all call for programs which can develop the language, literacy and numeracy competence of the job as part of vocational skills development.

Thus, the discursive construction of the 'new worker' includes the foregrounding of spoken and written language skills and the integration of these into competency standards (Australian National Board of Employment, Education and Training (NBEET) 1993). New education and training in these areas has developed into an industry of its own as government-funded language and literacy projects; industry-funded programs; university consultancies; and private providers all develop and offer diagnoses, curricula and training to help workers at all levels in the workplace attain the standards required to ensure increased productivity levels.

This is the background to the project. The development of our research methodology was appropriate to the government and industry agendas and desired outcomes. As academics, however, our research work was problematised by the tensions and ensuing collisions that became evident among the different players. Our principal research interest was to understand the complexities around the construction of workplace knowledge and practices in the context of the changing culture of work. On the other hand, the goal of the funding body was for us to provide a rational, linear description of the communication skills needed for productive and efficient work and of the training that would lead to these outcomes. The funding body saw the research as a task and product-oriented activity—identifying discrete spoken and written language competencies relevant to communicating in a range of job areas in the food industry and the subsequent development and delivery of relevant training based on the research. Changing work roles are often regarded as easily understood and able to be learned in short bursts of training, consisting of communication skills (negotiation, conflict resolution, assertiveness training and the like) and/or language and literacy skills improvement (spoken and written language for people with language backgrounds other than English and for people who have literacy 'problems').

The complexities around the reconciliation of the different goals of the various participants in this project will be discussed in the following section. First, however, some further discussion on the intersecting social, economic and political factors that contextualise the significance of collaborative research.

The participation of academics in commissioned workplace research can, in part, be understood in the context of economic rationalist discourse and its blurring of the 'distinction between educational and non-educational discourses and practices' (Usher 1997, p. 110). Educators, in contemporary universities, are not neutral disinterested seekers of workplace knowledge. Educational institutions, like their research sites, are workplaces. Academics in universities are not simply sociological observers of the effects of economic rationalism on contemporary workplaces and work practices. They are 'in business'—in this case business that involves the commodification and marketing of education. While academics might analyse or even struggle with the colonisation of education by managerial discourse, they too are in the marketplace. Their business needs more markets in order to be successful in the increasingly competitive global market.

Winning commissioned research contracts has its financial rewards, enabling the employment of academic staff, but also in terms of the higher education funding formulas, where a competitive index is used to distribute research funding. In other words, the previous year's research 'productivity' influences the funding allocation for the following year. Furthermore, academics have been involved in the construction of the workplace as a site of 'learning' and, therefore, a potential recruiting ground for new students. Thus, our complicity in commissioned research workplace projects has its own financial rewards, illustrating the inseparability of workplace reforms, research and educational practice.

This alliance forces us to consider two contrasting positions that are often taken in relation to academic compliance with the government agenda. The first is the critique from the Left that accuses academics engaged in commissioned research of 'selling out' to the economic rationalist agenda. Resistance, it is argued, in the form of non-participation, is needed to subvert the agenda. The second position is the strategic optimism argument which suggests that academic strategic intervention will make a difference. This position argues that we must exploit the opening provided in the new alliance in order to intervene and, thus, influence the agenda and the products to less performative ends (Luke 1995).

We argue that the first position fails to acknowledge the ambiguities and complexities that pull together academics, government and industry into activities centred on the dominance of economic goals. The second position, on the other hand, offers a useful point of consideration—useful in our commentary but also in the development of research tools for intervening in a way that unsettles the otherwise unproblematised realisation of economic rationalist goals.

Before examining the details of our project, first a brief discussion on the principle of performativity—a principle that underpins an economic bottom line explanation of productivity and one which makes the alliance between research, economics and the state almost inevitable. According to Lyotard (1984 p. 44), performativity is 'the principle of optimal performance: maximizing output (the information or modifications obtained) and minimizing input (the energy expended in the process)'. He further says that where:

> . . . the goal is no longer truth, but performativity—that is the best possible input/output equation. The State and/or company must abandon the idealist and humanist narratives of legitimation in order to justify the new goal: in the discourse of today's financial backers of research, the only credible goal is power. (Lyotard 1984, pp. 44–46)

Lyotard (1984, p. 47) goes on to speak of how a 'legitimation by power takes shape':

> Power is not only good performativity, but also effective verification and good verdicts. It legitimates science and the law on the basis of their efficiency, and legitimates this efficiency on the basis of science and law. It is self-legitimating in the same way a system organized around performance maximization seems to be.

Government commissioned research with its emphasis on performativity is an exemplary site, illustrating the way in which the spaces of contemporary educational research have been subjected to:

- intensification of research work through shorter contracts;
- greater formal control by state and quasi-state bodies;
- greater links between policy and research;
- funding competition which has led to a research economy where the emphasis is on competition and status display.

PAST COMPLIANCE: FUTURE DISRUPTION

What follows is a reflexive commentary on the commissioned research project that we were involved in: an examination of the language and literacy practices of three restructuring food industry enterprises (Joyce et al. 1995). Two years after completion, we have continued to discuss the research process and the outcomes. In particular, we want to re-examine our roles as researchers in relation to feelings of compliance and our struggles with this during the project and to explore ways of opening up this research space as a site of contestation. We want to re-present this and other commissioned research as areas where a number of positions can be taken up by researchers. The possibilities of taking up particular positions can only be seen if researchers enter the project recognising that the research methodology is a site of contention. Our commentary focuses on three written texts from that project—a predictable sequence of textual practices in commissioned research: the submission (i.e. the tender document), the final report (i.e. the text that signals the closure of the research project) and the training manuals (i.e. the desired textual outcome or product). These three texts provide the focus for the analysis of the research process. The discussion also includes a linguistic analysis of one of the 'meeting' texts gathered during data collection. We use this commentary on our own textual practices and those of the 'new workplace' to highlight the way in which a social and linguistic analysis of our work both reveals and constructs disruptive moments.

We are speaking from an academic position within the discipline of education. Our intellectual interest is in understanding the new kinds of knowledge about the contemporary nature of work and the meanings of 'education' and 'training' for contemporary work. We have been involved in many commissioned research projects on workplace communication and experienced the tensions around the need to find and then offer 'simple and relevant truths' that fit within the desired outcomes of government and industry. Moreover, these 'truths', it is argued, need to be articulated in a clear language that potentially empowers workers. Our concern is, though, that being complicit in this view of 'truth' also means surrendering to populist rhetoric about education—such as the belief that there are simple single solutions to, for example, the literacy 'crisis', if only we could 'get our education right'.

Conflicting desires regarding outcomes implicate methodological questions and concerns. For example, do we unsettle a 'positivist' approach and how might this be done without jeopardising the project or our reputations within the commissioned workplace research space? (The latter, of course, raises important questions of its own regarding any future involvement in this kind of research.) Another question might be, do we have two layers: one which meets the government agenda and another which speaks to academics? Can we then construct and make explicit a method for having two layers or a hybrid methodology? In understanding hybrid research we draw on the work of Stronach and MacLure who describe it as work that is not a 'rejection of previous methodologies or interpretative frames so much as an acknowledgment of their transgressive "other"' (1997, p. 112).

On the surface there was a congruence of our aims and the aims of the funding bodies. However, below the surface there was another logic operating, involving the dynamic between the research process and the expected product—competency-based training programs. This product is not disconnected from either the tendering processes or the research process. Our research questions were: How could we make explicit our interest in knowledge about the social identities of workers and their social practices in 'reconstructing' workplaces, given the lack of readiness of workplaces and industry bodies to engage in such complexities? How could we embed the complexities of workplace language and relationships within competency-based training modules with their prescriptive boundaries and organisation closing down the 'openness' of good learning?

The research practices themselves (the relationship between data collection, and data analysis) and their relationship to the development and trialling of the training manuals, shifted our focus and interest from simply reporting on what we found to examining the nature of what we, as government, industry and academic researchers, were doing. Our analysis and commentary are selective rather than exhaustive in considering the different research moments where we as researchers reflect on our performance and on our attempts to disrupt the 'positivist' research process. We see our work as a starting point for further exploration and development of alternative research practices.

The submission

The submission, the text that persuades the funding body of our expertise, unproblematically accepts the current economic agenda by complying with the promise that improving the communication skills of workers will increase productivity and that improved communication will result from the development of training programs focusing on the new communication demands. This message is reinforced by the title of one of the subsections: 'How the proposed project would increase worker productivity'.

The description of the research methodology reveals further compliance with government and industry's desired outcomes. It involved ethnographic studies of the sites as well as linguistic analysis of the collected spoken and written texts. The methodology, as reflected in the submission, provided a linear procedural description of tasks:

1   Collection of data, involving observation and taping of team meetings, consultative committees and training programs, interviews with employees and management, observation of job performance at the operator level.
2   Collation and analysis of findings.
3   Identification of oral communication competencies and strategies for relevant work contexts.
4   Development of 'Train the Trainer' modules.
5   Trialling and revision of modules.
6   Production of modules.
7   Delivery of modules in food industry enterprises around Australia.

This list describes certain kinds of research practices that resonate with a 'positivist' approach emphasising determinacy, rationality, impersonality and prediction, using the natural sciences as the model (Usher 1996, pp. 14–15). It is, therefore, the perfect match for the required outcome, that is, a rational, linear description of the communication skills needed for productive and efficient work and the kind of training that would lead to these outcomes.

Predictably, perhaps, the research methodology conceals one of our principal research interests which was to understand the complexities around the construction of workplace knowledge and practices. There was no suggestion in the methodology of the significance of local site-specific factors that might challenge the production of a generic list of oral communication competencies and generic training modules for trainers. Furthermore, our use of a positivist methodology reveals nothing of our own academic position on research: a position which challenges positivist epistemology. Our research paradigm (as practised in unaligned projects) recognises not only that the site of the research is a sociocultural construct but also that research is itself a sociocultural practice.

Thus, the complexities of the research process itself remained invisible. We presented the accepted model of commissioned research —enter workplace, collect data, analyse data, turn into desired training packages, then do the training (and perhaps evaluation). Implicit in this model is the rejection of anything that would thwart the process and anticipated outcomes. There is also no recognition that the researchers themselves influence the nature of the data collection. Researchers are hired because of their expertise (which includes a history of involvement, knowledge and getting the job done) but it is their 'technical expertise' that allows them to identify 'objectively' what is to be found.

There is a space which could be opened up here at the submission stage which would disrupt the rational, linear progression that appears so unproblematic and omits any human agency. The description of tasks could then include contributions by the participants as an integral part of the process, rather than full orchestration by the researchers. This would undoubtedly increase the potential for upsetting the seemingly simple progression of tasks and attendant outcomes. It would also mean that the unproblematic outcomes, as stated in the submission, should rather allow for a range of possibilities that are likely to emerge during a multiply layered research process.

The final report

There is little evidence in the report of the complexities of the research process or product. The focus is on the unproblematic, linear process. The report reveals the way in which we met the aims of the project, its rationale and its achievements. We succeeded; that is, our research was legitimate on the basis of its efficiency. We provided the proof and thus established the validity of the outcomes. The report reveals that we 'found' a deficit of language skills in the workforce (a consequence of most operator-level employees being from a non-English speaking background in combination with the introduction of new work practices that required more communication skills). We identified what was needed and we then developed and delivered training—implicit in this is the expectation that increased worker productivity would follow. In terms of the performativity principle, we performed well—'the best possible input/output equation' (Lyotard 1984, pp. 44–45).

The report was completed and presented long before any long-term outcomes could be assessed. We adopted the common practice of justifying our work by the inclusion of comments from the participants' evaluation forms collected during the trialling process of the manuals, for example:

'We've got to do this right across the site.'

'This is an excellent course and everyone, well 99 per cent of people, would get something out of it.'

'It taught us to communicate effectively.'

Such comments construct and provide proof, thus validating 'our success'. Yet this success, with its performative basis, should not be underestimated. The trialling did reveal a number of significant successes in our terms: the training helped participants consider the power relationships in their workplace and importantly understand better the way in which language is a resource for making meaning. This positive feedback can be seen, therefore, in two ways: providing validity for the funding body as well as affirming our own participation in the research.

The report does reveal some of the complexities of the introduction and implementation of new management and work practices. In outlining the findings we raised a number of issues, calling them 'general tendencies'. Some examples of the tendencies that were identified are:

- Meetings still *tend* to be hierarchically based if higher level management is present.
- Managers and supervisors still *tend* to dominate as they follow old and established patterns of communication.
- Men *tend* to take most turns at talk and often do not acknowledge the contribution of other members and often do not allow other members to have their full say.
- Non-English speaking background employees, especially women, *tend* to be disadvantaged in larger workplace meetings.
- Some middle managers *tend* to be threatened by the development of teams in the workplace.
- Operators now responsible for the maintenance of their machines *tend* to feel intimidated by fitters who may continue to insist that the operator is overstepping the boundaries.
- Employees *tend* to doubt the commitment of managers who remained distant from the shopfloor at a time of great change.
- Team members *tend* to be frustrated by the lack of response to their requests and suggestions which they made as part of a team.
- Lack of recognition for achievements *tends* to lead quickly to disillusionment.
- Many employees *tend* to criticise team training if it is undertaken

too soon or if the trainer does not relate the training directly to their workplace.

These 'tendencies' are significant in terms of the way in which they foreground the continuation of hierarchical power relations. But, interestingly, there is a lack of analysis of these in the report. There is an invisible assumption that managerial problems raised by the employees have been addressed (successfully) within the body of the training manuals and that the training program will be a site for raising and addressing them. Yet, many go beyond the training possibilities.

Our analysis of the report revealed to us that we did not make visible the relationship between these tendencies and the content of the training program. The absence of any discussion about the difficulties of the training manual genre, its discreteness and its potential impact, raises questions about our compliance in the very *writing* of the report.

Perhaps, the challenge here for researchers lies in a consideration of the following questions. Did the dominant genre, in which the final report was written, establish the boundaries of what could and could not be articulated? Could we have raised the dilemmas by writing the text in a different way? Could we have presented questions rather than resolutions, given the different histories and expectations of our partners, in a text that required very particular kinds of meanings? Could we have asked, with Robin Usher (1997, p. 9): 'Is it possible to use textuality against itself and write in a way which exemplifies openness and multiple meanings but which yet is still about something?'.

The training manuals

We met the desired outcomes in producing a training program that complied (both in content and design) with the expectations of those who commissioned the work—material that not only provides tight boundaries around each unit of competency but also one that renders invisible the politics and power relationships of workplaces that in many ways influence the effectiveness of communication more than discrete spoken or written language skills. Thus, the product, the training manuals, can be seen as a technology for regulating employees and their learning as well as an example of how we, as educators, have been regulated.

There was an enormous contrast between the ethnographic and linguistic richness of data that we collected and the concrete outcomes that were required by the project. The problems and case studies were presented as if they were easily resolved by following a number of procedures and steps using simple, clear and 'appropriate' language. The training manuals were presented in a way that rendered invisible the tensions, complexities and dilemmas around both the research process and the products. Thus, the workplace problems were silenced by the nature of their simple resolutions and, at the same time, the tensions around the research process itself were also silenced, shutting down the potential for detailed exploration of the complexities.

The prescriptive boundaries established through the content of the training manuals reveal an additional significant factor. The research process involved investigation of social and language practices at local specific sites, yet local knowledge about these practices was not integrated into the manuals. This absence perhaps can be explained in terms of Foucault's (1979) notion of disciplinary power exercised through the panoptic gaze. The prescriptive contents of the training manuals became part of the surveillance whereby workers regulate their practices 'automatically' according to 'anonymous' corporate power relations. The panoptic gaze is embodied in discursive practices which involve both the use of particular language (for example, 'team-work', 'empowerment' and 'self-direction') and particular kinds of activities which both shape and are shaped by training. This, therefore, becomes part of the technology involving the internalising of control and the imposition of 'self-discipline'.

It is important to note here that 'trialling' of the training manuals was part of the project. This was part of the 'invisible' research phase. Training sessions are a site where workers and their subjectivities, histories and sociocultural locations come to the fore. It was here that some of the tensions and differences in agendas became most apparent. In this context, in our dual role as researchers and trainers, we had a number of overlapping interests. We were interested in raising the consciousness of the workers about government/industry ideologies. We were interested in exploring with the workers the changing workplace as a postmodern site. At the same time, we wanted to complete the training days with 'success' stories to tell, of communication skills and strategies recognised, understood and learned!

Nevertheless, we do acknowledge that in some ways the training did disturb, if not challenge, the expected performative outcomes. As described earlier, the research methodology included a substantial amount of ethnographic and linguistic work. The data collected through our interviews and observations revealed the way in which power was played out in the workplaces. While we may have felt constrained by the genre of training, we did go beyond expectations by providing, as part of the activities, a number of transcripts that highlighted the complexities of the power relationships in the work-places.

As researchers with linguistic backgrounds, we were able to analyse the spoken texts at a number of levels and the outcomes of these analyses were then built into the training activities. In order to demonstrate the way in which we were able to do this, what follows is an example from the *Team Work* manual of a dialogue that is part of the unit entitled 'Acknowledging contributions'. This exchange is part of a weekly team meeting held to discuss issues, present ideas, find solutions etc. relevant to the production process in a particular section of the workplace. The team meeting demonstrates the new work order in action. It exemplifies the flattened hierarchy where power and responsibility should be shared and contributions from all workers are supposedly equally valued. This particular dialogue high-lights the presentation of ideas and how they are acknowledged by fellow workers.

1 L: John changed his mind he doesn't want to carry on any longer with cooling the lasagne—so I come up with a booklet which will be one page to one weekend and its shows who is working on that day—then I give a copy on Friday I give it to the gate house and booklet is always and the book is always next to the printer and the new bench next to the right hand side door of the computer—on the other side on the cover we've got phone numbers to everybody so—people who work—so if you need to ring them and chase another person for example for the shift. It would be easier . . .

2 C: Easier?

3 H: Can I make a suggestion—instead of leaving it on the table. Can you put it in the filing cabinet—put a file . . .

4 L: But that way—people who might not be sure whether—when what shift they're working cannot check—it's easy for us . . .

5 H: Why have the book sitting on the table for a full week—just in case somebody comes up and asks—put it in the filing cabinet!

6 L: But what is the harm of the book sitting there?

7 H: It's just that if all the books get left around—it makes the place untidy.

8 L: One little booklet.

9   H: They're going to come and ask you anyway, so they can go
        straight to the cupboard.
10 E: Even with that book—they'll—they'll still come and ask
        you.
11 H: So are you responsible for the packing on weekends now?
12 L: Yes—quite often—like John for example—Like John might
        have a person who doesn't show up—he could ring up
        somebody or check who he was supposed to . . .
13 E: Fine good system—well done.
14 L: So why—why hide it?
15 H: Just leave it out for the weekend.
16 L: Okay fine you win—you win.

An initial reading of this text reveals the significance of the
relationships between the workers involved in this exchange. The
dialogue is ostensibly an argument for the introduction of a new
booklet outlining rosters. However, the meeting site is also a contested
terrain where struggles for power are played out. The language of each
speaker constructs and reinforces the positions and powers of the
workers in their everyday hierarchical work roles: L is the operator,
bidding for the acknowledgement and valuing of his contribution—he
'fails'; H is the operations manager—he 'wins'; and the others are also
operators.

Our linguistic training has also given us insights and tools for
analysing the powerful role of language in either maintaining or
disrupting existing power relations—of benefit not only for us as researchers to reflect on and analyse our own textual practices, but also
for employees and managers in workplaces who struggle with new ways
of working and the communication practices they necessitate.

We did a more detailed analysis of the spoken text in order to
make explicit how the meanings glossed above are realised throughout
the text. We focused on the tenor of this text; that is, the social
relations being realised by specifically interpersonal language choices
including mood (relevant to the conversational role taken up by a
speaker and the complementary role assigned to another), modality
(relevant to deference and willingness to negotiate) and attitudinal or
evaluative vocabulary (relevant to the investments of speakers, both
emotional and ideological). What follows is a partial analysis that
informed the development of the activities that accompanied this
dialogue in the training manual.

L introduces his new idea speaking in unmodalised declaratives
(turn 1). At the end of his turn he moves to a modalised 'would' with

an evaluative comment 'easier' which allows space for an interruption in the form of a question from a co-worker. H, the manager, seizes the opportunity to enter the discussion. His comment, a modalised 'can' interrogative, changes in the third clause to the beginning of an imperative (turn 3). Further through the text, H's turns move from presenting two arguments against L's new idea (7 and 9) to an interrogative, shifting the ideational meanings from the booklet to L's work role (11). Here, the subject positions of H and L are made more explicit. What follows is a speedy 'resolution' where H's final turn is an imperative, albeit introduced by the modalised 'just', making clear to L and others that the matter is resolved (15). L understands this and his final comment reinforces his failure and thereby acknowledges the power and the hierarchy of the old workplace (16).

Within the dialogue L moves from statements (1 and 4) to interrogatives (6 and 14) and unfinished (somewhat incoherent) clauses (12) where, following his opening presentation, his turns are constrained (mainly by H). He shifts from a position of power in the exchange to one with no power. H begins by trying to construct himself as an equal participant by opening with interrogatives (3 and 5), then moves to declaratives (7 and 9) and finally uses a clear imperative (15). In other words, H's power becomes more overt as the dialogue progresses. This reading of the text highlights the fate of both efforts to challenge existing power relationships and to reassert them in this supposed flattened hierarchy.

The accompanying activity in the manuals focuses on the importance of the power relationships in the exchange of ideas in meetings. Participants can therefore begin to develop a language for reflecting on and understanding the new communication practices. In the actual trialling of the materials, when we moved from being academic researchers to trainers, the discussions prompted by this dialogue and accompanying activities ranged far beyond the simple linear development of language skills and strategies that is implicit in the manuals. The participants were able to explore the complexities and contestations of these new terrains, resulting in a discussion around the multiple possibilities of outcomes in 'acknowledging contributions'.

In reflecting on our research practices, the differences between the experience of training sessions and what appeared as written texts in the manuals were obvious: even though the manuals problematised communication practices in the workplace, the problems were presented as solvable in a linear, rational way—this is the genre of training manuals. The recognition that ideologies and sociopolitical locations underpin all the new (and old) ways of working is there, but the emphasis is on moving from this to successful ways of operating in the new culture as though the new identities are simply a set of skills and strategies to be learned. There is a kind of hollow reassurance that the skills and strategies have, as one of their bases, a valuing of (cultural) diversity.

CONCLUSION

A range of desires and goals will continue to exist in all collaborative workplace research, whether the research is commissioned or not. As researchers and educators we need to problematise 'collaborative' research and question the nature of collaboration and compliance, given the potentially opposing interests and goals of the various partners. Workplaces have become important sites for interdisciplinary research and academics are becoming more involved in workplace research. Our involvement is the result of: first, our 'academic' interest in theorising the nature of new workplace knowledge and the construction of 'knowledge workers' (Drucker 1993; Gee, Hull and Lankshear 1996) and in exploring the implications for education and training; and second for commercial reasons. A university is also a workplace and, therefore, also one of the sites of contestation around sociopolitical and educational discourses. We are implicated in and thus participants in blurring the distinctions between education and training.

We need to consider ways in which we can participate collaboratively and at the same time use research to extend understandings about the tensions and the contestations around the construction of knowledge. We need to resist surrendering to the need to find simple, accessible and immediately relevant truths and definitions of what counts as success—our challenging of these has to be visible and needs to be an explicit part of the collaborative initiatives among academics and government. One focus might be to develop a different theoretical perspective on what arises from the interviews, observations and training sessions. So, for example, instead of seeing the issues and problems of restructuring workplace practices as disruptions which either interfere with the linear, rational progression towards 'truth' or as texts which provide case studies or scenarios with problems to be examined, discussed and solved, issues and problems could be reconstructed as disruptions exemplifying the multiplicity of subjectivities and desires of the workers.

Research methodology can build in the disruptions within a

theoretical framework of transgressive validity that 'runs counter to the standard *validity* of correspondence: a nonreferential validity interested in how discourse does its work' (Lather 1993, p. 675). This methodology could then be described as hybrid research (Stronach and MacLure 1997), where modern and postmodern approaches intersect. The contract with its agreed products—texts and training—need not be abrogated, but the outcomes would include the training participants' explorations and disruptions disturbing the prescriptive single outcome. For example, the genre of the training manual would be challenged. Genres are often seen as closed and prescriptive, set in historical moments. A broader perspective sees genres as cultural constructs which evolve over time. They are efficient ways of 'getting things done' that often appear fixed and immutable. Yet, when the broader perspective is adopted, communications training in the workplace can be open, equity principles can operate and training can focus on social relations and multiple subjectivities. This contradicts the closed nature of training and training manuals. The opportunity for outcomes which recognise the complexities of the restructured workplace and restructured workers are opened up and valued. Researchers can come to play the role of those referred to by Gee, Hull and Lankshear (1996, p. 82) as 'language and cultural workers' who:

> . . . helped build trust between the researchers and people from whom they were separated by a vast cultural and social gulf. These relationships helped immeasurably as the researchers attempted to understand work activities and social positions on the shop floor. The goal was to understand workers by placing them within their historical, social, cultural and work contexts as fully as possible.

8 Feminist methodologies in discourse analysis: sex, property, equity

Penny Pether & Terry Threadgold

It should therefore be borne in mind throughout that a norm, or a law, is never something simply 'within' a closed system . . . the refusal to accept the closed terrains of conventional legal thought is an anti-conservative step . . . One such possibility, for instance, is the acceptance of multiplicity in social organisation rather than the simple division of social categories into the same and different . . . Like law, property is a mechanism of exclusion . . . (Davies 1994, pp. 17–19)

Rather than denying the orthodoxy, morality or reality of passion and love, the code addresses the kinds of practical and ethical problems that are faced by lovers and indeed by every remotely emotionally invested relationship. What is looked for in the casuistry of love is a certain justice in relationships, a justice that requires at the very least that the relation between lovers be the object of serious social speech . . . the *regulae amoris* work towards the notion of a jurisdiction which does justice to intimacy. (Goodrich 1996, p. 52)

The broad concepts and discretionary remedies of equity have enabled it to adjust readily to the different demands and conditions of modern society . . . this is a work which captures the spirit of equity and enables us to appreciate the shining virtues of a system of law, not based on custom and usage, but devised with vision and ingenuity by the judges themselves. (Mason 1996, pp. v–vi)

THERE IS NO OUTSIDE THE TEXT

The juxtaposition of these different voices at the outset of this paper allows us to locate *intertextually* some of the central sites and categories of contestation that a feminist discourse analysis of legal texts, in this case judgements involving equity, might hope to negotiate. It is worth noting here that Davies' feminist collocation of the lexical items *property*, *exclusion* and *legitimacy*, and her desire for *multiplicity*, have some resonances with Goodrich's desire for *serious social speech* about *intimacy* between lovers and a *jurisdiction* that would do justice to intimacy. It is also worth noting that these 'undisciplined' *ratio decidendi* (reasons for judgement) seem to bear little relationship to the visions of equity articulated by Mason. Contra the historical facts of equity as told by recent feminist scholars (Scutt 1990), for Mason, equity is still 'judge-made law' and still more flexible than the common law—not so encumbered with a weight of precedent and history. This seems a curiously ingenuous characterisation in the light of the operation of precedent which we will demonstrate in modern equity in the Australian context. And yet both sets of positions share a concern with change, the first desiring transgression (but not destruction) of the limits of the existing legal system (Davies 1994, p. 16), the second seeing change and adaptation as already contained within the *shining virtues* of equity and the *vision and ingenuity* of the judges.

What this small intertextual example demonstrates, then, is something of what Derrida means when he says 'there is nothing outside the text', namely that we cannot look 'directly' at the texts of equity, or of law in general, except 'through other frames, other horizons, other socio-historico-linguistico-political presuppositions, other "differential" relationships or networks', which, in Derrida's language, are the 'differential play' of the 'trace' or of *ecriture* (writing) (Derrida in Caputo 1997, p. 80). In other words, as texts which engage in discourse about equity and law, these are also texts which, as the traces of writings, produce and construct the things of which they speak, constantly *differing* with one another and *deferring* any final definition of equity itself.

Much of the most radical work that has been done on the critical discourse analysis of legal texts has been done with the aid of deconstruction (Derrida 1992; Cornell 1991, 1992, 1995), and modes of literary and rhetorical analysis (Goodrich 1990, 1991, 1996). There are strong connections between new historicist literary approaches which rely heavily on intertextuality (Levinson 1986), poststructuralist discourse analysis and aspects of deconstruction. Deconstruction itself, in its aim to understand as fully as possible the etymologies, the histories, the narratives embedded in words and the networks of other words in which words themselves are embedded, does textual work that is related to the work done by certain modes of linguistics.

The difference between these uses of linguistics and deconstruction is that, in the latter, the processes of analysis themselves are always profoundly historicised and always self-consciously subject to a certain 'dissension'—the struggle internal to meanings which always precedes any decision (Davies 1994, p. 95). Derrida's use of the neologism 'différance' is similar to the term 'dissension' and was developed contra Saussurean linguistics to suggest that sameness and difference within the system produce not 'value' but 'différance'—a constant struggle within meaning between fixity and deferral, a struggle engendered by the tendency of texts to wander, and thus to be *both* constantly at risk of being remade in new contexts *and* to be always at risk of bringing old contexts with them (Threadgold 1997a, pp. 89–90). Derrida also makes a distinction between 'repetition' and 'iteration' in order to emphasise the possibility of difference within what looks like textual, discursive or generic repetition. He argues that iterability or citation implies always *both* identity and difference:

> Limiting the very thing it authorises, transgressing the code or the law it constitutes, the graphics of iterability inscribes alteration irreducibly in repetition (or in identification) . . . (Derrida 1988, p. 62)

In the case of Derridean arguments about the discourse of law, judgement or decision is the moment which, like all iteration, always contains the 'discrepancy of a difference' and so might exceed the normative structures of the law and accomplish justice. But it is also true that Derridean scholars have accepted the other consequence of this argument, that the legal system, precisely because it is structured by the inevitable repetition of the same, as well as the difference of iteration, and because of the disciplinary and generic need to *appear* the same in order to be considered 'proper' law, changes slowly if it changes at all (Threadgold 1997a, p. 87). It may not then produce justice; lack of justice, in other words, may be systemic and this failure is seen as an inevitable consequence of 'iteration'.

There is then a difficulty with the Derridean argument and it relates to the questions of habitus, of corporeality and embodied experience. What we have to ask as feminists is whether 'iteration' is enough, whether there is not some need for something more, something that might make change happen more rapidly. Derrida has also argued that the process by which a text continues to work without the help of its producer (iteration/repetition) is only 'pseudo-mechanical', and the origin or producer is not purely mechanical. It seems to us then that this 'not purely mechanical' textual producer needs to be theorised.

Thus, for us, it is in the habitus in its interactions with text and discourse, not merely in a transformative poetics which would change only language, that possibilities for transformative justice might be located. This can be accomplished through different pedagogies, in making the habitus differently, or in making more than one habitus in law schools. Feminist initiatives in legal education in Australia have been designed precisely to intervene in the gendered process of making the body legally literate, and this in order to 'engineer' difference in repetition. Difference is also produced when those who are raced, sexed, and/or sexually-oriented differently, begin to experience and to question the white, male, heterosexual assumptions underpinning the habitus-forming institutional processes characteristic of the subject-formation of lawyers. Pether (1997, 1998) has theorised such 'difference' in terms of an Irigarayan, Levinasian ethics of alterity.

The theorising we have done here may help to explain differences in the ways in which specific judges take up or fail to take up new ideas, move or do not move towards change.

HISTORY AND DECONSTRUCTION

Historically, many claims have been made for equity, including that it was the court most open to the poor and the powerless, that it provided a necessary counter to the oppressions of the common law, and that it benefited women by shielding them 'from the harshness of common law principles which denied them a legal existence and a right to control property during marriage' (Loughlan 1996, p. 11). All these 'correctives' were imagined in terms of the judges' understanding of what was and was not *conscionable conduct*. Equity in its earliest forms was a 'supplement' to a 'common law' which might 'fall short by reason of its universality' (Aristotle, *Nicomichean ethics*, Book V, ch. 10, quoted in Loughlan 1996, p. 4). The earliest forms of equitable appeal from the common law courts were to the King through the Lord Chancellor, the King being perceived to retain the right to dispense justice outside the established courts (Loughlan 1996, p. 6). 'Adjudication in Chancery was therefore contextual and pragmatic', being able, it is claimed, to divorce itself from abstract rules and precedent and deal with the particular circumstances of a case if the application of common law rules alone seemed 'harsh and unjust' (Loughlan 1996, pp. 7–8). The early Lord Chancellors were trained in canon law, and the term 'conscience', as used in early equity jurisprudence, was influenced by its meanings in that context. Loughlan, however, also points to two rather different and more secular senses that the term came to have: the idea that the conscience of the King and the realm was actually enforced through Chancery in a form of conscience-based reasoning; and the alternative imperative to correct *other men's* consciences by ensuring that they did not act unconscionably (1996, pp. 9–10). Thus, Sir Anthony Mason refers to the 'ecclesiastical natural law foundations of equity' (1996, p. 1; Loughlan 1996, p. 4) as if matters such as 'nature', 'conscience' and 'morality' derived from such source are merely givens, not to be questioned. The issue of 'natural' to whom, whose 'conscience', and 'moral' when and for whom, it seems, has still not arisen as late as 1993 for this judge. Yet these are all corporeal and very specific questions, which elide the very great differences in power which may be at stake in courts of equity, and presume a patriarchal right to judge in the best interests of those less powerful, to 'protect' such people, according to the judge's conscience.

Goodrich, not so confident as Loughlan that all is for the best in this best of all possible legal worlds, rewrites the notion of equitable 'protection' as subjection and surveillance (1996, p. 21):

> The Crown, in one particularly striking definition, was a 'nursing father' whose ghostly power was to be used to the end of nurturing the inner subjection or spiritual obedience of both institutions and individuals within the Commonwealth.

It is possible to see in Mason's pronouncements the ghostly traces of the 'nursing father' and all the attendant dangers of such paternal protection (Threadgold 1997a, pp. 154–60). We will have good reason below to return to these intimations of immortality and to the priestly divinations of judges.

Meanwhile recent feminist work has also been deconstructing conventional histories of equity, arguing that precisely because equity law developed beyond these ghostly origins to cover property cases, and often specifically the case of marital assets, the principles were devised not to protect wives, as the judges argued (see Loughlan 1996, p. 11 above) but to 'keep the property in the family' or to protect a father's or male relative's rights (Scutt 1990, p. 238; Pether 1991). In this disjunction between judicial narratives of 'vision and ingenuity', critical accounts of power and feminist tales of male property interests, we begin to see habitus at work: 'embodied history, internalised as second nature and so forgotten as history' (Bourdieu 1990, p. 57). We also begin to see that what is sometimes taken for 'agency', 'intention' and 'conscience' is in fact produced through 'the investment, the desire, the pain, the memories, and the possibility of negotiating the multiple positions which have interpellated the body in those histories' (Threadgold 1997a, p. 101).

In the Australian context, the *English Juridicature Act* of 1873 and its statutory counterparts in the Australian States effectively merged the common law and equitable jurisdictions while still enshrining 'in statutory form the principle that where there is a conflict between the rules of the common law and the rules of equity, the latter prevails over the former' (Loughlan 1996, p. 21). Thus despite Mason's preference for equity over the 'custom and usage' of the common law, and as we shall show below, it is clear that equity is now as dependant on precedent and written law as is the common law. The difference is that equitable doctrines do not affect all areas of law in the same way: 'Copious glosses' on the law of property and contract, for example, have yielded many substantive equitable doctrines such as trusts, advancement, undue influence and relief against penalties and forfeitures, while other areas of the law such as crime, tort and public law have remained relatively free from equitable rules (Loughlan 1996, p. 16). There are kinds of matters which are 'equity' matters, including many 'high status' commercial disputes, but also those with which we will be concerned here, involving the adjustment of interests in assets after the end of non-marital relationships.

These histories, which we will find to be crucial to our readings of the equity judgements, have material effects on the possibilities of justice in these different legal arenas (Threadgold 1996). In the case of equity, its very supplementarity—the fact that it is already in excess of, or claims to be in excess of, the common law—demands a reading of the 'flaws and silences, the marks or traces of other discourses, the breaks and seams of the circle' (Goodrich 1990, p. 239) which constitute its 'imagery of filiation and descent' (Goodrich 1996, p. 108).

MINOR HISTORIES: 'THERE IS (STILL) NO OUTSIDE THE TEXT'/*STARE DECISIS*

The case we want to explore in this paper is contextualised by a series of Australian judicial decisions which fall in the period 1982–92. They involve family relationships which have broken down ('the end of love'), in the main between de facto partners. The case we will look at in most detail involves the breakdown of a relationship between a mother and two sons but it inevitably 'implicates', through the citation of precedent and the cultural and gendered baggage that it brings with it, all the other kinds of relationships with which equity currently deals. All of the cases involve equity and speak in various, often problematic, ways to the claims of Equity to be a court of conscience and to have benefited women in respect to property rights.

The period covered by these cases has been a critical one in terms of changes of attitude on the part of the Equity Division of the Supreme Court, the NSW Court of Appeal, the High Court and the NSW Legislature. It has also been a period of considerable 'dissension' in the sense discussed above, a period which has seen a critical ideological split between and among the judges of the Equity Division of the Supreme Court and the NSW Court of Appeal in relationship to questions of gender and power, what Gatens has called 'inter-sexualities':

> Spinoza's immanent and monistic theory of being is attractive to me because it allows one to theorize the interconnections between sexed bodies and other body complexes, such as the body politic or other institutional assemblages (the law for example). It is only within these complex assemblages that sexed bodies are produced as socially and politically meaningful bodies. (Gatens 1996, p. 149)

All of the cases that will be implicated here centre on a small number of legal doctrines and categories which are either equitable 'as such', or upon which the relevant equitable principles and remedies rely. Chief among these would have to be the 'de facto relationship' (defined in opposition to 'marriage'), 'the public good/interest', 'property', 'constructive trust', 'presumption of advancement' and 'conscionability'. All but the case we will focus on frame, or are framed by, the NSW *De Facto Relations Act 1984*, which is in most cases sharply distinguished from the Australian *Family Law Act*, just as the property rights of married women are constructed as other than the property rights of women in de facto relationships. Transgressing and marking all the judgements is evidence of more than the judgement purports: that is, certain commonly repeated, discursively constituted sets of statements and attitudes which trace the ideological underpinnings of the judgement, and the habitus and investments of the judge.

There are several moments in this intertextual chain where judgement changes legal meanings and thus lived realities for some people. In 1982, in *Seidler v Schallhofer* (1982) 2 NSWLR 80, judge-made law in NSW crosses a rubicon and decides that de facto relationships are not immoral and that recognising them in legal ways is not against public policy. In 1985 and 1987, *Baumgartner v Baumgartner* (1985) 2 NSWLR 406; [1987] 164 CLR 137, establishes grounds, on the basis of her contribution to family finances, for a de facto wife to share in the property accumulated during a relationship. It is argued that it would be rewarding 'unconscionable conduct' not to so allow.

Brown v Brown, a 1993 decision of the NSW Court of Appeal, is the case we will explore in detail here. It relates to a different set of gendered relationships (and the adjustment of property interests) after these relationships had 'broken down'. What is of interest to us is that in this case a new and complicating gendered ideological division among the judges on the Court emerged.

This case concerned a mother's contribution to property registered in the names of adult sons, equity's imposition of a *resulting trust* and the operation of the *equitable presumption of advancement*. The latter principle had previously been applied to fathers who were presumed by equity to intend to benefit the property interests of their children (this is what is called 'the presumption of advancement') such that property bought in a child's name belonged to the child equitably as well as legally (this is 'the resulting trust'). The *obiter dicta* (incidental words) of the majority judgement in this case contemplated extending the principle to mothers. The minority judgement found that the extension of the principle should occur. This is significant at face value both because it indicates a change beginning in the way in which the High Court is thinking about the position of women and because minority judgements can become precedents in later legal argument. However, the stakes here are not quite what they seem, as we will demonstrate below.

REASONS FOR JUDGEMENT: DISCOURTEOUS FEMINIST READINGS

One of the tasks of feminist discourse analysis in these legal contexts is to make visible and audible the networks of meaning and representation, and the corporealities, that dominate the scene of writing. This is done in feminist contexts with the explicit aim of changing the law's patriarchal and discriminatory discourses and practices, but also the law's bodies, the bodies who perform the discourses and practices, the bodies that are folded into them. In a common law system like the Australian one, judge-made law has a central and privileged position. Indeed, if one accepts that statutes and constitutions do not actually mean until they are brought into meaning by judicial interpretation in the context of adversarial proceedings, judge-made or common law is the essential legal discourse. The written judicial decision, known as the 'judicial opinion' in the United States and 'Reasons for Judgement' in Australia, has had a privileged status in the formation and transmission of the law. To give one example, the casebook, made up of edited selections from written judicial decisions, generally appellate decisions (from courts of appeal) has been central to the education of lawyers in the common law system. It is thus central to the replication of a more or less covertly gendered law (Frug 1985).

Drucilla Cornell (1991, p. 30) aligns deconstruction with the making visible of the essential metaphoricity of language and representation, its literariness, if you like. In this chapter we will use a literary/rhetorical approach to the reading of the legal texts, because, as Goodrich proposes (1996, p. 113), 'in the most radical of senses', and in ways that are quite closely aligned to deconstruction, 'literature demands the end of law' (Goodrich, 1996, p. 5). Following Goodrich here, we propose to employ

> . . . techniques of interruption in interrogating and criticising legal texts and institutions through the use of historical and literary techniques. The interruption of law (*ius interruptum*) thus refers first to a suspension of the strict protocols of legal reading and genre . . . the interruption is dangerous . . . [it] . . . is a form of minor jurisprudence. (Goodrich 1996, p. 5)

Our strategic discourtesy is directed at the excessive insistence on the centrality of the doctrine of precedent and the techniques of case analysis and statutory interpretation which mask an unprincipled and generally unselfconscious performance of judgement as a species of priestly divination. It will involve reading precedent improperly—as intertextuality, as traces of bodies at work.

SOLIPSISM, 'INGENUITY AND VISION': A LITERARY EXCURSION

Marjorie Levinson's 1986 reading of Wordsworth's 'Lines Written a Few Miles Above Tintern Abbey, on revisiting the banks of the Wye during a tour, July 13, 1798' provides a helpful model of the techniques we want to use here. Levinson's reading opens with an economical gesture towards her reading politics: she uses as her epigraph a passage from Mary Moorman's biography of the young Wordsworth which draws attention to the evidence of both industrialisation and the persistent presence 'of beggars and the wretchedly poor' at the then contemporary site of Tintern Abbey on the day Wordsworth writes about it. Levinson then juxtaposes this biographical and intertextual information with an exhortation of the poet's to the reader about the interpretation of the poem. It is this explicitly preferred interpretation, the interpretation signed by the author, which she proceeds to transgress, following the clues that Moorman has discovered:

> In a note to *Tintern Abbey*, 1800, Wordsworth calls attention to the poem's odal transitions and versification; he hopes that the reader will find in these features 'the principal requisites of that species of composition'. (Quoted in Levinson 1986, p. 14)

Levinson ignores the instruction to read the poem as an ode. She rejects the lessons in reading embedded in Wordsworth's own *Lyrical Ballads* (Levinson 1986, pp. 55–56). She is purposefully discourteous in explaining the poem intertextually, situating it in a network of other contemporary texts from outside the literary canon, indeed notably from contemporary popular culture—tourist guidebooks, journalism, the interdisciplinary perspective offered by economic history—using these to explore the resonances between the poem and its textual others. Levinson (1986, p. 45) argues that:

> . . . the poem's abstraction, its representation of the 'still, sad music of humanity', its construction as pastoral prospect, serves to drown out the noise produced by real people in real distress.

Thus it is that: '*Tintern Abbey* finally represents mind, and specifically memory . . . as a barricade to resist historical change and contradiction . . . it betrays his [Wordsworth's] flight from something that he dreads' (Levinson 1986, pp. 53, 55).

Now it perhaps does not need saying that no reading of the poem itself, or of the merely linguistic patterns in the poem, could produce such a reading. These patterns may, of course, be used to motivate the reading. There is a metonymic relationship between the words of the text and the intertextual histories and resonances Levinson locates, but there is also Levinson herself, her corporeality and habitus, *as* and at the scene of writing, now intervening between Wordsworth and his text. Far more is gained, in terms of understanding the social and historical constitution of Romanticism, in this one reading, with resources that have largely always been available to Wordsworth scholars, than most of those scholars have ever actually read while focusing on the poem itself. This 'iteration' then of Wordsworth criticism is specifically different because of the discourteous way in which the feminine author exceeds but does not ignore dominant reading practices, the way in which she produces the scene of writing differently, the way in which she refuses the constraints of the 'closed system'.

There are parallels here with judgements in equity. Rather like Wordsworth, judges are able to withdraw into a carefully constructed space which allows them to perform *their* writings too in denial of the realities around them, a space where mind and memory also build barricades against historical and social change and contradiction, a space where selectively constituted legal categories allow them to perform as if 'serious social speech' about love, personal relationships and the end of love had not occurred.

BROWN V BROWN

Both majority and minority judgements in *Brown v Brown* yield to the same kind of purposeful reading against the grain as Levinson's. The narrative of this case which, as usual, forms the first part generically of both the majority and the minority judgements, is about a family struggle over property. An 89-year-old woman, who dies three days into the first trial, leaving a signed affidavit as evidence of her side of the story, had in about 1958, contributed all her assets, on the sale of the family home after the death of her spouse, to the purchase price of a new home, bought jointly with her two sons. The sons jointly (£2675) and the mother (£2125) contributed roughly equal amounts to the purchase price. The title of the property was in the name of the sons. Some thirty years later, the sons subdivided the property and some later-acquired land and made $600 000 dollars on the deal. This seems to have been what precipitated the family dispute. Mrs Brown claimed that she only then became aware that the house was in her sons' names only, and began proceedings claiming a beneficial interest in the sold property equivalent to her proportionate contribution to its purchase. She moved into a nursing home shortly after she began proceedings. The sons claimed during these proceedings that their mother had agreed to pay all her assets towards the purchase price of the house in return for the right to reside in the property for the rest of her life. Mrs Brown was unable to be cross-examined and died three days into the trial. Only Kirby J's minority judgement mentions that it was when the land was sold that Mrs Brown claimed that she wanted her two daughters to share in the benefits of her estate, and that she changed her will to benefit only her daughters. Among other things, she claimed that her sons had stopped visiting her in the nursing home.

In the interstices of this legal story (already not quite the same story in the two judgements) it is possible to read the traces of immense family pain, of the end of the love of a mother for sons, or of sons for a mother, of the shadowy role of daughters, of a mother who spent her last years in a nursing home, a place where she was never 'at home', of social histories enacted as personal pain. This is not of course what the law sees. It sees a clear choice between the presumption of advancement and a resulting trust: and yet there is very little clarity or even agreement in the way in which the case is argued in the majority and minority judgements.

THE MAJORITY JUDGEMENT

The majority judgement cites a series of English, Australian and New Zealand cases between 1879 and 1932 which hold that the presumption of advancement which applies when fathers buy property in the name of their children does not apply to mothers. The presumption of advancement is an equitable doctrine which counters another equitable presumption that when a person buys property in the name of another person, there is a resulting trust of the property in favour of the person who pays for it. The majority judgement fails to overturn the precedent that the presumption of advancement does not apply to mothers, citing United States authority which extends it to mothers, noting that the Canadian position is 'unresolved', and referring to *obiter dicta* from a single judge of the NSW Court of Appeal in *Dullow v Dullow* (1985) 3 NSWLR 531, and a 1990 textbook on trusts. The status of a degendered presumption of advantage remains similarly *obiter dicta* in this case.

The precedents cited are used as authority for the proposition that 'the state of the authorities would seem to leave it open for judicial decision to allow the same presumption to be made in the case of a gift by a mother to her child as is made in the case of a gift by a father to his child'. *The majority, however, does not rule on this question,* effectively finding that *if the presumption applied in this case* there was evidence to rebut it, both on the basis of the trial judge's findings and on their own appellate reading of the world. Here are the final lines of the majority judgement (Gleeson CJ, majority judgement, 59IC–E, emphasis added):

> We are here dealing with a transaction that occurred in 1958. In the social and economic conditions which apply at the present time the drawing of a rigid distinction between male and female parents, for the purposes of the application of the presumptions of equity with which we are concerned, <u>may be accepted to be inappropriate</u>. I <u>would be</u>

prepared, although with <u>rather less conviction</u>, to say the same about conditions in 1958. I <u>would therefore not decide this case</u> on the basis that, Mrs Brown being a mother rather than a father, <u>the presumption of advancement did not apply</u>. However, the facts as found by Bryson J, and <u>the objective circumstances</u>, rebut a presumption of advancement. His Honour found that Mrs Brown <u>did not intend</u> to make a gift (or loan) to her sons. Moreover where a <u>widowed mother, of modest means</u>, makes a payment of substantially the whole of her assets to contribute to the purchase of real estate, and legal title to the real estate is vested in her <u>adult, able-bodied sons</u>, the facts <u>seem to me to point against an intention</u> of advancement. Mrs Brown had <u>no moral obligation</u> to make such provision for her sons <u>at the expense of her estate</u>. The sons, it may be remembered, alleged that she was making a bargain with them that was partly <u>for her own benefit</u>, but that allegation was rejected by the trial judge. Since there was no operative presumption of advance- ment, *the basic presumption of resulting trust applied.* That is the presumption advanced by Bryson J. The appeal should be dismissed with costs.

The underlining above is ours, as are the italics below. Bryson J made the judgement that is on appeal in this case. Gleeson CJ here finds no reason to regard the earlier judge as having erred in law. The decision then stands (*stare decisis*) and the law with respect to resulting trusts is still here considered to uphold Mrs Brown's claim. Gleeson J accepts Bryson J's assessment that the confusion and the lack of documentation in the original case 'suggested that in truth no agree- ment about the matter of ownership of Gladesville had been made at all' (586E). What Bryson J did regard as clear-cut however, was the fact that Mrs Brown in her affidavits 'made *unqualified statements* which would establish *that she did not intend to make a loan or gift'.* He therefore argued that 'there is no reason in substance why I should not accept what she says and I do accept it' (589C). It is significant here that both judges, Bryson and Gleeson, show some anxiety but no real hesitation in allowing the evidence in an affidavit *signed by a dead women to stand*—despite the fact that that evidence could not be subjected to cross-examination.

Bryson J believes that Mrs Brown may have been wrongly or inadequately advised in 1958 (586F–G). It is clear that he is aware of the kinds of gendered advice that might have been given to the benefit of the sons. Class is also an issue here, however, and the judge's reference to the 'modest means' of these people, and his narrative of the widowed mother and able-bodied sons in the final section of the judgement quoted above, appears to be the sole basis for his decision that Mrs Brown would not deliberately give away the only 'modest means' she had. The underlined pattern of modality and negation in the final lines of the judgement—'may be accepted', 'would be pre-pared', 'with rather less conviction', '**would** . . . **not** decide . . . on the basis that the presumption of advancement **did not** apply'—actively construct here the uncertain, ambivalent position of the judge who really doesn't think old ladies should be made to give all their property to their able-bodied sons *and* who thinks the sons were morally despicable for taking it if she did, and thus decides, on very shaky grounds, that she never intended any such thing. The embold-ened doubly negated refusal to de-gender the presumption of advancement follows as a direct consequence of this very personal narrative—to de-gender the presumption of advancement would, in this case, force the judge to decide in favour of the sons.

The processual construction of gendered relations of power here is very complex, but it has much more to do with the majority judges' positioning in an everyday narrative of masculinity brought up to protect its womenfolk, than it has to do with abstract legal categories. And yet there is a connection, because it is precisely the challenge to patriarchy, which a change to the gendered presumption of advance-ment would signal, that the majority judges, via Gleeson C J's judgement, here reject. The majority judgement almost incidentally protects *one* woman from *some* men but fails altogether to change the system which potentially oppresses women *as a category* in questions of property relations.

The majority in this case imply that overturning the gendered presumption of advancement in relation to parents and children (as demanded by liberal feminist legal reform) might not be inappropriate (*I would not decide—it did not apply*). This opinion *is based on no evidence*. We are told that the gendered assumption is probably in-appropriate now and probably was in 1958. These assertions belong to the world of 'judicially-noticed' facts, that is, facts that don't need to be proven in evidence because judges know them to be true (as opposed to listening to 'the still sad music of humanity'). We would suggest that this passage from the judgement invites a reading against past and contemporary texts about women's social and economic conditions, statistics on male and female earnings or patterns in ownership of family assets, some sociology, or fiction or history or advertisements: an intertextual reading to bring law's opinions back in touch with some wider reality. Such contextualisations would demonstrate the essential subjectivity of this monologue which claims objectivity, and would insist that it enter into dialogue with what it currently ignores and excludes—that indeed it provide *evidence* for itself and stop relying on *hearsay*.

The pattern of citation and argument we have outlined above almost cries out for a Derridean reading of the signature and of *destinerrance*, the 'tendency of texts to mistake their destinations' (Threadgold 1997a, pp. 89–91). We have here the signature which cannot be relied upon to guarantee the meaning of the text it signs, the readers (the judges) who nevertheless 'sign for' what has been delivered by the signing—and the tendency for texts, which become unreliable in the absence of the guarantee of the signature, to wander into other contexts where *the only thing that is certain* is the impossibility of recovering *just what the signer intended*. And yet that is what the judges proceed to decide.

THE MINORITY JUDGEMENT

Kirby P's (Kirby was the President of the court at this time) minority judgement starts from a different position and is precisely adversarial to the majority. In fact it is in Kirby P's judgement that the connection between property ownership and masculinity, the inheritance rights of fathers and sons, together with a different version of the protection of womenfolk and some striking assumptions about Mrs Brown, her husband and their family relations are played out. Kirby P's minority judgement recommends a re-trial to be heard before the primary judge, Bryson J. The grounds of this appeal are to be that the presumption of advancement *should have been degendered* and that the sons should have benefited from it.

Kirby proceeds to trace a substantially similar line of precedent to the majority judgement but emphasises, for its own purposes, the fissures in the doctrine which argues that the presumption of advancement *does not apply to mothers equally* with fathers. Kirby J notes that in *Dullow v Dullow* both he and McHugh JA agreed with Hope JA's proposition, which he quotes (597 B–C, emphasis added):

> . . . it is not necessary for me to consider what the correct principle is as to any presumption of advancement when a mother places property in the name of a child. I should say however, that, as at present advised, I think that *if the law is to be left constrained by presumptions, the same presumption should apply to gifts to children by both mother and father* . . .

Kirby cites the majority judgement in *Calverley v Green* which applied conventional views of both the presumption of resulting trusts and the presumption of advancement *to the detriment of a de facto wife* whose de facto husband had bought a property in the couple's joint names. The presumption of advancement by a husband of a wife was not deemed to apply in the case of de facto relationships. In referring to this judgement, Kirby P locates his minority opinion in a controversy among the members of the court about property rights deriving from de facto relationships. Thus at the outset of his judgement, while his concern may appear to be with the de-gendering of the presumption of advancement, that desire is already embroiled in this debate, and turns out to be a very gendered and located attempt to use a doctrine in which he himself does not believe (as is later made clear when he quotes Murphy J), and to de-gender it (something one might imagine to be in the interests of women), in order to support the interests of the sons in this case (601E):

> If, for example, the position had been that the late Mrs Brown had pre-deceased her husband and that it was he, and not the wife, who made the gift to the sons in 1958, it cannot be doubted that the presumption of advancement would have been invoked.

READING PRECEDENT: INTERTEXTUAL HISTORIES

Kirby P complicates the question of his adherence to or departure from precedent by indicating that he would have preferred, if unconstrained by precedent, to have substituted *both* the resulting trusts presumption *and* the presumption of advancement (the issues at stake in *Brown v Brown*) with an approach proposed by the influential judicial radical, Justice Murphy, in a minority judgement in *Calverley v Green* (595C–E, Kirby JA quoting Murphy J in *Calverley v Green* (1984) CLR 242 at 264, underlining added):

> The presumption of advancement, supposed to be an exception to the presumption of resulting trust, has always been a misuse of the term presumption and is unnecessary. Transfer of the title of property wholly or partially to another is commonly regarded as of great significance . . . The notion that such a deliberate act raised a presumption of trust in favour of the transferor, would astonish an ordinary person.

The relevance of this for our purposes, is that Murphy J in this minority judgement in *Calverley v Green* provides a significant critique of judges making their particular view of the world ('false presumptions', 'a misuse of the term') count as 'fact' through the use of the doctrine of presumption. At the same time, like Kirby P, Murphy believes that if presumptions continue to constrain the law, they must reflect 'common experience', operate according to 'standardised inference' and reflect changing social conditions. As in the majority judgement, there is absolutely no evidence supplied of what or whose 'common experience' or which changing social conditions are being referred to here. But this will become the grounds in Kirby P's judgement for arguing that the presumption of advancement should be degendered in line with the changing role of men and women in society.

Kirby P is engaging here in a strategic rereading of precedent in order to be able to argue authoritatively that there are 'legal authorities, principles and policies' which demand the degendering of the presumption of advancement:

> So long as it survives as a tool of legal reasoning, it should be grounded not in the gender of the parties making and receiving gifts, but in the relationship between them. It is from such relationships, in *the ordinary experience of human existence*, that substantial gifts may be grounded in the presumption of advancement. (*Brown v Brown* at 598 C–D)

Here the (white masculine middle-class) liberal abstraction of 'the experience of human existence', apparently now also de-gendering experience itself, is in fact a reinstatement of the universal in the form of the masculine—a reference to the specifics of this case, and Kirby P's concern for the men in it. On these grounds of liberal equality, the existing 'gendered' presumption of advancement (which only allows fathers to leave gifts to their children) *is read as discriminatory against men*. This is then the end to which Kirby P has erected an apparatus of legal history and precedent (from New Zealand, United States and Canada) to support the 'removal of gender discrimination in the expression of the presumption' (598C)—that is, to make it apply to women too so that these very particular sons will have another right of appeal.

Kirby P's approval of this majority position in *Calverley v Green* is supported by a pattern of representations of women that can be seen clearly in his use of two additional and also remarkably gendered precedents:

> . . . the better view in the past was that where the payment was made by a mother—who in those days had no obligation to maintain her child or children—there was no presumption of advancement . . . (596D quoted from Powell J in *Oliveri v Oliveri* (29 March 1993, unreported) at 31, emphasis added)

One wonders just when it was that women had no such obligations. The second case is a Canadian one which decided for the degendering of the presumption of advancement. It is the section that Kirby P chooses to quote that is interesting:

> *The common law* has never been held to be fixed in time. As times changed so did the common law. There is no reason at this point in time where women play such an important role in the workplace that they cannot make a gift to a child resulting in the presumption of advancement. (Kirby P 598F–G quoting *Dagle v Dagle Estate* (1990) 70 DLR (4th) 201, Canada, Prince Edward Island Court of Appeal, emphasis added)

These extraordinary generalisations, for which no evidence is adduced, which show a remarkable forgetting of the historical realities of women's lives (Threadgold 1997b, 1997c) and a memory constructed out of partly remembered chunks of *textual* precedent and *legal* narratives, are what Kirby P adduces as authoritative 'legal policy'. In these utterly 'positioned' and subjective remarks, clothed as legal apparatus, Kirby P is at the same time asserting his compulsion by the legal (the obedient citation of precedent) and his *equitable* (because not gender-discriminatory *and* responsive both to contemporary social contexts and advanced judicial opinion) *breaking with precedent.*

That position purports to be anti-patriarchal, in its liberal model of gender equality—yet it perpetuates and compounds the law's systemic gender discrimination. These examples also provide a stark example of the contingency of the doctrine of precedent. The same citations produce radically different conclusions in the majority and the minority judgements. And Kirby P's judgement, which rejects 'stereotypes concerning able-bodied sons' and removes what it describes as 'gender discrimination', in the end applies a presumption which may, depending on evidentiary considerations, have resulted in a finding that 'a woman of fifty-seven, with a continuing need for a home, effectively gave all of her most substantial asset away to her sons. She reserved nothing for her daughters' (594F)—*a de-gendering with a strangely gendered outcome.*

CITATIONS OF THE FEMININE

This judgement also explicitly cites contemporary documents about Australian law and gender, appropriating these for its own uses. Kirby P cites dismissively the single most important Australian feminist legal reference on gender discrimination in law:

> . . . it would be an impermissible approach to the development of either common law or equitable principles to accept the removal of stereotypes

only where this resulted in advantages to women. (Graycar and Morgan 1990, pp. 118, 317)

Page 317, referred to above, deals with a decision by a federal court judge which held that an anti-harassment law that dealt only with sexual harassment of women did not fail a relevant requirement that the law in question should accord women 'equality with men before the law': that is, that the anti-harassment law was not biased against men. Even taking into account the federal constitutional context in which the case was decided, this decision clearly turns on the con-textual prevalence of sexual harassment of women, rather than on the liberal assumption of formal equality, or on an anxiety about men's position before the law, on which Kirby P's stance depends. He thus 'misreads' the feminist text. The reference to page 118 is puzzling, as this section of the Graycar and Morgan text deals with domicile and marital rape. A psychoanalytic reading here might begin to explore the unconscious which sees these issues of (un)equal treatment for men and marital rape as connected. We will not pursue this here.

What is clear is that Kirby P's reading of Graycar and Morgan is at least as discourteous as our reading of his judgement and that his use of the precedent of feminist scholarship in this judgement is enlisted in the interests of a thinly disguised masculine 'backlash' against gender-based legal reform, in the tradition of David Williamson's play *Dead White Males* (see also Davis 1997).

CONCLUSIONS

We would argue, then, that our reading of *Brown v Brown* makes strikingly evident the preference of judges for personal narratives and for the property interests of sons and fathers over those of mothers and wives. But the differences between and among judges are also very legible here: the significance of their own white, middle-class and masculine imaginings of the world, and the ways in which these intimations of specific positioning in the world mediate and constrain their use of the law and its categories and the kinds of contingent judgements they are likely to make.

The most powerful resource we have for a critical feminist dis-course analysis of equity judgements is the judgements themselves. Read as the judges read them, they provide 'evidence', 'authority' for particular 'legal' arguments which relate the specificity of a case to generally accepted legal principle. Our reading of *Brown v Brown* has already deconstructed that position by using precedent itself, and the judge's own use of it, to explore some of the repressed investments, desires and subjectivities that haunt the legal imagination. In doing this however we have not been reading precedent as precedent, but rather as intertextuality, as part of the network of texts, material conditions and embodied experiences which are precisely the historical conditions of possibility for the contingent opinions that judges come to hold. In our writing, precedent has become evidence of something other than itself. We have also been reading the judges' words as metonymic of larger legal, social and cultural contexts and of their own limited because disciplined habitus.

Legal processes involve the contestation and the making of gendered subjectivities and realities, but there can be no easy or simple articulation of particular discursive realities with a totalising concept like 'patriarchy'. The complexities of these judgements perform the tensions between tradition and change characteristic of the law as social process. They offer a timely reminder of the scene of writing as corporeography, of the need for ethnography and history as well as theory and linguistics, in both discourse analysis and law, to ensure 'a very thorough understanding of the contexts, both material and discursive, in which we write, very detailed understandings of the materiality of texts (and the resistances they offer to the meanings we want to make)', and a researched sense of the social, personal and ethical implications 'of the new discursive spaces, the unthought and the unspoken that we are trying to make visible and audible' and thus effective, through our writing (Threadgold 1997a, p. 56).

CASE LIST

Baumgartner v Baumgartner (1985) 2 NSWLR406; (1987) 164 CLR 137.
Brown v Brown (1993) 31 NSWLR at 582.
Calverley v Green (1984) 1555 CLR 242 at 264.
Dullow v Dullow (1985) 3 NSWLR 531.
Seidler v Schallhofer (1982) 2 NSWLR 80.

9 Disciplining the body: power, knowledge and subjectivity in a physical education lesson

Jan Wright

The body has become a social and cultural site of increasing interest within feminist and social theory in recent years. The dominant discourses in Western society have traditionally emphasised the body as a physical and biological given, to be understood, like other 'natural' phenomena, through empirical investigation. Philosophical, feminist and poststructuralist discussions around the body (Foucault 1979, 1981; Bartky 1988; Bordo 1990; Grosz 1994) have demonstrated how our knowledge of the body—and the body itself—is constituted in specific cultural and historical circumstances and in the context of particular relations of power. This happens in many different sites including the print and electronic media, schools, public spaces, and in and through institutional discourses associated with the law, medicine, education, sport, religion and so on.

Particularly important to current social theory is an understanding of the body not as separate from the mind—the mind/body dichotomy of Western thought—but as integral to 'the self'. In poststructuralist terms, this is understood through the concept of 'embodied subjectivity', where those social practices which form selves work through language and material practices to locate individual subjects in relation to institutional and cultural discourses. The body is thus produced by and exists in discourse, the term referring to 'sets of deep linguistic principles incorporating specific 'grids of meaning' which generate what can be spoken, seen and thought' (McWilliam 1996, p. 18). While discourse in this sense is differentiated from language, choices in language (as social practices) provide indicators as to how those discourses are being drawn upon by writers and speakers and to the ways in which 'users' position themselves and others. Questions can therefore be asked about how language works to position speakers in relation to what discourses, and with what effects.

Foucault further understands discourse as 'practices that systematically form the objects of which they speak . . . Discourses are not about objects; they constitute them and in the practice of doing so conceal their own intervention' (Foucault 1972, p. 49). It is through discourse that meanings, subjects and subjectivities are formed. Much current semiotic work focuses primarily on reading bodies as they are inscribed with meaning—in performance, the electronic media, photographs, art, dance forms and written texts, both literary and non-literary. What this chapter offers is a different set of insights which overlap but also extend this work. Drawing on poststructuralist and linguistic theory and methodologies, it first provides a set of tools to examine how the body is represented in texts derived from spoken language. Second, the chapter examines the effects of that talk as it acts on bodies, to promote certain kinds of bodily behaviour and social relations. The chosen site is a physical education lesson but the analysis could be extended to many similar sites where talk is central to the constitution of the body and promotes 'bodywork' in different ways—for instance, coaching sessions, aerobics, tai chi, bellydancing and yoga classes.

Schooling, as a set of practices specifically intended to shape and train bodies, becomes a fruitful site to examine this process of subjectification. As Shilling (1993, p. 22) points out, 'the moving, managed and disciplined body, and not just the speaking and listening body, is central to the daily business of schooling'. Focusing on how bodies are managed through disciplinary practices—such as expecting children to sit still and quiet, to control their toileting behaviour—does not take into account how teachers' talk, together with the practices it expects, constitutes particular notions of the body.

In physical education, a site within schooling specifically focused on the body, teacher talk works both to manage/discipline bodies and to inscribe the body with particular meanings, that is, to (re)produce particular discourses which determine how bodies can be thought about and, consequently, how they can act in space and in relation to other bodies. For instance, teacher talk constitutes notions of the skilled/unskilled body, as well as the way the body learns (through the acquisition of skills broken down into their component parts). 'Bodywork' can thus be used to describe teacher talk both as it constitutes knowledge about the body and as it affects the way bodies work.

While this chapter does go beyond the language of the lesson to other material practices, it will focus on the spoken language of the teacher. It is important to acknowledge that there are problems with a singular focus on language. Bodies are certainly not only, or indeed mostly, produced in and through language. Rather, material practices such as dress, the organisation of space, the work done by bodies through exercise and by paid labour are all implicated in the construction of bodies as cultural products. Language, however, in both written and spoken forms, influences how we can think about/conceive of bodies. It categorises and associates value with certain kinds of bodies rather than others and it can be employed to evoke bodily movement. For instance, through medical, legal, psychoanalytic and educational discourses, bodies are described and positioned in relations of value. School physical education is a site which, because of its focus on the body, brings a number of discourses and material practices to bear on the bodies of teachers and students. The questions, then, which motivate this analysis are as follows:

- What kinds of bodies are being constituted in physical education lessons?
- What discourses and material practices are drawn on to constitute bodies and in what relations of power?
- What are the consequences of such bodywork for individual subjectivities and social relations?

A METHODOLOGY

To make a closer study of how language use is implicated in the construction of knowledge and subjectivities, a finegrained tool of analysis is required, one which is able to provide a systematic analysis of spoken language going beyond mere 'insightful interpretation'. It might be argued that the analysis described below could result from a close non-technicalised reading of the texts. While this may be true for some texts, a systematic analysis of the grammatical and lexical patterns leaves such a reading less to chance and can provide insights into patterns of use which would otherwise have been unavailable. The analytic tools I use are derived from systemic functional linguistics (Halliday 1994), a system of grammar which recognises the ongoing social constructedness of meaning.

Language does not make meaning, nor can it be interpreted in isolation. Any poststructuralist analysis of language must take account of the social and cultural contexts in which texts are constructed.

It must also consider the ways in which language use is constituted in the context of particular discursive relations which predict certain power relations. While Michel Foucault eschewed a close analysis of language, his work provides a means of understanding and interpreting the ways in which language and other social practices work to constitute specific relations of power. Such relations are not monolithic but are pervasive and negotiated and, through their subtle operations, work to form subjectivities. Foucault puts it thus (1980, p. 39):

> But in thinking of the mechanism of power, I am thinking rather of its capillary form of existence, the point where power reaches into the very grain of individuals, touches their bodies and inserts itself into their actions and attitudes, their discourses, learning processes and everyday lives.

In a somewhat controversial move, Jennifer Gore (1995a, 1995b) has sought to construct an empirical technology which provides a means to examine the practices of power in pedagogy. While not using a linguistic approach, she has developed the following eight coding categories—derived from a careful reading of Foucault's *Discipline and Punish*—with which to analyse her data. These are: surveillance, normalisation, exclusion, distribution, classification, individualisation, totalisation, regulation (Gore 1995a, 1995b). What I have attempted to do in this paper is to go beyond Gore's examples, mostly recorded through fieldnotes, to focus on linguistic realisations of the categories identified through close analysis in a spoken context. The intention here is to be neither exhaustive nor prescriptive. Rather, through an examination of the way Gore's coding categories function in a specific text in a particular situational and cultural context, I will demonstrate the link between those categories and specific language choices. As Gore (1995b) points out, no one category is exclusive of the others. Many of the examples provided below could and should be coded in terms of several other categories. All categories cover the exercise of power in relation to knowledge, interpersonal relations and subjectivities. The examples cited below specifically relate to the physical education text and are clearly not exhaustive for this text or any other. Non-verbal examples are taken up in the analysis of the lesson as a whole.

Surveillance

Surveillance is defined as 'supervising, closely observing, watching, threatening to watch or expecting to be watched' (Gore 1995b, p. 169). Linguistic evidence of surveillance includes the use of those processes which implicate the gaze of teacher, students and teacher, and students together: 'I am watching you'; 'let's see . . .' and 'Start to look at how you are doing things'. This last command explicitly instructs the students to become involved in the monitoring of their own performance, but they are already implicated by moves like 'let's see'. I would suggest that evaluative statements such as 'that was good' are also indications of surveillance, the outcomes of a close monitoring of behaviour.

Normalisation

Normalisation is defined as 'invoking, requiring, setting or conforming to a standard—defining the normal' (Gore 1995b, p. 171). Normalisation suggests the correct and proper way, often in comparison to another way of being or acting. Grammatically this may be signalled by words such as 'normally', 'usually', or 'the best/better' or 'right' way of being or performing an action. For instance, in the lesson the teacher says 'normally we do co-ed'. This suggests that co-education physical education is the/a normal practice in contrast to single sex physical education. Most of the descriptions of how skills should be done are also examples of a normalising practice: they suggest that there is only one, correct way to perform the skill. Conditional clauses such as 'If you keep your knees into your chest, then you will roll over' arguably also have a normalising function.

Exclusion

Gore describes this category as 'the reverse side of normalisation—the defining of the pathological' (Gore 1995b, p. 173). In this physical education lesson the female and male students have been separated. The separation is presented as a consequence of effects produced by the short skirts the girls wear as part of their physical education uniform. These effects include the girls seen as preoccupied with being looked at. Though the girls have no control over the choice of such a uniform, much less the gaze of the boys, they are the ones whose behaviour is effectively pathologised.

Classification

This category is defined by Gore as 'differentiating groups or individuals from one another, classifying, classifying oneself . . . the classification of knowledge, the classification of individuals or groups' (Gore 1995b, p. 174). The most obvious examples in language are those attributes which work in binaries such as physical/mental, hard/ easy, strong/weak and attributive relational clauses such as 'girls are . . . '. But any language choice which divides the world into groups functions as a form of classification. Examples include differentiating boys from girls and linking particularly ways of acting and being with one group in comparison with the other; differentiating gymnastics and dance by their specific attributes from other forms of physical activity.

Distribution

This category deals with the distribution of bodies in space. Most of the organisational directives in the lessons fall under this category, for instance, the separation of girls from boys and commands which organise the class such as 'we'll have a line down here giving lots of room for girls to bring the mats out . . .', 'we're separating you . . .' and 'one at a time please'.

Individualisation

This category is defined as 'giving individual character to oneself or another' (Gore 1995b, p. 178). This is recognisable when individuals are named or addressed using the singular 'you' (maybe ellipsed (deleted) in commands) and their behaviour or appearance singled out for comment, for instance, 'Allison, if you face me you'll know what is going on'. It also covers situations where individuals are requested to answer questions or perform actions and where the individual speaking uses the first person pronoun singular (see Wright 1990 for a more detailed discussion of the functions of person pronouns in spoken texts). While the following example is not included in the texts below, it does come from the same lesson. It provides an example of how individualisation can often have a totalising effect as well: 'I'm a woman and women are allowed to change their minds'.

Totalisation

Totalisation is defined as 'the specification of collectivities, giving collective character', often achieved through the use of 'we' (Gore 1995b, p. 179). The collective 'we', where the teacher includes him or herself as a member of the class, is a very common feature of teacher talk generally. It is rarely a strategy that students have at their disposal. In the texts below it is employed frequently, for instance, 'we're not going to start with forward rolls today' and 'we'll have our usual partners please'. Totalisation also occurs when a particular group is linked to a set of attributes, for instance in the statement: 'we're particularly aiming at you people being more conscious of what you are doing instead of who's looking at you doing it'.

Regulation

As Gore points out, while all the categories could be seen to have regulating effects, this category was used where regulation was most explicit so that regulation was defined as 'controlling by rule, subject to restrictions, invoking a rule, including sanction, reward and punishment' (Gore 1995b, p. 180). Linguistic examples of this include particularly statements which include 'must', 'need to', 'have to', 'should', as in 'have to get the blood circulating' and 'You should turn your feet out so little toes go to the floor'.

THE CONTEXT: PHYSICAL EDUCATION AND THE BODY

As teachers in the texts below make linguistic choices that constitute meaning and social relations, they draw on existing cultural and institutional discourses or sets of meanings already circulating and contribute to the (re)production of those discourses as they speak. To interpret any text it is necessary to be able to identify the intertexts from which it may be constituted, the cultural resources which are available (and, at times, not available) to the participants—both listeners and speakers—to be able to make meaning. The physical education lessons are constituted intertextually by drawing on a complex range of institutional discourses from education, sport, the academic disciplines associated with the study of human movement and, most recently, discourses linking exercise and fitness with health. These intersect with broader cultural discourses around gender, sexuality, ethnicity and bodies widely circulating through day-to-day interactions and particularly through the media.

Physical education, in comparison with other curriculum areas of contemporary schooling, provides the optimum opportunity for a detailed attention to the disciplining of the body and the production of embodied subjectivities. Physical education is centrally concerned with 'work' on the body, with the regulation and control of the body through the ritualised practices of both sport and physical education lessons (Hargreaves 1986) and through the scientific and medical rationales that underlie these practices (Kirk 1990). In Australia the physical education curriculum is profoundly implicated in constructing gender differences and patriarchal/dominant versions of heterosexual femininity and masculinity. This happens primarily through the dominance of the curriculum by activities traditionally associated with men and boys and with the construction of hegemonic masculinity (Connell 1995), namely sports and team games, and the consequent marginalisation of gymnastics and dance.

As well as discourses which constitute the body as gendered, there are many other systems of values and meanings which affect the body and are embedded in the practices of physical education. Richard Tinning (1990), for instance, has identified the influence of the sets of values and beliefs associated with technocratic rationality, individualism, compulsory heterosexuality and mesomorphism. The two most prominent beliefs which need to be mentioned here are those which equate health with fitness and those which define physical activity in terms of performance and achievement. In Western society the commodification of the body, through the fashion and fitness industries and through the popular media, together with a prevailing anxiety about death through heart disease, has led to the equation of health with fitness. This healthy/fit body is a slim toned body, the apparent product of hard work through exercise and diet. The pursuit of fitness and a 'healthy lifestyle' has also been promoted by the state (for instance, the New South Wales 'Life be in it' campaign) as the practice of the responsible individual. The rationale for physical education as a legitimate subject in the school curriculum has often been argued on the basis of its presumed contribution to children's fitness through their participation in physical activity. Most physical education teachers would argue that one of their main aims is the promotion in their students of a commitment to a healthy lifestyle and regular exercise.

A further set of relevant discourses are those which promote the acquisition of skills and the improvement of performance as the primary purpose of school physical education. These outcomes are achieved through teaching practices based on the principles and understandings of the body derived from research in the human movement sciences, for instance, exercise physiology, biomechanics and motor learning. Learning is then taken as requiring the teaching of specific skills by experts who can demonstrate them, break them into their component parts for easier acquisition, organise activities which provide for repetitive practice, analyse skill performance and offer corrective guidance. This skill acquisition and training approach stands in opposition to other approaches which promote learning through movement. These emphasise the *process* of learning rather than the end product (performance). Movement education, a form of physical education developed by women in Britain and popular in girls' schools in the late nineteenth and early twentieth century, is an example of one such approach where the emphasis is on problem-solving through movement and body awareness (Kirk 1992, Wright 1996).

The metaphor of the body as machine is prominent in both the healthy lifestyles and performance discourses. In one, the body is to be exercised and cared for, to be worked on to accrue health benefits; in the other, the body is to be trained to perform effectively and to achieve in competitive situations. Neither stands alone, both have many elements of compatibility with each other and with dominant discourses informing physical education. All are evident to some degree in the text which will be discussed below.

A TEXT ANALYSIS: A GIRLS' GYMNASTICS LESSON

The text to be analysed comes from a Year 9 (fourteen years old) girls' gymnastics lesson taught by a female teacher. In many ways this is not a typical physical education lesson since physical education classes are increasingly co-educational. Classes including boys have differences which can be linked to the differences in the positioning of boys and their male teachers in relation to the discourses and practices associated with sport. However, the structure and more general features of this lesson still serve to demonstrate how language use produces particular notions of the body, including the gendered body, in the context of specific pedagogical technologies of power.

The transcript of the gymnastics lesson was made as part of a larger study in which teachers agreed to wear a microphone and were recorded using a professional Sony Walkman. Lessons were also video-taped and observational notes made. It is usual in physical education lessons for the teacher to do most of the task-related talking and there is usually little verbal interaction between teachers and students; consequently, most of the linguistic material that is available is from the teacher.

Physical education lessons, as a result of their organisation and use of space, lend themselves to the constant exercise of power through the techniques of surveillance and distribution. Students are frequently organised into differing configurations—singles, pairs, groups, teams—

in the space available according to directions from the teacher. Similarly, the open space of the gym or field provides the teacher with the opportunity to constantly monitor the students' behaviour. The very teacher-directed approach of most physical education lessons, marked by the dominance of commands, also indicates the regulatory potential of physical education: teachers determine where students will move, what they will do and how they will do it. While not all students concur, and many find subtle ways of resisting and engaging in their own forms of regulation and normalisation, the structure, organisation and typical interaction patterns of traditional physical education lessons lend themselves tò the constant enactment of these techniques of power on the part of the teacher.

The roll-call: classification, surveillance and normalisation

The lesson begins with a roll-call. The students are seated on the floor in front of the teacher while the teacher calls each name in turn and waits for the student's response. Students are allocated marks according to the completeness of their uniform. By Year 8 (thirteen years old), many of the girls can supply their own mark. In other words, they have by now internalised the effects of surveillance and can regulate their own behaviour (technologies of the self). Like most schools, the appropriate dress in this class means a specific uniform which goes beyond the necessity of safety—in this case, a short brown skirt or brown tracksuit pants with a pale blue t-shirt. These are clothes that the girls would not by choice wear on any other occasion and serve as an indication of compliance with school and class rules.

The roll-call provides an opportunity for surveillance and for remarking on the students' uniforms as an indication of their attitude to the lesson, of defining the standard and of establishing rules (normalisation). It serves to divide students into those who comply —those whose bodily inscriptions fit with the range of expectations— and those who do not (classification). Like most of a physical education lesson, the monitoring goes beyond uniform to an obseravation of body types—those who are slim and/or appropriately muscular, and can be taken to have an appropriate attitude to physical activity, and those who do not, and are presumed not to have.

Following the roll marking, the teacher (T) makes a number of statements which establish that the arrangement for this lesson has been changed (distribution). The change has taken place because the teacher was concerned that the girls may have been inhibited by the boys' scrutiny of their bodies (exclusion). In articulating her concern, she constructs the girls as objects of the boys' gaze—under male surveillance. She also clearly differentiates 'boys' as a category with different attributes from 'girls' (classification) and characterises all the boys and all the girls as possessing the attributes described (totalisation).

> T: With the 9B 2 girls you weren't with us last week, but what we've decided very briefly is with Year 9s we're separating you for gymnastics as I explained, from the boys in your class, whereas you normally do co-ed physical education. Doing that particularly in gym because of skirts, and you'll see that the girls who were here last week have been told that they're able to wear light pants, um tights, something suitable they consider to gymnastics, (someone talking in class) Listen please, (pause). Something that you consider to be suitable for gymnastics.
>
> What will happen, Mr P and Mr S are taking all the boys in the three classes. At the moment they're going outside, but at times, . . . we're doing gymnastics from now until the end of the term, they will be using half of the hall in here. So what we're particularly aiming at is you people being more conscious of what you're doing instead of who's looking at you doing it.

In this quote the teacher establishes the normality of relations where girls' bodies are subject to the scrutiny of the male students and where the girls are so preoccupied with this scrutiny that they cannot concentrate. It is also taken-for-granted (as normal) that female teachers will teach female students and male teachers will teach male students.

The warm-up: the fragmented body

In the next section of the lesson the teacher, through a series of commands, organises the arrangement of the warm-up. The teacher has some linguistic choices about the way she does this: her commands can take a variety of linguistic forms including imperatives, declaratives or interrogatives.[1]

This particular teacher tends to use declaratives when giving general instructions to the whole class. For example, rather than saying 'Find a partner and the two of you bring the mats out and place them in this half of the hall', she uses what could be understood as the less powerful 'we'll have *our* usual partners please'. In this quote, she also uses the communal 'we' and 'our' instead of 'you' and 'your' when she is clearly referring to activities in which only the girls will be involved (choosing partners). These grammatical strategies paradoxically provide examples of regulation and totalisation, as the teacher uses language which can be construed as an attempt to construct a teacher–student relationship which is more inclusive and less marked for unequal power relations. At the same time, she is involved in the technique of classification—joining herself with the group—a strategy which is less likely to be available to the students. Its success as a strategy depends on how the students make sense of what she says in the context of the lesson, their experiences of teachers, and of this teacher, and what else the teacher does and says in this lesson.

The following excerpts from the gymnastic lesson are typical of the more general linguistic features usually identifiable in a physical education warm-up but they also provide some further illustrations of how gendered bodies are constructed in physical education. The basic unit of analysis in systemic functional linguistics is the clause, so the text has been 'claused' for easier analysis.

Teacher, Student

T: What's the purpose of doing a warm-up?.
S: Stretching our calves.
T: Stretching and,
S: (Unclear)
T: No, what else do we have to do other than stretching?
   (Pause)
   Have to get the blood circulating.
   All right.
   So that all those fibres, muscle fibres are being fed with oxygen, so that we're prepared to do physical work.
   Right standing up very quickly. (Pause)
   Right, just on the spot, just jogging.
   (Pause)
   [sound of girls jogging]
   Right keeping those ankles right up off the floor. (Pause)
   Don't have to come very high.
   Right rolling wrists,
   make a wave with your forearms and your wrists,
   (Pause)
   [Giggling and talking in background]

and pressing against each,
hands against one another.
. . .
And point those little toes to the floor.
When you do gymnastics or dance,
Allison if you face me
you'll know what's going on.
You should turn your feet out
so little toes go to the floor.
Not big toes,
but little toes. (Pause)

As is the case in most physical education lessons, the teacher does most if not all the talking, generally as a series of ellipsed commands realised by material processes ('press', 'stretch') and circumstances of place or manner. In many cases, commands are ellipsed to the point that only circumstances remain ('up', 'there', 'quickly'). The students are positioned as the recipients of a constant flow of talk to which they must respond by moving their bodies in specific ways. The students ('you') are the main subjects and actors in the clauses, with the body or parts of the body positioned as the object/goal to be moved in specified ways and in specified directions. The warm-up is based on the principles of movement derived from exercise physiology and from pedagogical imperatives about safety—students must go through a warm-up, that is, move parts of their bodies in specified ways, so that they can participate in a skill practice without injury. The activities thus draw on particular knowledge regimes which are translated into specific practices by the teachers and the students.

Of all the segments of the lesson, the warm-up would have to provide the most potential for the expression of the regulatory practices and technologies of training that Foucault (1979) describes in relation to the disciplining of bodies in army training. Bodies are divided into component parts (calves, ankles, wrists, feet, elbows, toes) which must move or be placed in specific ways and within specific time frames. The physical organisation and the predominance of commands in the warm-up provides an optimum environment for creating relations of authority and control. Divergences from the appropriate execution of the activity provide the means for the assertion of the teacher's authority and her right in this lesson to regulate all behaviour pertaining to the body. Students are physically organised to facilitate surveillance by the teacher. They face the teacher and the pace of the instructions means that all students have to be paying attention so that they are performing the activities at the same time as the rest of the class.

In this text, what is of particular interest is the close attention to the positioning of parts of the body, to the placement of the feet and toes. The request to place the feet is explained in terms of the standards appropriate to gymnastics and dance, realised by the use of the obligatory form of the verbal auxiliary, for example: 'When you do gymnastics or dance . . . you *should* turn your feet out so little toes go to the floor. Not big toes, but little toes'. The 'you' both carries the meanings of *you* the specific students in the class and is a statement of rule—'one should', this is 'how things are done', drawing on a set of values and behaviours appropriate or 'normal' to a specific field of movement (normalisation, classification). This attention to the aesthetics and proper comportment of the body is taken up again in other parts of the lesson, for example when the teacher says:

> Form, how we do things in gymnastics is important . . .
> Let's now start to get legs together if they're supposed to
> be together; straight if they're supposed to be straight.
> Think about your feet, and instead of having this big blob
> on the end of your leg, right, your foot becomes the same
> line as your leg. Start to look at how you're doing things.

Practice: classification; standardisation

Having completed the stretches, the practice stage is introduced by statements about the skills that will be practised in the lesson that day:

> T: Rolls,
>   we're not going to start with forward rolls today,
>   we're going to start with backward rolls.
>   (Pause: a few groans from girls)
>   Backward rolls don't necessarily have to go over your head.
>   What are the things to remember in a backward roll?
> S: Keep your head tucked in.
> T: Keep your head tucked in, yes,
>   in any roll you have to keep your head tucked in
>   'cause basically you're trying to become like a ball
>   aren't you.
>   Something else,
>   Yola? (Pause)
>   What about your knees,

where do your knees have to go in a backward roll
if you're going to,

S: under (rest unclear)

T: Well under your chin or up to your chest.
You've got to keep your back rounded and
your knees into your chest.
If you keep your knees into your chest
then you will roll over.
If you're going to do a shoulder roll,
keep your knees tucked
and they go over your shoulder to one side,
and then you don't get that stretch of the neck that you
do in a backward roll.
What about hands
if you're going to do a backward roll?

S: (unclear)

T: Right,
where you just put them in that back arch,
where your hands went underneath you in the back arch,
that's where they go.
Keep your elbows in,
don't have them flying out to the side,
elbows in,
knees tucked to your chest and backward rolls.
Let's see,
one at a time please,
longways, along your mat.
Don't have to tell you that
you know that one already.

The text above begins with a set of statements which classify rolls into backward rolls and forward rolls and goes on to set up the criteria for successful backward rolls (normalisation, classification). In this case, the students are invited to recall (presumably from a previous lesson) what they already know about the execution of backward rolls (an opportunity for surveillance since the teacher can note who remembers and who doesn't). The teacher reiterates student responses in a linguistic form which is characteristic of this section of the lesson: that is, a rule-like statement realised grammatically by modulation (meanings of necessity and obligation). Such meanings are realised through the use of modal auxiliaries such as *have to*, *must*, *got to*, *should*, as in: 'you have to keep your head tucked in' and 'you've got to keep your back rounded'. It is also realised in imperatives which encode correct procedures rather than demanding an immediate response, for example 'keep your elbows in', an enactment of a regulatory process by which certain rules of behaviour are invoked. In this way specific knowledge about the body is meant to be acquired through a process of learning which assumes that direct instruction together with appropriate teaching points drawn from exercise physiology and bio-mechanics are the best (and only) ways of learning socially valued skills.

The number of questions in this section is rather unusual for a typical physical education lesson and is indicative of the ways this particular teacher draws upon a movement education discourse, where students are expected to think about the elements of time, space, weight and flow in relation to their movements. A movement education approach is ostensibly intended to place more emphasis on student-centred learning and problem-solving. In Gore's terms it shifts more to mechanisms of the self. However, movement education classes still provide contexts for constant surveillance and for the processes of normalisation. What has changed is what is regarded as normal. In traditional physical education classes standardised performances are valued as normal; in movement education classes expressions of creativity and variance are valued.

Material ('doing') processes predominate, with the body or body parts as objects to be moved in particular directions, in a particular manner (circumstances of place) to achieve a specified skill. It would seem that the body is taken primarily to be a tool or instrument, whose skills can be honed in response to directions from the teacher/expert, but that learning and thinking *about* movement is generally not part of the physical education process.

DISCUSSION

Returning to the questions posed at the beginning of this chapter, it is clear from the analysis that it is the teacher who is primarily involved in the processes of regulating what can be done, how it can be done and where it can be done. She is embodied as the expert through her capacity to ask questions to which she knows the answer, to demonstrate skills, to assist others through directions and by supporting and moving bodies. Through her use of language, the teacher constructs particular notions of female embodied subjectivity, concerned with how one looks. On the one hand this is constituted in terms of male scrutiny and, on the other, in terms of the female body as an aesthetic object where close attention to the positioning of body parts is important.

The lesson illustrates those assumptions about the body, about physical activity and about bodies and gender that are taken-for-granted, that is, that are dominant/hegemonic. What we have in both gymnastics and sport more generally is adherence to the idea that there is a hierarchy of skills, with the basics having to be mastered before moving on to skills of a higher order. Not only is a hierarchy of skills assumed, but there is also a profound conviction that certain skills are valuable in themselves and need to be part of each student's repertoire, for example, the forward and backward roll in gymnastics. While this is rationalised by arguments of safety, the whole configuration, the way of thinking about the body, the existence of these activities and not others in the syllabus, speaks to a particular historical set of circumstances and not the universality of these activities and skills and the ways of acquiring them.

The analysis above demonstrates that, as Foucault points out (1979, p. 176):

> . . . a relation of surveillance, defined and regulated, is inscribed at the heart of the practice of teaching, not as an additional or adjacent part, but as a mechanism that is inherent to it and which increases its efficiency.

But as Gore (1995b) points out, inherent in Foucault's notion of power is its capacity to be productive—to bring into being that which it names. This is of particular relevance to pedagogy, in which the exertion of power is inescapable. In physical education, the exertion of mechanisms of power on the body is particularly evident: the physical organisation of the lesson lends itself to constant surveillance of the students by the teachers, and vice versa; the knowledge and skills which constitute the content of the lesson are taken as given, with the teacher as expert. This provides a context in which the practices that regulate the body, and which determine normal and appropriate ways of behaving, are constantly reiterated. At the beginning of the lesson students are categorised in terms of different 'naturalised' characteristics. The students' practice of the set activities and their ability to judge their own rating in relation to the uniform requirement both speak to the successful operation of the various technologies of the self that are in keeping with their positioning as students and as students of a physical education lesson.

What this means for the teachers and students involved is that certain ways of thinking about the body and moving the body become naturalised and other ways remain hidden—impossible and inconceivable. Students may, outside the school, encounter alternative ways of moving the body, such as yoga, as well as different discourses of femininity. They may not. There is no evidence of student resistance to the discursive regime in operation in this class, only the co-operative performance of required movements. Such compliance may indicate an only too successful outcome to bodywork as the means of production of feminised subjects according to dominant discourses.

NOTES

1   Imperatives are the most overt way of coding commands: *Do this, Put your arms like this, Stop that.* Other choices initially associated with other speech functions, such as question or statement, can also be used, particularly when being polite or not wanting to be too direct. Examples of commands realised as interrogatives include *How about trying a backward tumble now? Are you going to behave?* Examples of commands realised as declaratives include *That's a good height for you, There's too much noise in here.*

10 Writing without ink: methodology, literacy and cultural difference

Jennifer Biddle

The editors of this collection have asked that I write an introduction to this chapter on the methodology that I have employed. They have asked that I make explicit the methods I've used in order that these might be repeated, followed, learned; in order that this introduction might serve a pedagogic purpose; in order to shed light on how to write about what I have written about here. Reasonable enough request. But I baulk. Freeze. Resist. Why would anyone want to emulate this idiosyncratic, perhaps even mad writing project? Who would want to—who even could?—repeat the disparate, if not desperate, set of mishaps and circumstances of my pre-, during and post-fieldwork experiences which have led to this work I call my own? Is there method here? What if there isn't? How can I justify my position in this collection of works on methodological approaches?

Method. An ugly word. And my *Shorter Oxford* concurs, simultaneously convincing me of my deepest fears, and confounding them, demonstrating as it does the necessary relationship between method, methodical and Methodist. 'Procedure for attaining an object', 'a way of doing anything, esp. according to a regular plan', 'excessive regard for methods'. Help. How can I turn my eclectic, eked-out-of-experience and necessarily experimental scribblings into procedures, plans, regularity? Can I write about what belies my own practice? Am I expected to lie?

Of course, I could hide behind professional platitudes and institutional commonplaces. That is, after all, what they are there for. 'Without the experience of fieldwork I could not have written this chapter. The immeasurable generosity, patience and intelligence of

Lajamanu Warlpiri made this research possible'. And of course, these statements, like all discursively dominant ones, are necessarily true. And I don't for an instant want to underplay the enormity of fieldwork as a pedagogic, a life experience. Nor, worse, would I want to disavow particular Warlpiri individuals' efforts in both tolerating, and teaching me throughout the ongoing process of my 'fieldwork'.

But equally true, and far less easily uttered, is the artifice of writing itself. Writing can never simply capture or represent my own—let alone Warlpiri—experiences. And it is a deeply suspicious view of language, of writing particularly, that also informs this paper.

Alternatively, I could speak of the 'methodologies' of Jacques Derrida which, along with the exigencies of fieldwork, do serve to shape this chapter, at least in part. Only I am not convinced that Derrida's 'deconstruction' offers a clear-cut methodology. To outline as I might, as indeed, Jonathan Culler (1983) and Christopher Norris (1982) before me have, deconstructive 'approaches' and 'formulas' for reading a text, is, of course, possible. One could, undoubtedly, identify in my work certain 'deconstructive' propinquities: the identification and subversion of taken-for-granted ways of thinking about historically entrenched binaristic logics—speech and writing, orality and literacy, colonised and coloniser, Aborigines and Europeans; the tenacity of these ways of thinking, and the violence of their effects; the enactment of a systematic reversal and displacement of the assumed hierarchies between the terms while continuing to work in and through them or, as Spivak (1976, p. lxxv) writes, quoting Derrida, the aim is 'to dismantle the metaphysical and rhetorical structures which are at work . . . not in order to reject or discard them, but to reinscribe them in another way'. Yes, I could locate these types of operations for you throughout this chapter, ergo, I have done so by listing them here.

But to do so is to miss the point.

Edward Said has called Derrida's work a 'technique of trouble', a phrase I love precisely because it gets at what is altogether too often overlooked in 'methodological' discussions about deconstruction—that is, as Cordelia Chavez Candelaria (1994, p. 191) has noted, the profoundly anti-authoritarian nature of Derrida's project. This may also serve to explain why, when Derrida is taken-up by women theorists, they do so in terms of explicitly politicised, explicitly anti-authoritarian agendas, be these feminist, sexual, postcolonial or otherwise. Gayatri Spivak, Judith Butler, Barbara Johnson, Jane Gallop, Eve Kosofsky Sedgwick, Trinh T. Minh-ha and Elizabeth Grosz are names which come immediately to mind. Men who take-up Derrida tend to do so in more strictly philosophical and/or literary ways. Gasche and Rorty represent the former, Culler and Norris, the latter. (I generalise of course: Irene Harvey's work is profoundly philosophical, not particularly political, and, on the other side, Homi K. Bhabha's implicit use of Derrida is anything but politically benign.)

In other words, it is more an orientation, an attitude to my subject matter, that describes whatever 'Derridean' inflections and influences are operant here. If I may be so bold as to insert myself in this genealogy of feminist theorists, it is precisely these kinds of anti-authoritarian attitudes that coincide with, and inform, my own. And it is this which, above all else, from my perspective, typifies the 'method' at work in this chapter, if method I must call it. A refusal to accept the terms in which literacy, in which the alphabet and, in turn, Aboriginal difference itself, has been constructed and construed; a disregard for the supposed 'neutral' terms of writing combined with an imperative to rework the pernicious consequences of conceptualisa-tion itself; a belligerent conviction that writing is a culturally specific material practice with no little effect.

The universal embracing of literacy cross-culturally makes the effects of writing particularly difficult to trace. Thus, the historically absented identity of the writing subject—that is, (universalised) European cultural conceptualisations and practices—is as much under interrogation here as are the terms of Warlpiri differences. In short, my paper works to enact what it seeks to describe: to find a form to figure cultural differences differently. Or—because that sounds al-together too idealistic, too hopeful, given the immutable legacy of language as I have inherited it in semiotic and poststructural defi-nitions—at least to avoid reinscribing the same kinds of differences.

But I ask myself: can refusal be a method?; does irreverence count?

This chapter is an investigation into writing and cultural identity. It is concerned with the way in which alphabetical writing, as a culturally specific mode of representation, is actively involved in the production of cultural difference(s). Nowhere are the effects of writing more apparent, and simultaneously disavowed, than in the writing of a language and the teaching of literacy to people assumed to be 'without writing'. The dominant portrayal of Australian Aboriginal people as either pre-literate or illiterate—a portrayal reinforced rather than countered by the contemporary heralding of traditional 'oral' Aborig-inal practices—is here refuted. I argue that it is not the case that Warlpiri Aborigines are pre- or illiterate but, on the contrary, Warlpiri use the alphabet in terms which not only demonstrate a profound appreciation of literacy, but ultimately the inadequacy of literacy, of the alphabet, to represent literate subjects.[1]

I rely here on a specific conceptualisation of writing as a mimetic form of representation. As I explore below, the alphabet is commonly understood to represent speech. It purports to mimic—to imitate, to copy, to liken—the sounds of speech. Even if unsuccessful, as I will argue, this purportedly mimetic relationship between graph and sound produces important social and political effects which this chapter seeks to discern.

In order to trace the mimetic effects of the alphabet as it moves to write, and to name, Warlpiri differences, I use a notion of mimesis derived from a number of sources. Adapting from Walter Benjamin (1969) and Michael Taussig (1993), I argue that mimesis can be understood as 'effects produced by the copy'. It is the partial and virtual force mimesis produces as it moves to copy and reproduce European models and methods of writing and, in turn, Warlpiri mimetic responses, which I examine below. The attempt to create colonised subjects mimetically, through the use of writing and naming techniques, is shown to have both succeeded and failed. Following the work of Homi K. Bhabha (1994), I examine the ways in which colonial mimicry produces an ambivalent authority. The colonised are kept at a distance, becoming only ever partial resemblances, partially reformed, both miming and menacing the colonial order or, as I explain below, 'almost the same but not quite' (Bhabha, 1994, p. 86). Or, as Warlpiri might say themselves, 'same but different'. Mimesis, Paul Carter (1992, p. 168) argues, while 'designed to minimise difference, exacerbates it'.

A proviso: the material under consideration in this chapter is of a highly sensitive nature. I have taken great care to limit potential offence by employing circumspect renderings of the proscribed or *Kumanjayi* names I refer to in order not to violate the taboo on their usage. When the actual sound of the name is important for the purposes of discussion, I have used International Phonetic Alphabet (IPA) letters. As I discuss below, it is the use of Roman alphabetic letters to write out a name in its entirety which is potentially taboo for Warlpiri. In my understanding, the use of IPA letters to represent a name in full, as I do here, is less likely to cause offence. Unlike the letters of the Roman alphabet, IPA letters are not a commonly held or utilised code; they are not recognised or identified as being 'names' as such. These variant renderings of taboo names will undoubtedly affect reader accessibility, and I apologise in advance. However, these variant forms represent my attempt to remain in keeping with taboo restrictions. I do not want to cause offence or 'sorry'.

In order to appreciate the use of literacy, of the alphabet, in Warlpiri figurations of the proper name, it is necessary to understand something of the complex system of personal appellation Warlpiri possess.[2] But this is not easy. There are no generalisations without qualification here; no tendencies which aren't seemingly belied by others. The unassuming proper name is anything but simple. Nowhere are the 'bewildering' effects of mimesis that Taussig (1993) describes more evident than in contemporary Warlpiri names. The name is no mere signifier of identity. Nor has the name simply been one thing among others exchanged between Europeans and Aborigines in the ongoing attempt to encounter, to comprehend, the difference of the other. Both groups have moved—and continue to move—to rename the other throughout the colonial endeavour. The terms in which Europeans have re-named Warlpiri make definitive differentiations between contemporary European and Warlpiri naming practices difficult to sustain.

To make matters even more complicated, it is through the name itself that Aboriginal cultural specificity has been understood. Aboriginal societies are renowned for their intricate and varied naming practices. Numerous names for any one person are common, and a tacit principle of non-disclosure operates regarding personal names. An absolute quantification—a typology of personal address and reference forms—is perhaps impossible in Aboriginal context(s). As von Sturmer (1981, p. 14) puts it, the use of names in Aboriginal societies is 'subject to extreme variability'. Dixon (1980, p. 28) suggests, following Stanner (1937), that Aboriginal peoples have so many names because there needs to be at least one or more name(s) available at any given moment which are not proscribed by prevailing taboos (kin-avoidance, polite deference, death). This is, however, a somewhat functionally reductive explanation, in that it assumes a singular identity which pre-exists and, in a sense, supersedes the very complex notion of identity that multiple nominal forms suggest.

The avoidance of the use of personal names is combined with a marked preference for the use of 'class' terms, that is, terms which indicate membership of socially determined groupings based on age, gender, kinship, moiety and country. This preference for the use of class terms over that of personal names is what Sutton (1982, p. 187) calls the 'Principle of Generality' (see also Stanner 1937; von Sturmer 1981).

This Principal of Generality—and the potential 'danger' of personal names—has been understood as resulting from particular configurations of the Aboriginal social, primarily 'avoidance relationships' and the taboo on speaking the name of the dead. Circumspection with regards to others is something of a cultural imperative among Aborigines (see Haviland 1979; von Sturmer 1981; Sutton 1982; Rumsey 1982; Liberman 1982; Kendon 1988; Eades 1988). The overt identification of others is eschewed. Identifying another too closely in a particular context—using a personal name—may act, or enact, a certain identification of, and/or with, the name bearer and, in turn, serve to closely identify the name user. One should avoid 'presenting oneself too forcefully' and 'linking oneself too clearly with one's ideas', von Sturmer (1981, p. 29) claims. Instead, a highly diplomatic tendency towards 'self-effacement', as Kendon (1988, p. 458) describes it, prevails in many Aboriginal societies.

Personal names may also be considered dangerous because they do not specify identity in terms of publicly recognisable classificatory categories of 'being' and 'relating'. As Lévi-Strauss (1972) argues, personal names threaten classificational systems because they push, and define, the limits of classification. Class terms may be privileged in societies like Warlpiri because they 'name' and group persons in terms of structured categories of kinship, age, moiety or gender. Thus, they prescribe and proscribe certain relationships—modes of behaviour—accordingly. Class names are organised, and in turn organise, in terms of the external dictates of *Jukurrpa*, the Dreaming, Law: the regulatory body of Warlpiri society. By contrast, personal names are said to individuate and simultaneously *de*-differentiate because they do not encode in terms of the prevailing dictates of external authority. Personal names may be considered 'dangerous' because they do not entail the externalised authority that class names necessarily possess. They may, in turn, pose a certain threat to the Law because they do not necessarily circumscribe an order of relations and relating.

Here, distinguishing between types of personal names becomes important. For, while Lajamanu Warlpiri may concur with this Principle of Generality, there is also evidence of a more free use of European personal names than the literature maintains. That is, there appears to be a movement towards the favouring of the more sociocentric, stable names over those of the egocentric, situationally specific and necessarily variant, class terms (with due variation across the Warlpiri nation, as Dussart (1988, p. 59) preliminarily outlines). Stanner (1937), Sutton (1982) and von Sturmer (1981) seem to suggest that class terms *always* predominate over personal names. But, in my experience at both Lajamanu and Dussart's (1988) at Yuendumu, European personal names are commonly used in both reference and address.

I want to suggest that this movement can be understood in relation to the dissemination of the 'proper' European name—effects of writing—in and on and by Warlpiri. In other words, there appears to be a growing correlation between the proper name and the actual terms of address and reference Warlpiri currently use. But not without a difference. Let me explain.

Warlpiri currently hold names which are very like European proper names: first name, surname, and subsection term or skin name (with the skin name located in either 'middle' or 'last' name position). For example:

Michael Nelson Jakamarra

Jimmy Jampijinpa Robertson

Norah Nelson Napaljarri

Lady Nungarrayi.

Europeans imposed both first and last names on Warlpiri throughout the period of early contact for a variety of identificatory and administrative purposes. Warlpiri themselves currently confer European personal names on their children at birth, unlike the much later conferred Warlpiri personal names.[3] The more unusual, the better, for example, Azaria, Lava, Basil and Attrina are names recently conferred. In my experience, the naming of children explicitly does *not* involve naming through inheritance practices as happens with Warlpiri personal names. In short, Warlpiri appear to have been diligent students of the lessons that the 'proper' name teaches, in their movement to employ the unique, highly individuated, personal name.

The conjoining of the skin name in the making, the marking, of the proper Warlpiri name is significant. The sixteen 'skins' are one of the more complex systemic features of Warlpiri society and have been subject to much debate and commentary (see Laughren 1982; Nash 1982; Meggitt 1962, pp. 165–187; Scheffler 1978, pp. 327–384). Crudely formulated, skin names serve to define kinship relations between each and every member of Warlpiri society, structurally and, potentially, genealogically. They also position members of society in relation to one another in broader organisational terms by moiety (patrimoiety and matrimoiety), semi-moiety (patri-couple) and subsection. Skin provides terms commensurate, on the one hand, with both the egocentric kinship and the sociocentric classificatory dictates of *Jukurrpa*, the Dreaming, Law. On the other hand, skin provides terms which are simultaneously commensurate with the absolute terms required by the dictates of the proper European name—that is, names which can be used 'equally' in address or reference, which remain the same regardless of referent, addressee or propositus (the technical term referring to the person from whom a given relationship is reckoned— see Scheffler 1978). Proper European names, like the skin names, are *not* circumscribed by speaker, topic, gender or social state, as are all the other names which Warlpiri potentially hold and use: kinship terms, age–mate and social status terms, nick-names, and Warlpiri personal names. Sutton (1982) and Rumsey (1984) provide detailed discussions of the enormous variation in usage of personal names and kinship terms.

Skin names have come to form part of the Warlpiri proper name. They occupy the space between the European first name and the surname and, consequently, have been used by Europeans as both. The ongoing presence of an 'Aboriginal' signifier has been maintained in the Warlpiri proper name. Skins are positioned as, and thus likened to, both European middle names and surnames, although the latter may be becoming the more common position. For example, Peggy Napaljarri Rockman (Ryan 1990, p. 58) has more recently been written as Peggy Rockman Napaljarri (Napaljarri and Cataldi 1994). So, too, Jimmy Jampijinpa Robertson (Ryan 1989, p. 94) is more recently found as Jimmy Robertson Jampijinpa (Ryan 1990, pp. 25–27).

Whether this Aboriginality is figured as middle or last name, the inclusion of the skin necessarily positions Warlpiri names ambivalently in relationship to European names, creating a recognisably similar but nevertheless different name from the proper name, a point I return to below.

The increasing standardisation of this form of the proper name is evident in the use of initials in both 'death taboo' and graffiti practices. One of the more serious offences, widely reported in the literature and witnessed time and again in my experience, is the speaking aloud of a recently deceased person's name. Warlpiri fervently avoid the presence of the recently deceased. Mortuary ceremonies and bereavement practices are organised by and around certain ritualised avoidances or 'erasures'. For instance, camp is moved from where the deceased has lived; places frequented by the deceased are avoided; clothing, shoes, blankets, mattresses, furnishings belonging to the deceased are burned; cars of the recently dead are dumped; photographs, tapes and videos showing the deceased are destroyed, covered or stored; ceremonial songs/dances associated with the person and/or their birthplace are not performed; brands of alcoholic drink that the deceased preferred will not be purchased. All these avoidances ensure that a certain erasure of the deceased's presence takes place. In this way, erasure operates with no mere symbolic force.

The erasures I describe here also ensure that a certain re-inscription will ensue. Thus, a new camp, car and cassette player; new blankets and sheets etc. will accrue to relatives of the deceased (and many of these items are part of mortuary exchanges). That is, to erase is also to re-mark. In a more general sense, one could also then speak of the erasure as the mark making the re-mark possible.

Eradicating the presence of the deceased must also occur verbally. The presence of the dead, the potential evocation of their presence, persists in their personal name. For Warlpiri, personal names bear material witness. Not unlike the marks that ancestral beings left behind in their travels through country—the same marks which are put, traced and retraced by Warlpiri in inscriptive practices of acrylic painting and other ritual contexts (Biddle 1996)—names also bear the trace of a presence.

Stanner (1937, p. 301) likens the Aboriginal personal name to a shadow:

> The personal names by which a man is known are something more than names. The name seems to bear much the same relation to the personality as the shadow or image does to the sentient body. To stab a man's shadow with a spear is not a friendly action. Names are not symbols so much as verbal projections of an identity which is well known in the flesh.

This figure of the shadow is wonderfully apt. We understand the shadow as a material repetition of the body's silhouette which, in reproducing the sentient body, simultaneously conjures its essence. Likewise, the name can be understood as a vocal silhouette, a repetition that literally bears vestige, a sentient, sounding, embodiment of person. Person is of primary concern in Warlpiri inscriptive practices generally. What matters is not so much *what* but *who* left the mark ancestrally; ancestors are always specified by name, be it by skin, kinship, place, site, species term or personal name (or, more frequently, a combination of each). And, in turn, it is through person, through the names of the ancestors, that Warlpiri are named and affiliated with others and with country accordingly. In short, the trace, the material remainder of another's presence, identifies, and is identified, in terms of *person*. The name, as part of a more general inscriptive emphasis on trace, can be understood as a sonorous, material evocation of an identity already existent. The name both traces and bears the trace of a presence which precedes and supersedes any given instance of its use—even if every use is (also) its manifestation.

This evocative potentiality of the personal name may help to explain the taboo on speaking the personal name of the deceased. To avoid the literal conjuring of another likely in the evocation of the personal name, Warlpiri employ a certain name replacement, *Kumanjayi*. *Kumanjayi*, it needs to be understood, is *not* a name for the deceased. The deceased are not, at least, in my experience, ever referred to by a name of any sort, personal, class, or *Kumanjayi*. When they need be referred to, as when passing on the sorry-news of death, it is only through extreme forms of circumlocution and circumspection. It might be said to me, for instance, if I asked in the inordinately circumspect manner one must, who the signs of the sorry-news in the community concerned—the instantaneous stopping of work, the movement of persons west, the wailing of women—'You know that one Ruthie Nangala who works for Shop? Well her husband got no brother now'.

Rather than a means of referring to the deceased, *Kumanjayi* is instead a replacement name for someone who bears the same personal name as the recently deceased. Thus, when someone passed away at Yuendumu with the same name as a school-age boy I worked with at the time, he became *Kumanjayi*, as his family, friends and teachers, as well as his written school work and name tags, proclaimed. He (name, person) became literally *Kumanjayi*, re-inscribed both verbally and in writing. Nash and Simpson (1981) provide a shorthand definition of *Kumanjayi* as meaning, following Warlpiri, 'no name'. However, their longer definition (1981, p. 173) points out that *Kumanjayi* is itself necessarily a class name. It does not become taboo upon death of its bearer, more than one person holds it at any time, and it necessarily indicates membership in a social/linguistic category. But here they also specify a more subtle rendering of the term which is commensurate with my appreciation: *Kumanjayi* also functions as a proper name in both address and reference, as can all the sociocentric class names. So thorough is its erasure, that one does not have to be aware of whom or what name *Kumanjayi* replaces in order for it to function as a name. Children and anthropologists, for example, who share much in common in the field, are often not aware of the proscribed name of a person who has passed away.

It is not only the name itself which *Kumanjayi* replaces; it also replaces words which potentially sound like the proscribed name. But—and this should be stressed—only words which sound like the proscribed *English* personal name. Nash and Simpson (1981, p. 171) suggest that this is because English, unlike Warlpiri, has a particularly high degree of common words which are near 'homophones' of personal names, resulting in a certain stretching of the taboo practice. Thus, the death of the above mentioned person resulted in a common English word also becoming *Kumanjayi*: the word used to refer to the object which starts a car or unlocks a door. This word became *Kumanjayi* because it is an almost direct homophone of the *Kumanjayi* name of the deceased. Phonetically, they would both be rendered, pronounced in Warlpiri, [kid3]. The common word, sounding the same as the personal name, is likely to evoke the (same) potential presence as the name, and hence, it also becomes taboo. Accordingly, one could not say 'Where're my ____?' or 'Gimme my____' without causing sorry. The polite form, the only form available for those considered 'inside' the boundaries of the social—a boundary Europeans are never expected to respect in full, as I return to below (see also Stanner 1937, p. 309)—was instead: 'Where're my *Kumanjayi*?' or 'Gimme my *Kumanjayi*'.

In short, sound itself is considered a vehicle for the material trace of the deceased's presence. It is here that the Warlpiri use of the alphabet in name avoidance becomes of interest: the usage suggests that the letters of the alphabet do not sound, nor sound-out, the proscribed name. This implies a very different understanding of alphabetic writing, and of writing generally, but one which may still be in keeping with the larger Warlpiri principle of trace. Let me explain.

First, younger Warlpiri may use the alphabet to spell-out the taboo name. This is likely to occur in the presence of a non-Aboriginal who is unfamiliar with other forms of circumlocution and/or who may require, for Land Claim genealogies, social security, or other bureaucratic reasons, explicit identification of the deceased in European terms. That is, spelling indicates a certain Warlpiri familiarity with European naming expectations, and a willingness to comply. Nash and Simpson ascertain that this recourse to spelling is a permitted violation of the taboo on speaking the name. As they (1981, p. 168) put it: 'reference to the proscribed name is tolerated, in that literate Aborigines sometimes communicate a proscribed name by spelling it aloud or writing it down'.

However, I think Nash and Simpson may suffer from a certain phonocentrism, that is, an assumption that the name of the letter 'sounds' the same as the proscribed name uttered aloud. They would not speak of a 'tolerated' reference to the name in spelling if they did not perceive of spelling as a violation of the taboo. To return to the above mentioned example: the assumption is that the five letters (five names of letters) used to spell this name *aloud*, that is [kɛ i aɪ ti ɛtʃ] sounds-out, and therefore, sounds the same as the name itself pronounced aloud, that is [kidʒ]. Hence, spelling would break the taboo. The names of the letters are (implicitly) thought to bear a necessary relation to sound: letters sound the same as the names they spell. But this kind of assumed relationship between letter and sound is not evident in Warlpiri use of spelling.

For Warlpiri do not only employ letters to spell *Kumanjayi* names. They also use letters to initial *Kumanjayi* names. For example, the name of the 'man who slew Goliath' was taboo at Lajamanu during my fieldwork 1989–1991 (see also Nash and Simpson 1981, p. 170). But rather than the particular man who bore this name being called *Kumanjayi*, he instead became *DCJ*, or rather, *Dee-See-Jayi*, as Warlpiri pronounce it. A letter stands for each of his names: *D* (first initial of the name of the 'man who slew Goliath'), Campbell, Japaljarri (names changed to prevent identification). This new 'name' is used freely in both address and reference.

It is not only personal *Kumanjayi* names which follow this pattern of initialling, but potentially, other proscribed proper nouns (names) may also be initialled. For example, the fifth day of the week was taboo at Lajamanu during my stay, and has also been proscribed at both Warrabri and Tennant Creek since 1977 (Nash and Simpson 1981, p. 170). A Warlpiri or English synonym has not been used to replace the proscribed term, as in Sunday being *Wapirra-kurlangu* (belonging to God); Thursday being *Ironum-jayi* (Ironing Day), dating from the period the Warlpiri call 'Welfare Days', when the community was organised according to various assigned group tasks by days of the week; and Wednesday being 'Warlpirised' as *Ngunjalpa*. The fifth day of the week instead has become *F-ngirli*, pronounced [ɪɛpɲɪali] as Warlpiri has no sound equivalent to *f*, and English *f* sounds generally take the bilabial p/b form. The suffix added here, *ngirli*, is what Nash (1980, p. 256) identifies as a noun case enclitic, the elative, meaning *from* (as in *-ngurlu*, the *u* changing to *i* because of vowel assimilation). Thus, the fifth day of the week in the form of *F-ngirli*, means literally, *from F*, indicating that the source of the word, following the alphabet's teaching, is its initial point of articulation, the first letter, *F*. Again, this name is used freely with clearly no transgression of the taboo.

Not unlike the anagram, initial letters are transposed to form a new personal name: a name significantly not taboo; a name of the order of *OJ* or *JR*, where what the initials stand for is, like the term *Kumanjayi* itself, irrelevant to the function of the letters as a name. The name is literally the names of the letters pronounced aloud.

Unlike acronyms such as NASA or ATSIC, the Warlpiri principle of initialling retains the original pronunciation provided by the names of the letters themselves. In short, the names of letters are clearly freed from the taboo on speaking the name of the deceased. And this freedom, I'd like to suggest, implies a radical severance of the letter from its sound; a radical reappraisal, in short, of the very relationship which constitutes the alphabet's raison d'être.

Alphabetic writing is based on the premise that sounds of speech *are* the same sounds that name each letter: A is for Apple, Artichoke and Aardvark; B is for Bee, Balloons and Bicycles. The alphabet is defined in fact by the very one-to-one relationship assumed between letter name and speech sound: grapheme and phoneme. I do not mean simply to draw attention here to the more usual argument that would find fault with the notion that letters stand for sound. But rather, I am more interested in noting what is usually not discussed: the deeply effective nature of the names of the letters themselves. I understand this is a counter-intuitive argument. We do not tend to think of letters as really having names but merely consider them to be sounds. Letters, it is assumed, are named simply by the sound of themselves in the alphabet: sounding like, sounding out, pronouncing, what it is they are. Spelling is taught through the reiteration that the name of the letter corresponds with the spoken 'sounds' it represents (A is for Apple, Artichoke and Aardvark). Thus, the name of the letter and the sound itself become bound. The direct link between the proper name and its rightful identity is here undiminished in the alphabet: one alphabet letter name equals one sound. The proper name function is ensured when the signifier possesses the signified one on one: the ultimate union, the perfect match. For the name of the letter literally announces, pronounces aloud, its singular identity in utterance. The letter A does not stand for—but operates as—the proper name, the only name of the sound [ɛ].

This sovereign association is one Warlpiri do not appear to honour. Clearly letters are *not* considered homophonous to spoken sound. [kɛ i aɪ ti ɛtʃ] and [kidʒ] do not sound the same. Letters do not trace the name. Letters—initials—do not name.

Now this is impossible. A tautology. A short-circuit in the mindset of the literate. What Warlpiri practices suggest is that 'this is not a name' despite the fact that every single form is in place to designate precisely a name. Initials belong to the proper name alone. The repetition and the severance of the first letter in capital form is the very mark in English orthographic practices differentiating the proper name from common nouns. The initial is the very essence distilled, as it were, from the alphabet's teaching—to represent sounds of spoken words by naming their 'initial' point of articulation. This very power, this very purpose of the letter, is at once asserted and denied. Warlpiri introduce chaos into a stringent regime of resemblance. They draw on and cite the letter's authority in repeating the initialling practice and also usurp that authority in so doing. What appears a name is not a name.

I intentionally repeat myself here, like Michel Foucault (1982) before me, to evoke Magritte and the effect(s) of his painting entitled in English 'This is not a pipe'. For a similar impossibility is made manifest by Warlpiri who, in their use of initialling, draw attention to the very taken-for-granted terms of the letter's habitual identity, the place where representation bears resemblance, ultimately, to its referent. Where initials name. And where, more to the point, they clearly do not.

Homi K. Bhabha's (1994) notion of mimicry as 'menace' is perhaps useful here for figuring Warlpiri initialling practices. For, in this repetition, this doubling, this mimesis of spelling and phoneticism and initialling of the 'proper' name, a certain scandal is introduced. At the very point that authority is respected in repetition, as Bhabha describes colonial mimicry, it is also effaced. The same phonetic principle which makes it possible for the initial to represent the name is broken in *not* representing the name. The very repetition of the letter, volunteered by Warlpiri in initialling, serves to assuage the narcissistic authority of colonial rule. For here, the 'civilising' movement to create literate colonial subjects is assured. Warlpiri appear to be particularly 'good' literate subjects who so clearly understand the imperative that they take initialling the proper name on-board themselves. But the gap that makes mimesis possible, also makes it productive, performative—an anti-authoritarian posture—and menaces the very principle which privileges the phoneme in and of writing in the first instance. The same authority which authorises the force of initialling dissimulates in its effects.

What is most revealing, most threatening, perhaps, in the Warlpiri use of initialling is the potential upset to one of the greatest myths of Western sensibility: that the alphabet is phonetic. A myth supported by the very names of the letters. Warlpiri here appear to 'work the weakness in the norm', as Judith Butler (1993b, p. 26) has described a perhaps parallel repetition in the performative re-claiming of certain names by women, gay and queer subjects. Warlpiri uses of the letter demonstrate the very precarious claim the alphabet has on speech. For, of course, the letters of the alphabet *do not* bear necessary relationships to sound. The familiar twenty-six letters are a conventional series of graphic assignments which hold at best a conventional, and unsystematic at that, relationship to sound. According to Fromkin and Rodman's (1978, pp. 56–64) calculations, minimally, forty-one differing graphic symbols would be necessary to even approximate the sounds of 'standard' spoken English (whatever that is!). Even were a one-to-one relationship between letter and sound ever agreed upon— unlikely as this is, given the historical disagreements over what constitutes the 'distinctive features' of the phoneme's identity (Lyons 1968, pp. 99–132; Chomsky and Halle 1965)—it would still require the learning of a necessarily arbitrary associative bond between the two, as we know from Saussure (1959). And this requires, following Derrida (1976), the de-privileging of sound in writing. This is an almost impossible task given the very prima facie relationship between alphabet and speech sound—between writing and speech generally— which continues to assail the thinking about, and the practice of, alphabetic writing.

In short, the Warlpiri death taboo is not violated by initialling. Indeed, alphabet initials provide the same erasure of presence that *Kumanjayi* itself does. To put it succinctly: initials, first, introduce a substitute for the taboo name which are themselves already existent independent names and, second, initials provide a class name substitute and thus, like all other class names, including *Kumanjayi*, they cannot become taboo. Letters belong instead to an independent code held in common potentially with all other names. Letters are classificatory names already and are used to represent what amount to class names in the very process of initialling.

But even more importantly, perhaps, initials provide a further purpose that the use of the name *Kumanjayi* cannot. They provide a means of replacing a taboo name in the terms dictated by the proper name. Proper names are increasingly mandatory in a context where the function and effects of proper identification are no small matter. And by *proper* here I mean a form of name *recognisable* as proper— readable, write-able and pronounceable—by those who continue to define the terms of identification.

It seems to me that, in the spelling aloud of *Kumanjayi* names and in the recourse to initialling, Warlpiri involve themselves not in a simple acquiescence to the terms of the proper name, but to something more like an active pre-empting. The conflicting values between the two systems of appellation, Warlpiri and European, are not unappreciated by those who bear the consequences. To put it bluntly, Warlpiri appear to have completely given up any expectation of proper

WRITING WITHOUT INK 185

avoidance respect behaviour from non-Aborigines. Spelling out a name in advance may serve to avoid having the non-Aboriginal 'guess' which person is deceased by calling out the personal name and hence causing sorrow and shame. Initialling provides a shorthand form of the proper name in contexts saturated with the proper name and its effects. It provides a way out of having to employ a Warlpiri name altogether, including the name *Kumanjayi*. In short, the names of the letters provide a means of assigning identity in terms which meet with European expectations and demands regarding the proper *pronounce-able* name. It repeats the proper name form and function (even if with differing effects).

Indeed, one might almost say the Warlpiri principle of trace is *protected* by the use of the letter precisely because it prevents in advance the possibility of taboo violation, perhaps protecting in the sense of camouflaging, as Homi K. Bhabha (1994, p. 85), following Lacan, identifies the function of mimicry. Like the UN trucks I watched on my television last summer making their way into Sarajevo covered in wood and sticks and mud mimicked the hillsides they drove through in order not to be subject to attack, Warlpiri initialling has tactical functions. And effects. The taboo on speaking the name of the dead remains intact *because of*, not in spite of, the use of initialling. Initialling facilitates the more general movement involved in death, where the person moves literally from the individuated in life, back to the great undifferentiated categories of the ancestral realm at death. That personal names become *Kumanjayi*—that the initial can be used to replace the personal name—likewise moves to assure that identity moves from the individuated to the undifferentiated status of the pre-given categories of the class name. Writing possesses the double ability to encode both individually on the one hand, and generally, on the other. In short, writing, while it may identify specifically, does so generically.

It is here that I think Lévi-Strauss (1972) underplays the role of writing in relation to the name's movement to 'generalise'. For, as Warlpiri initialling practices show, writing plays a determinative role in the proper name. And, in turn, writing plays a determinative role in showing precisely the conditions, the limits and the movements of classification. The written proper name—and its pronunciation in the form of lettered initials—precisely provide 'class indicators'. First-name–middle-name–last-name is an order immutable. There is no other narrative of proper identity available in the proper name of English alphabetic writing. The proper name provides forms 'repeatable, imi-table and durable', the absolute conditions of writing, Derrida claims

(1988, pp. 20–1). The repetitious similarity of the form of the proper name in writing, Derrida (1988, p. 9) argues, 'corrupts' the claim to unambiguous individuation that the proper name lays claim to. What may be understood as individuation is, in fact, a necessary classification. Writing makes for the distinctions 'we' recognise as 'proper' to the name—discrete, readable, pronounceable, repeatable units in order, in space and time.

Clearly, the reiteration of the letter in Warlpiri practices exposes at once, as Judith Butler (1993b, p. 22) identifies a perhaps similar strategy at work in the renaming of 'queer', the 'binding power of the law and its expropriability'. For the phonetically bound letter serves very differing ends in Warlpiri *Kumanjayi* practices. The Warlpiri citation of the letter exposes the 'failure of the law to control its own terms' (Butler 1993b, p. 23). A sign of a name is produced but it distinctly breaks with its 'proper' function. The very laws subscribed to in the 'proper' writing of the name are disavowed by the system itself. Warlpiri in 'working the weakness in the norm' usurp authority for their own purposes.

Warlpiri use the very loss of identity inherent in writing to contend with literal loss. Initialling works to assuage the likely loss conjured by too literal, too homophonous a repetition of the name in *Kumanjayi*; of the loss of the person present in the name as trace. Initialling protects—it camouflages—the principle of tracing. Initialling also serves to reinscribe class names potentially at risk in the 'proper' name (I think here of the subsection, the skin particularly). This strategy demonstrates the necessary incommensurability between graph and sound, word and object, name and self—the more general loss which necessarily constitutes the identity of the subject in/of writing.

Acknowlededgments

I would like to thank Alan Rumsey and Jane Sloan for their close readings of earlier versions of this text. The collaborative environments of the Department of Anthropology, Macquarie University, and the *Culture & Text* workshop, convened by Alison Lee and Cate Poynton, where I delivered versions of this chapter, helped clarify my thinking. The research on which this paper is based was conducted with assistance from the Australian Institute of Aboriginal and Torres Strait Islander Studies (AIATSIS) and the Carlyle Greenwell Bequest of the University of Sydney. Finally, I would like to thank my Yapa family and friends, who I hope can countenance the grandiose extent of my interpretations.

NOTES

1   For further discussion of the problematic assumptions of the pre-literate or illiterate 'Aborigine' see Biddle (1991, 1996).

2   My interest in this chapter is not to describe the intricate details of Warlpiri nominal forms and usages but, rather, to provide an interpretation of one aspect of these: the mimetic effects of the alphabet, of writing, in and on the Warlpiri name. Unfortunately, this requires that I generalise here far more than I would like, particularly in this first half of the chapter, where I gesture towards providing the reader with an overview of current Warlpiri naming practices in order to locate the ensuing analysis of the alphabet's effects. Details of the name forms I describe here could easily fill a chapter, if not an entire book. Where available, I have indicated further references.

3   Unfortunately, the complex differences, and relationships between Warlpiri and European names, cannot be contended with in a chapter of this size. See Dussart (1988) for a preliminary discussion.

11 Discourse analysis and cultural (re)writing

Alison Lee

> It depends . . . what your agenda is in doing the work. What do you
> want to get out of this? Who are you trying to convince? Who are you
> talking to? (Threadgold in Kamler 1997, p. 450)

Discourse analysis is most often conceived of in terms of what someone
does *to* a particular site or text. There is assumed a relationship of
exteriority with regard to that site, an 'etic' relationship (Kline 1995),
where the analyst's tools, whatever kind they might be, are applied in
the production of an authoritative account *about* the site. There is,
in general, within the field of discussion and debate about discourse
analysis, a paucity of commentary concerning the relations of power-
knowledge, that obtain between the analyst and the object domain of
analysis. In particular, there has typically been a tendency to assume
the capability of analysis, given the truth-revealing capabilities of
particular methods, to strip away what might, admittedly provocatively, be inferred as the 'false consciousness' of the text or object of
analysis, its failure to know itself, and to reveal a better truth about
that object (Hodge and McHoul 1992; Patterson 1997).

At the same time, discussion about discourse analysis enters
into another, rather oppositional, relation with the term 'text'. Discourse analysis is analysis of discourse, or text, the precise emphasis
differing according to different analytic traditions. Yet discourse analyses, or the results of such analyses, are themselves texts. As Luke
(1997, p. 346) notes: '[a]s intellectual work, all forms of discourse
analysis generate texts about texts, regardless of the particular analytic
metalanguage or rewrite and parsing rules used'. These new texts are

written and read, and rewritten in discussion and debate, just as are the texts and objects they purport to write about.

Together, the question of analytic authority, the question of textuality and writing, and the attendant underpinning oppositions which structure the field, form a major complex of issues that discourse analysis as an emerging scholarly field needs to address. Indeed, in the search for 'method', in the eager and sometimes surreptitious search for, and exchange (among neophyte researchers in particular) of, exegetical texts which appear to offer some light upon what it means to 'do' discourse analysis, many of these questions go unasked. While 'discourse analysis', of whatever tradition, is grounded in matters of language and signification and hence appears to avoid most of the worst forms of naive realism, there nevertheless appears to be a dearth of discussion of precisely those questions that have long been debated within the social sciences, as well as cultural studies, feminisms, and forms of postcolonial theorising. Within the more linguistically and generally technically oriented approaches to discourse analysis, in particular, such questions remain largely unaddressed.

This chapter seeks to add to current discussion about the practices of discourse analysis by raising a series of questions concerning its failure to date to take up the challenges that are thrown out by broader debates concerning the practices and politics of representation within the humanities and social sciences. Such literatures might offer discourse analysis a great deal at this point in its development as a methodological field. Through an examination of critical aspects of what Hodge and McHoul (1992) term 'the politics of text and commentary', and issues that have emerged through recent debates within the social sciences and cultural studies, I hope in this chapter to contribute to a problematisation of the emerging 'disciplinary' scene of discourse analysis.

Many of the matters raised in the following sections of the chapter are not in themselves new. In what is often referred to as the 'textual turn' in the human sciences, forms of theory have been mobilised that attend closely to questions of representation and writing (e.g. Clifford and Marcus 1986; Game 1991; James, Hockey and Dawson 1997). These questions are fundamentally questions of power—of who it is that produces which account of the social world. They are also questions of desire and pleasure—of which texts persuade and convince, of whom they persuade and convince, and to what desired ends. Yet the field of discourse analysis has by and large not participated reflexively in discussion about these matters in relation to its own research and representational practices. This is true of the emerging 'family of text analytic practices' (Luke 1997, p. 346) with which I provisionally align my own research and writing, that of 'critical discourse analysis'. The point of this chapter for this volume is to (re)assemble some key questions concerning the practices and politics of text and commentary, in the light of Terry Threadgold's question in the epigraph with which I began.

ON ANALYTIC AUTHORITY

In the title of this section I make an intertextual reference to the canonical paper originally published by James Clifford in 1983: 'On ethnographic authority'. In deciding to make this reference explicit, I provide a partial answer—at least with respect to my construction of a reader for this chapter—to Threadgold's question: who are you talking to? It is not at all certain that contemporary readers of texts about discourse analysis will have passed through major debates within the social sciences and cultural studies concerning representation and writing, such as the 'writing culture' debates within social anthropology, within which Clifford's paper, and the controversial collection of chapters in Clifford and Marcus (1986), mark a 'watershed' for that discipline and more broadly. Similarly, it would seem that *practitioners* of discourse analysis have not in recent years widely participated in such debate. Anthropology and other social science disciplines have engaged the 'textual turn' and have been significantly influenced by rhetorical theory, semiotics and discourse analysis (Clifford 1986). Discourse analysis as a field in its own right, perhaps even an emerging discipline, has not at this stage in its development substantially engaged in reflexive discussion about its own knowledge-producing and representational practices in specific social, political, and legal contexts (James, Hockey and Dawson 1997).

A further, related, observation is that there is, in much of the literature about discourse analysis, a tendency towards monodisciplinarity. That is, while it is customary for definitions of discourse analysis to name the many disciplines within which discourse analysis has been developed, in general, texts within disciplinary fields tend to 'talk to' other texts and writers within that discipline. The following two recent assemblages of the constitutive disciplines and theoretical frameworks of discourse analysis are quite characteristic of the collection of such accounts I have assembled for the purpose of discussion here:

Discourse analysis, the study of the use of language for communication in context, is a rapidly-expanding field which is characterised by proliferating analytical methods and continuously renewed tools. Its scope embraces a broad range of disciplines from sociology to anthropology, and from education to psychology, among others. At the same time, discourse analysis has built a significant foundation for itself in linguistics—theoretical, descriptive and applied. (Georgakopoulou and Goutsos 1997, p. vii)

[Accounts of discourse analysis] invariably refer to families of text analytic practices based on various schools of psycholinguistics, sociolinguistics, systemic functional linguistics, ethnomethodology, sociological pragmatics, poststructuralist, feminist, psychoanalytic and, most recently, postcolonial theory. (Luke 1997, p. 346)

In many cases, the primary purpose of discourse analysis appears to be field-building, according to the logics and imperatives of disciplinarity. That is, discourse analysts, like all publicly licensed scholars in the modern university, are responsible and responsive to the regulatory practices of their peers through peer review and citational practices. Discourse analysts write and speak to discourse analysts. In the following summary comments of a very careful and scholarly book on method in discourse analysis, Deborah Schiffrin makes clear the primary disciplinary reference point for analytic work in her field (1994, p. 419):

In a sense, then, the need to combine the study of structure with that of function, to understand the relationship between text and context, and to make clear how discourse is related to communication, is actually a single need. This need bears directly on the interdisciplinary nature of discourse analysis. I have said that it is difficult to always know how to separate (and relate) structure and function, text and context, discourse and communication. But what I am really saying is that it is difficult to separate language from the rest of the world. It is this ultimate inability to separate language from how it is used in the world in which we live that provides the most basic reason for the interdisciplinary basis of discourse analysis. To understand the language of discourse, then, we need to understand the world in which it resides; and to understand the world in which language resides, we need to go outside of linguistics. When we then return to a linguistic analysis of discourse—to an analysis of utterances as social interactions—I believe that we will find that the benefits of our journey have far outweighed its costs.

Here, in a striking visual image of the discipline and the university as 'enclosure' (Deleuze 1992), the analyst brings back the fruits of her journey (language and the rest of the world) to the laboratory and her community of linguists, in order to analyse them and to come to 'know' them through her tools. McHoul and Luke (1989, p. 324) write

of the desire for scientificity, the driving 'will to know' which characterises linguistically oriented forms of analysis. This point is not
necessarily made in critique of such practices. Rather, it might add a
corrective to some of the more unreflexive of the claims for discourse-
analytic work to *correspond* in some sense to the world it writes about
(Game 1991). There is a sense in which the *stance* of the researcher
in much linguistically oriented discourse analysis remains a positivist
one, notwithstanding the theoretical understandings about language
that might be supposed to destabilise and undermine such a stance.
There is a profound sense, in the many textbooks on methods in
discourse analysis, whether linguistic, ethnomethodological, or 'critical', that the research practices which produce the texts, that are then
subjected to analysis, are not to be themselves subjected to reflexive
scrutiny concerning the conditions of their production. Books about
discourse analysis do not, by and large, contain discussions on epistemological and methodological dilemmas about representation within
contemporary social science and cultural research.

This absence is in many respects almost as characteristic of
traditions in discourse analysis that are overtly 'critical' and politicised
in relation to agendas of social justice and change. That is, much work
in critical discourse analysis is curiously inexplicit about the necessary
assumptions upon which its 'heuristics' are based (Josephides 1997).
Instead, critical discourse analysis has been concerned with the
question of advocacy and effect. For Luke (1997, p. 345):

> . . . whatever the aspirations for scientific or disciplinary legitimacy it
> might harbour, discourse analysis is itself a kind of public speech act—
> with a will towards (re)constituting the very objects about which it
> purports to speak.

It is for this reason that questions of the material effects of analysis
must be a primary reference by which discourse analyses must be
judged. That is, critical discourse analyses, for Luke (1997, p. 345),
must be judged as 'social actions'—'textual interventions in the public
sphere which attempt to make material differences for particular
constituencies and interests'. For example, Kress recently notes (1996,
p. 15) that:

> . . . critical studies of language, Critical Linguistics (CL) and Critical Dis-
> course Analysis (CDA) have from the beginning had a political project:
> that of altering inequitable distributions of economic, cultural and polit-
> ical goods in contemporary societies.

Yet there are other questions to be asked of analytic work in these
fields: questions concerning the construction of the objects of analysis

and the attribution of knowledgeability in relation to the 'text' or 'object' of analysis and the analyst. These questions are all the more important to ask since critical work is often expressly concerned to redistribute 'agency', as one of the 'goods' referred to by Kress. Ann Game (1991), in writing about advocacy research in sociology, cautions against a too-easy elision of the agency of the analyst in this formulation. 'Agency' in sociology, she says, is used to refer to 'others', 'oppressed groups'—women, working classes etc. Game proposes, however, that there is a need for a critical reflection on the agency of the analyst—'the agency of the *subjects* of sociological knowledge'. This desire for agency, she says, is suppressed through the focus on the agency of the oppressed. The constitution of oppressed groups as 'objects of knowledge' effects a 'return to self' of the researcher (Game 1991, p. 6). Game further requires of social researchers (1991, p. 10) that they ask:

> What is the itinerary of desire in my knowledge, and in the choice of my objects of study? Who is the other to whom desire is addressed, and how is this other constituted in relation to (one)self?

What many models of discourse analysis have in common, together with a tendency to under-theorise their own representational/ research practices, is an associated tendency towards a monologistic stance in the sense that predominantly 'etic' accounts of texts are produced. The analyst speaks *about* a text (largely) *to* a community of other analysts. This is a dominant feature of much of the work in discourse analysis, notwithstanding more or less careful attempts to theorise and account for 'context' of production and reception of the texts in question, such as in systemic functional linguistic theory (e.g. Halliday and Hasan 1985/1989) or the work of Fairclough and Kress (e.g. Fairclough 1995a; Kress 1988). And, notwithstanding the 'condition of doubt' noted by Patterson (1997, p. 425) as an identifying hallmark of the critical discourse analyst vis-a-vis the 'target of scrutiny', there does not appear to be a similar calling-into-doubt of the figure of the researcher, as author, as advocate, as producer of the 'public speech' (Luke 1997, p. 65). While a politics of representation might be enjoined by commentators such as Luke in terms of the material effects of public texts of critical discourse analysis, what yet remains to be engaged is a questioning of the positionality and 'itinerary' of the analyst, in relation to the many meanings of the term 'representation': 'interpretation, communication, visualisation, translation and advocacy' (James, Hockey and Dawson 1997, p. 2).

This analytic stance has two key dimensions. First, in relation to the imperative for field-building, ever-finer systems of distinction and discrimination are produced, with a view to accounting, with ever-more delicacy, for the mechanisms for the production of meaning or the achievement of social relations. Second, the relationship to the object domain, whether text or subject, is one of speaking *about* and even *for*. What such analytic practices do not adequately account for is a set of relationships between 'etic' and 'emic' perspectives, the relationship between 'insider' or 'practitioner' or 'native' perspectives and those of the analyst. Nor is there an accounting for the way in which such knowledge becomes articulated in terms of the exposure brought about through the analysis, in what Giddens (1986) names the move from 'practical consciousness' to 'discursive consciousness'.

Within the 'writing culture' debate, the critique of monological authority in social science writing produced an imperative towards a 'democratisation' of representation. For the purposes of briefly re-staging some of the crucial moves in that debate, Clifford's historical account of the emergence of the dialogic as a principle in ethnographic writing is instructive here. According to Clifford (1983, p. 132), the 1950s ushered in mounting criticism of 'colonial' forms of rep-resentation, 'discourses that portray the cultural realities of other peoples without placing their own reality in jeopardy'. In response, Clifford, citing Dwyer, examines models of dialogue between re-searcher 'self' and researched 'other' that stress a hermeneutics of 'vulnerability' (Clifford 1983, p. 134; Dwyer 1977). Such a stance stresses the 'ruptures' of fieldwork, the 'divided position' and 'imperfect control' of the ethnographer, and represents the experience of research in ways that 'tear open the textualised fabric of the other, and thus also of the interpreting self' (Clifford 1983, p. 134).

The work of Dwyer and others in the 1970s promoted collaboration and dialogue with informants. Yet, as Clifford insists, ethnographic texts are always *representations* of dialogue and not the dialogue itself. Hence, the monological authority of the writer can be displaced but not eliminated. It is important to stress that a necessary problematisation of monologic practices in textual analysis can no longer lead inexorably towards a romantic idealisation of the dialogic or the multi-vocal: terms forming around the other arm of a binary. The terms of the 'writing culture' debate referred to above have permanently destabilised the claim to a new 'democracy' of representation through a 'multivocality' of representer and represented. The argument I am developing here is that it is instructive to read the contemporary scene of dis-course analysis, particularly critical discourse analysis, within the terms of the 'writing culture' debates about the practices and politics of representation. The aim of such a reading is to suggest ways in which the discourse analyst's gaze can be directed more reflexively towards their own representational practices, including their own will to truth or, in Hodge and McHoul's (1992) terms, to 'mastery'.

Hodge and McHoul write of two extreme types of disciplinary formations of the text-commentary relation, which they refer to as 'mastery' and 'liberty'. The first formation coheres around the notion of commentarial dominance over, and colonisation of, the object-text. The second is characterised by a more 'humble' gesture by which the commentary allows the object-text the position of dominance— to 'speak for itself'. In relation to the position of 'mastery', the text is positioned as containing a 'mystery', available only to the skills of the analyst:

> What is paradoxically interesting about the approach . . . is that it flatters the text equally with itself. The two, as it were, look as if they are in a conspiracy to defraud 'ordinary' readers. The text's meaning is 'deep'—but the commentary's skill is more than equal to that depth. This is the characteristic mode of explanation and owes some allegiance to traditional (Baconian) natural science models. The text, like nature, is an infinite mystery. But the commentary, like the mathematical gesture, presumes to unlock that mystery, privileging, in one move, both itself and, to a lesser extent, its object. (Hodge and McHoul 1992, p. 190)

At the opposite end of this binary formation, 'libertarian' approaches to 'letting the text speak for itself', dating from the 1960s, involve such traditions as those Hodge and McHoul refer to, following Garfinkel and Sacks (1970), in terms of 'ethnomethodological indifference'. In von Wright's (1971) terms, this approach is signalled by the move from 'explanation' (*Erklärung*) to 'understanding' (*Verstehen*). Letting the text 'speak for itself' ranges from various traditions within 'non-intrusive' sociology, to approaches within phenomenology and ethnography. The text 'becomes the master: it "teaches" the analyst', who remains silent, acting as a medium through which the 'text emerges to full consciousness' (Hodge and McHoul 1992, p. 194).

Hodge and McHoul point out, however, that text-libertarianism is a 'panopticism under another name'. The silence of the analyst is 'far from innocent and is in fact part of a very effective strategy of power'. Here they refer to, among other things, the issues of which texts are to be selected and which excluded. As they note, 'libertarians who self-consciously take the side of the victim still face the dilemma of which particular victim to choose' (Hodge and McHoul 1992,

p. 195). This point connects importantly with Clifford's caution against the tendency in 'fictions of dialogue' in ethnographic writing for the ethnographer's counterpart to appear as a representative of his or her culture:

> . . . a type, in the language of traditional realism—through which general social processes are revealed. Such a portrayal reinstates the synecdochic interpretive authority by which the ethnographer reads text in relation to context, thereby constituting a meaningful 'other' world. (Clifford 1983, p. 135)

The troublesome question of representativeness, of the imperative in anthropology to be concerned with 'whole cultures', is instructive for a critical discourse analysis which requires of itself a practice of advocacy. The 'constituencies and interests' for/to whom critical discourse analysts want to speak must themselves be discursively constituted through the epistemological frames and attachments of the analyst. There is a need here to critically examine the relationship between epistemological standpoints and modes of analysis.

Instead of fictions of representativeness, shielding a will to mastery in commentary, it is important to ask, following Foucault, under what institutional and historical conditions do writers come to be authors? Under what constraints is a particular speaking and writing taking place? Hodge and McHoul go on to a fascinating account, drawing on Foucault and Lyotard, of some of the politico-theoretical problems of textual commentary that seek to displace the problematic binary of text/commentary, self/other, leaving the intensive scrutiny of the 'insides' of texts and taking into account such matters as the conditions of their production and circulation. Ultimately, they want to insist on the notion of text as 'spectacle', as performance and as *writing*.

METHOD AND WRITING

> *analysis*
> separation of a whole, whether a material substance or any matter of thought, into its constituent elements: a 'breaking up'—from Greek. (*Macquarie Dictionary*)

> The resolution of something complex into its simple elements. (*Shorter Oxford Dictionary*)

> In PHILOSOPHY, the discovery of verbal forms of expression for complex ideas and PROPOSITIONS which make explicit the complexity that is hidden by the more abbreviated character of their usual verbal formulation . . . it was a kind of defining process, in which the defining terms

are more elementary and unproblematic than the terms being defined.
(*Fontana Dictionary of Modern Thought* 1988)

All forms of discourse analysis generate texts about texts (Luke 1997,
p. 346). Yet the status of discourse analysis as itself *writing* is problematic. Typically, it seems, the textuality of the object text is foregrounded,
while the textuality of the analytic text is not. That is, there appears
to be a tension between the imperatives of analysis and those of writing.
These may in part be connected to a prior epistemological binary,
prevalent in modern disciplinary economies, between science and
literature. 'Method' adheres to the principles of science. The principles
of 'analysis' require the 'breaking up' of complex textuality into simpler
parts. Much linguistic analysis, for example, offers a systematic way of
'breaking up' a text in the manner referred to in the *Macquarie
Dictionary* definition above. Judgement of analysis is concerned with
systematicity. Literary writing, on the other hand, is characteristically
subject to evaluation on quite other grounds: on aesthetic and formal
grounds, etc.

Addressing the problematic historical divisions between science
and writing, in relation to textual analysis, Roland Barthes notes
the opposition between language-objects (texts) and their metalanguage (method) which, he says, must be transcended. For
metalanguage remains ultimately subject to the 'paternal model of
science without language' (Barthes 1986, p. 10). Here Barthes is
referring to science's refusal of language as distinct from literature's
central relation to language. For science (by which he refers to 'all of
the social sciences'), 'language is merely an instrument, which it
chooses to make as transparent, as neutral as possible' (Barthes 1986,
p. 4). On the other hand, 'language is the *being* of literature, its very
world: all literature is contained in the act of writing' (Barthes 1986,
p. 4). Since Barthes, there has been close attention dedicated to the
necessary contingency and the textuality of science in general, to its
status as 'narrative' (Geertz 1983; Lyotard 1984; Harré 1990; Van
Maanen 1995), as 'fiction' (Game 1991; Graff 1981), as rhetoric
(Burke 1984; Bazerman 1988). In certain domains of theory, at least,
a binary has been destabilised. Nevertheless it is productive to explore
the now often residual but nevertheless potent call to science in much
discussion of 'method' in discourse analysis.

There are two related features pertaining to such discussion. First,
the notion of 'breaking up', identified in the definitions above as
integral to analysis, construes texts in terms of part–whole relationships, such that the 'reductionist' logics of science (Scott 1995,

pp. 42–143) work to produce 'more elementary and unproblematic' terms than those in which the text is couched. These are the terms of 'commentary', which enter into and produce the 'text-commentary binary' identified in the introduction to this chapter. Second, the rhetorical appeal of science works to secure trust in the reader (Harré 1990). As Barthes (1977, p. 196) puts it, 'Method certifies'. It acts as a kind of rhetorical guarantee, persuading the reader of systematicity and trustworthiness: a guarantee that the work has been done and that the work is adequate to the claims to be made on behalf of method to have accounted for the text in the manner indicated.

In critique of this position, poststructuralist readings of science—and indeed of all research—view research and knowledge production as always and inevitably an enactment of power relations (see Harding 1986). Patti Lather (1991), for example, drawing on Cherryholmes (1988, p. 14), construes research practices more as 'inscriptions of legitimation' than procedures that help us get closer to some 'truth' that is capturable via language. This notion allows an understanding of the force of textuality, its formalised strategies for convincingness, its speech acts.

The point being developed here concerns the meanings of the search for method in discourse analysis, the desire for tools that will 'unlock' the mysteries of texts, which drives researchers to seek out exegetical texts such as those cited in the first section of this paper. A focus on 'writing' in this section has a two-fold purpose: first, to explore possible meanings of a binary opposition between 'analysis' or 'method' and 'writing'; and second, to point to the ultimate task of the discourse analyst—once 'Method' has been called forth and applied—to write.

It is at this point that I turn to work that has been radically formative of my own understandings of what is in question here. In 'Writers, intellectuals, teachers' (1977, p. 201), Roland Barthes directly and provocatively lays out a challenge:

> Some people talk avidly, demandingly of method; what they want in work is method, which can never be too rigorous or too formal for their tastes. Method becomes a Law, but since that Law is devoid of any effect outside itself (nobody can say what a 'result' is in the 'human sciences') it is infinitely disappointed; posing as pure metalanguage, it partakes of the vanity of all metalanguage. The invariable fact is that a piece of work which ceaselessly proclaims its determination for method is ultimately sterile: everything has been put into the method, nothing is left for writing; the researcher repeatedly asserts that his text will be methodological but the text never comes. No surer way to kill a piece of research and send it to join the great waste of abandoned projects than Method.

Having secured his reader's attention through a typical strategy of provocation, Barthes goes on to acknowledge the necessity and inevitability of Method in answer to the demand for 'responsibility' in research:

> Here Method is inevitable, irreplaceable, not for its 'results' but precisely—or on the contrary—because it realises the highest degree of consciousness of a language *which is not forgetful of itself.* (1977, p. 201, original emphasis)

In insisting finally on *writing*, however, the 'space of dispersion of desire, where Law is dismissed', Barthes ends this short piece with the following:

> At *a certain point*, therefore, it is necessary to turn against Method, or at least to treat it without any founding privilege as one of the voices of plurality—as a view, a spectacle mounted in the text, the text which all in all is the only 'true' result of any research. (1977, p. 201, original emphasis)

It is this juxtaposition of the power of the insistence on the irreducibility of writing with the acknowledgement of 'responsibility' in research that provides the tension and the productiveness of Barthes' discussion here.

Within poststructuralism, an expanded notion of writing is available, through the work of Barthes and, significantly, Derrida (e.g. 1976). In drawing on poststructuralist understandings of writing, Game and Metcalfe (1996, p. 90) provide a helpful gloss on two levels in which writing might be understood: what they term the 'literal and the metaphoric'. The literal notion of writing refers 'in the narrower sense [to] a specific form of signification or medium'; they refer to writing in the broader sense, drawing on Clifford and Marcus (1986, p. 90) as 'cultural production'. In its expanded and elaborated sense, within poststructuralist theory, 'writing' becomes a metaphor for all forms of textual and discursive practice. Research and knowledge production are seen in terms of the play of conscious and unconscious forces within a symbolic economy. Rather than being understood as representation, as was discussed in the previous section of this chapter, Game and Metcalfe (1996, p. 91) note that 'writing specifically and signification more generally are understood as processes of transformation rather than representation'. Writing produces and positions; texts are 'social facts' (Rabinow 1986). Here questions of desire and the unconscious in textual practice connect to questions of public accountability and the material effects of texts: who texts are speaking to and for.

Barthes' work allows a revisiting of practices of 'analysis' as, in the first instance, practices of *reading* and of *writing*. Such practices, as Barthes has pointed out, yield up 'not a "result" nor even a "method" . . . but merely a "way of proceeding"' (Barthes 1977, p. 127). Barthes is writing here against a particular 'scientific view of the text' as it was constituted within certain disciplinary/methodological regimes—notably structuralism. While his injunctions are no longer new nor particularly radical within cultural studies, feminisms and postcolonial theorising, they typically still await substantive debate *within* the field of discourse analysis. In particular, as newcomers to the field recognise the currency of discourse analysis as a new and increasingly influential research (writing) practice, there is a crucial need to engage histories of debates concerning the 'politics and poetics' (to evoke the subtitle of Clifford and Marcus' 1986 collection) of representation and signification.

DISCOURSE ANALYSIS AND REWRITING

How might the relationship between method and writing be productively engaged in the contemporary moment, bearing in mind earlier exhortations that discourse analysis, and 'critical discourse analysis' in particular, is 'social action', text intended to produce material change? And what of the notion of '(re)writing' referred to in the title of this chapter? In summing up contemporary theorising within cultural studies concerning this point, Terry Threadgold (1997a, p. 1) begins her recent book thus:

> It is now both a feminist and a poststructuralist/postmodernist catch-cry, in some places, that one does not analyse texts, one rewrites them, one does not have an objective metalanguage, one does not use a theory, one performs one's critique. Critique is itself a poiesis, a making . . . I want to suggest that there are also seductions involved in allowing oneself to be positioned totally by the discourses and genres of rewriting and refusal of metalanguages, the seductions of an anti-science metaphysics.

The metaphor of 'rewriting' emerges from feminist and postcolonial refusals of the patriarchal narratives of modernity. In Threadgold's account, plots and endings that worked against the interests of women and other marginal groups were rewritten; new narratives were produced. In contrasting the notion of 'rewriting' with discourse analysis, Threadgold comments in a recent interview that critical discourse analysis 'has never talked enough about the making. The generative nature of the meaning of texts, the process and the metaphor of performativity' (Threadgold in Kamler, 1997, p. 442). She goes on (pp. 443–444):

> The notion of rewriting and performativity and performance and the making of texts from cultural studies, feminism etc. is different from what you do with critical discourse analysis which is somewhere to stop the process—or even understand that there has been a process—you think about the ethics and the consequences—real social consequences of a text. But to do that, it seems to me, you've actually got to stop it somewhere . . . I was trying to 'perform a rewriting', critically, and at the same time to stop the process every so often to do the critical discourse analysis.

This account accords in several respects with recent calls by Kress to 'turn around' the emphasis of critical linguistics, critical discourse analysis and social semiotics to 'become an enterprise focused, engaged on making'. By this he does not advocate an abandoning of the project of critique; rather, Kress proposes a 'critical language project [that] can pursue both aims through the recognition of the need for its own reconstitution as a fully developed theory of communication, of cultural, social, semiosis' (Kress 1996, p. 19).

These accounts of discourse analysis by Threadgold and Kress explicitly engage the relationship between analysis and writing, at least in the expanded sense of the term writing, to refer to 'cultural production'. For Kress (1996, p. 18), the task of the discourse analyst in a multicultural society resides in the responsibility to 'conduct an ethnography of representational resources, across all the major identifiable groups in a society'. Kress' project for discourse analysis is a grand and sweeping one, and it brings us back to the concerns of the earlier parts of this chapter. Who will such an ethnographic project be 'talking to', in its production and its eventual distribution? In the light of such a call, the revisiting of relations of analytic authority produced within the 'writing culture' debates in anthropology and in feminist and more recently postcolonial theorising is timely. The task of the analyst, in developing such a 'theory of communication', might be productively engaged in questioning the conditions of its production, its assumptions and ascriptions of agency in research practice and in the 'itinerary of desire' of the analyst.

In Threadgold's accounting for her own project, there remains the distinction between analysis and writing which might, for the purpose of discussion here, be brought into question. Threadgold's book is a *tour de force*, a performance in many parts, some of which draw on the 'metalanguage' of systemic functional grammar to attend closely to the micro-politics of representation within the clauses of English grammar, some of which are more overtly 'poetic' in their weaving of the 'metalanguages' of different theoretical literatures into a highly textured work. In what sense the clearly analytic moments of the book are not 'writing' remains unclear, unless certain premises concerning the boundaries between writing and not-writing are sustained. In many respects, this apparent distinction might work to do this multifaceted text an injustice. Threadgold's book remains an instructive example of what Threadgold herself has argued over many years, that there 'cannot *not* be a metalanguage' (Threadgold in Kamler 1997, p. 440). She argues that, even in the most radical of refusals of metalanguage on the grounds of the denial of subjectivity involved in the objecti-fying effects of metalanguage, new metalanguages are produced. Even Derridean notions of writing, presented in terms of a refusal of method and metalanguage, have become institutionalised and, as a conse-quence, formalised. It is useful to juxtapose this point with the position taken up by Biddle in this volume.

In drawing the threads of this discussion together, then, the project of engaging in the search for method is both necessary and inevitable. The need for 'responsibility' in research brings a corre-sponding requirement for systematicity, of some kind or another. Yet the search for method, of itself, is never sufficient to produce or account for the texts of analysis. Discourse analysts need to be able to account reflexively for the textuality of their own texts. The notion of 'poesis' used by Threadgold is not merely a 'literary' one, not merely performative or aestheticised, but is also crucially situated inside relations of power. The notion of advocacy needs to be placed along-side the issue of agency, the 'politics and poetics' of speaking for, about, and to, others, that is, the question of addressivity in relation to disciplinary formation.

References

Aers, David, Hodge, Bob and Kress, Gunther, 1981 *Literature, Language and Society in England 1580–1680*, Gill and Macmillan, Dublin

Alcoff, Linda M., 1996 'Dangerous Pleasures: Foucault and the politics of pedophilia', *Feminist Interpretations of Michel Foucault*, ed. Susan J. Hekman, University of Pennsylvania Press, Philadelphia, pp. 99–135

Alcoff, Linda M. and Potter, Elizabeth, eds 1993 *Feminist Epistemologies*, Routledge, New York and London

Althusser, Louis, 1971 'Ideology and Ideological State Apparatuses', *Lenin and Philosophy and Other Essays*, New Left Books, London, pp. 121–176

Anderson, Benedict, 1983 *Imagined Communities: reflections on the origin and spread of nationalism*, Verso, London

Austin, J. L., 1962 *How to Do Things with Words*, Oxford University Press, Oxford

ANTA (Australian National Training Authority), 1994 *Towards a Skilled Australia: a national strategy for vocational education and training*, ANTA, Brisbane

Baker, Carolyn D. and Freebody, Peter, 1987 'Constituting the Child in Beginning School Reading Books', *British Journal of Sociology of Education* vol. 8, no. 1, pp. 55–76

Baker, Carolyn D. and Keogh, Jayne, 1995 'Accounting for Achievement in Teacher–Parent Interviews', *Human Studies* vol. 18, nos 2/3, pp. 263–300

Bakhtin, Mikhail M., 1981 *The Dialogic Imagination*, ed. Michael Holquist, trans. Caryl Emerson and Michael Holquist, University of Texas Press, Austin

——1984 *Problems of Dostoevsky's Poetics*, ed. and trans. Caryl Emerson, Manchester University Press, Manchester

——1986 *Speech Genres and Other Late Essays*, eds Caryl Emerson and Michael Holquist, trans. Vern McGee, University of Texas Press, Austin

Barthes Roland, 1974, *S/Z*, trans. Richard Miller, Hill and Wang, New York

——1977 *Image–Music–Text*, trans. Stephen Heath, Fontana, Oxford

——1986 'From Science to Literature', *The Rustle of Language*, trans. Richard Howard, Basil Blackwell, Oxford, pp. 3–10

Bartky, Sandra Lee, 1988 'Foucault, Femininity and the Modernization of Patriarchal Power', *Feminism and Foucault*, eds Irene Diamond and Lee Quinby, Northeastern University Press, Boston, pp. 61–86

Bazerman, Charles, 1988 *Shaping Written Knowledge: the genre and activity of the experimental article in science*, University of Wisconsin Press, Madison

Bell, Allan, 1991 *The Language of News Media*, Basil Blackwell, Oxford

Bell, Philip and van Leeuwen, Theo, 1994 *The Media Interview: confession, contest, conversation*, University of New South Wales Press, Sydney

Benjamin, Walter, 1969 *Illuminations*, ed. and with introduction by Hannah Arendt, trans. Harry Zohn, Schocken Books, New York

Bennett, Tony, 1998 *Culture: a reformer's science*, Allen & Unwin, Sydney

Benveniste, Emile, 1966 *Problèmes de Linguistique Générale*, Gallimard, Paris

Bernstein, Basil, 1971 *Class, Codes and Control 1: theoretical studies towards a sociology of language*, Routledge & Kegan Paul, London

——1973 *Class, Codes and Control 2: applied studies towards a sociology of language*, Routledge & Kegan Paul, London

——1975 *Class, Codes and Control 3: towards a theory of educational transmissions*, Routledge & Kegan Paul, London

Bhabha, Homi K., 1986 'Signs Taken for Wonders: questions of ambivalence and authority under a tree outside Dehli, May 1817', *'Race', Writing and Difference*, ed. H. L. Gates, University of Chicago Press, Illinois, pp. 163–184

——1994 *The Location of Culture*, Routledge, London and New York

Biddle, Jennifer, 1991 'Dot, Circle, Difference: translating Central Desert paintings', *Cartographies: poststructuralism and the mapping of bodies and spaces*, eds Rosalyn Diprose and Robyn Ferrell, Allen & Unwin, Sydney, pp. 27–39

——1996 'When Not Writing is Writing', *Australian Aboriginal Studies* no. 1, pp. 21–33

Bloor, Thomas and Bloor, Meriel, 1995 *The Functional Analysis of English: a Hallidayan approach*, Arnold, London

Bordo, Susan R., 1990 'The Body and Reproduction of Femininity: a feminist appropriation of Foucault', *Gender/Body/Knowledge*, eds Alison Jaggar and Susan Bordo, Rutgers University Press, New Brunswick, pp. 13–33

Bourdieu, Pierre, 1990 *The Logic of Practice*, Polity Press, Cambridge

——1995 *Outline of a Theory of Practice*, trans. Richard Nice, Cambridge University Press, Cambridge

Brown, Penelope and Levinson, Stephen, 1978 'Universals in Language Use: politeness phenomena', *Questions and Politeness: strategies in social interaction*, ed. Esther Goody, Cambridge University Press, Cambridge, pp. 56–311

——1987 *Politeness: some universals in language usage*, Cambridge University Press, Cambridge

Brown, Roger and Gilman, Albert, 1960 'The Pronouns of Power and Solidarity', *Style in Language*, ed. Thomas A. Sebeok, MIT Press, Cambridge, Massachusetts, pp. 253–276

Burke, Kenneth, 1984 *Permanence and Change: an anatomy of purpose*, 3rd edn, University of California Press, Berkeley

Burman, Erica and Parker, Ian, eds 1993, *Discourse Analytic Research: repertoires and readings of texts in action*, Routledge, London and New York

Butler, Judith, 1990 *Gender Trouble: feminism and the subversion of identity*, Routledge, New York and London

——1993a *Bodies that Matter: on the discursive limits of 'sex'*, Routledge, New York and London

——1993b 'Critically Queer', *GLQ* vol. 1, no. 1, pp. 17–32

——1997 *Excitable speech: a politics of the performative*, Routledge, New York and London

Button, Graham, ed. 1991 *Ethnomethodology and the Human Sciences*, Cambridge University Press, Cambridge

Caldas-Coulthard, Carmen Rosa and Coulthard, Malcolm, eds 1996 *Texts and Practices: readings in critical discourse analysis*, Routledge, London and New York

Cameron, Deborah, 1995 'Rethinking Language and Gender Studies: some issues for the 1990s', *Language and Gender: interdisciplinary perspectives*, ed. Sara Mills, Longman, London and New York, pp. 31–44

——1997 'Theoretical Debates in Feminist Linguistics: questions of sex and gender', *Gender and Discourse*, ed. Ruth Wodak, Sage, London, Thousand Oaks and New Delhi, pp. 21–36

Carter, Paul, 1992 *Living in a New Country*, Faber, London

Cherryholmes, Cleo H., 1988 *Power and Criticism: poststructural investigations in education*, Teachers College Press, New York and London

Chomsky, Noam, 1959 'Review of Skinner, *Verbal Behaviour*', *Language* vol. 35, pp. 26–58

——1965 *Aspects of the Theory of Syntax*, MIT Press, Cambridge, MA

Chomsky, Noam and Halle, Morris, 1965 'Some Controversial Questions in Phonological Theory', *Journal of Linguistics vol. 1, pp. 97–138*

Christie, Frances, Bunbury, Rhonda, Dawkins, Sue, Morris, Don, Maclean, Rod and Share, David, eds 1984a *Children Writing: study guide*, Deakin University Press, Geelong

——1984b *Children Writing: reader*, Deakin University Press, Geelong

Churchill, Ward, 1986 'Review of Michael Castro's "Interpreting the Indian: twentieth century poets and the native American"', *Journal Of Ethnic Studies* vol. 13, no. 4, pp. 138–142

——1993 'Another Dry White Season—Jerry Mander's "The Absence of the Sacred"', *Indians Are Us: culture, genocide in Native North America*, Common Courage Press, Maine, pp. 139–165

Clark, Katerina and Holquist, Michael, 1984 *Mikhail Bakhtin*, Harvard University Press, Cambridge, MA

Clifford, James, 1983 'On Ethnographic Authority', *Representations* vol. 1, no. 2, pp. 118–146

——1986 'Introduction: partial truths', *Writing Culture: the poetics and politics of ethnography*, eds James Clifford and George Marcus, University of California Press, Berkeley, pp. 1–26

Clifford, James and Marcus, George, eds 1986 *Writing Culture: the poetics and politics of ethnography*, University of California Press, Berkeley

Colorado, Pam, 1988 'Bridging Native and Western Science', *Convergences* vol. 21, nos. 2–3, pp. 49–68

Connell, R. W., 1995 *Masculinities*, Allen & Unwin, Sydney

Cook, Guy, 1992 *The Discourse of Advertising*, Routledge, London and New York

Cornell, Drucilla, 1991 *Beyond Accommodation: ethical feminism, deconstruction and the law*, Routledge, New York

——1992 *The Philosophy of the Limit*, Routledge, New York

——1995 *The Imaginary Domain: abortion, pornography and sexual harassment*, Routledge, New York and London

Courtney, Marianne and Mawer, Giselle, 1995 *Integrating English Language Literacy and Numeracy into Vocational Education and Training*, TAFE (Foundation Studies Training Division), Sydney

Culler, Jonathan, 1976 *Saussure*, Fontana/Collins, Glasgow

——1983 *On Deconstruction: theory and criticism after structuralism*, Routledge and Kegan Paul, London, Melbourne and Henley

Davies, Margaret, 1994 'Feminist Appropriations: law, property and personality', *Social and Legal Studies* vol. 3, pp. 365–383

206 CULTURE & TEXT

Davis, Mark, 1997 *Gangland: cultural elites and the new generationalism*, Allen & Unwin, Sydney

Deleuze, Gilles, 1992 'Postscript on the Societies of Control', *October* no. 59, pp. 3–7

Deleuze, Gilles and Guattari, Félix, 1987 *A Thousand Plateaus: capitalism and schizophrenia*, trans. Brian Massumi, University of Minnesota Press, Minneapolis

Derrida, Jacques, 1976 *Of Grammatology*, trans. Gayatri Chakravorty Spivak, Johns Hopkins University Press, Baltimore

——1981 *Dissemination*, trans., introduction and notes by Barbara Johnson, University of Chicago Press, Chicago

——1982 'Signature, Event, Context', *Margins of Philosophy*, trans., with additional notes by Alan Bass, The University of Chicago Press, Chicago

——1988 *Limited Inc*, trans. Samuel Weber and Jeffrey Mehlman, Northwestern University Press, Evanston, Illinois

——1992 'Force of Law: "The Mystical Foundation of Authority"', *Deconstruction and the Possibility of Justice*, eds Drucilla Cornell, Michael Rosenfeld and David Gray Carlson, Routledge, New York, pp. 3–67

——1997 *Deconstruction in Nutshell: a conversation with Jacques Derrida*, ed. John D. Caputo, Fordham University Press, New York

Diamond, Irene and Quinby, Lee, eds 1988 *Feminism and Foucault: reflections on resistance*, Northeastern University Press, Boston

Dittmar, Norbert, 1976 *Sociolinguistics: a critical survey of theory and application*, Edward Arnold, London

Dixon, R.M.W., 1980 *Languages of Australia*, Cambridge University Press, Cambridge

Drucker, Peter, 1993 *Post-Capitalist Society*, HarperBusiness, New York

du Gay, Paul, 1996 *Consumption and Identity at Work*, Sage, London

Duranti, Alessandro and Goodwin, Charles, eds 1992 *Rethinking Context: language as an interactive phenomenon*, Cambridge University Press, Cambridge

Dussart, Françoise F., 1988 'Notes on Warlpiri Women's Personal Names', *Journal de la Societe des Oceanistes* vol. 86, no. 1, pp. 53–60

Dwyer, Kevin, 1977 'On the Dialogic of Fieldwork', *Dialectical Anthropology* vol. 2, no. 2, pp. 143–151

Eades, Diana, 1988 'They Don't Speak an Aboriginal Language Do They?', *Being Black*, ed. Ian Keen, Australian Studies Press, Canberra, pp. 97–115

Easthope, Antony, 1986 *What a Man's Gotta Do: the masculine myth in popular culture*, Paladin, London

Eco, Umberto, 1979 'Peirce and the Semiotic Foundations of Openness: signs as texts and texts as signs', *The Role of the Reader: explorations in the semiotics of texts*, Hutchinson, London, pp. 175–199

Eggins, Suzanne, 1994, *An Introduction to Systemic Functional Linguistics*, Pinter, London

Eggins, Suzanne and Slade, Diana, 1997 *Analysing Casual Conversation*, Cassell, London and Washington

Eglin, Peter and Hester, Stephen, 1992 'Category, Predicate and Task: the pragmatics of practical action', *Semiotica* vol. 88, nos 3/4, pp. 243–268

Fairclough, Norman, 1989 *Language and Power*, Longman, London

——1992 *Discourse and Social Change*, Basil Blackwell, Oxford

——1995a *Critical Discourse Analysis: the critical study of language*, Longman, London

——1995b *Media Discourse*, Edward Arnold, London

——1996 'Technologisation of Discourse', *Texts and Practices: readings in critical discourse analysis*, eds Carmen Caldas-Coulthard and Malcolm Coulthard, Routledge, New York and London, pp. 71–83

Fairclough, Norman and Wodak, Ruth, 1997 'Critical Discourse Analysis', *Discourse Studies, A Multidisciplinary Introduction: volume 2, discourse as social interaction*, ed. Teun A. van Dijk, Sage, London, Thousand Oaks and New Delhi, pp. 258–284

Feit, Harvey, 1973 'The Ethno-Ecology of the Waswanipi Cree: or how hunters can manage their resources', *Cultural Ecology*, ed. B. Cox, McClelland and Stewart, Toronto, pp. 115–125

Firth, J. R., 1957 'The Technique of Semantics', *Papers in Linguistics 1934–1951*, Oxford University Press, London, pp. 7–33

Fontana Dictionary of Modern Thought, 1988, revised edition, eds Alan Bullock, Gunnvor Stallybrass and Stephen Trombley, Fontana, London

Foucault, Michel, 1971a *The Order of Things: an archaeology of the human sciences*, trans. Alan Sheridan, Tavistock, London

——1971b 'Orders of Discourse', trans. Rupert Swyers, *Social Science Information/Information sur les Sciences Sociales* vol. X, no. 2, pp. 7–30

——1972 *The Archeology of Knowledge*, trans. A.M. Sheridan Smith, Tavistock, London

——1975 *I, Pierre Riviere, Having Slaughtered My Mother, My Sister, and My Brother . . . : a case of parricide in the nineteenth century*, trans. Frank Jellinek, Pantheon, New York

——1979 *Discipline and Punish: the birth of the prison*, trans. Alan Sheridan, Penguin, Harmondsworth

——1980 *Power/Knowledge: selected interviews and other writings 1972–1977 by Michel Foucault*, ed. Colin Gordon, Pantheon Books, New York

——1981 *The History of Sexuality: an introduction*, trans. Robert Hurley, Penguin, Harmondsworth

——1982 *This Is Not A Pipe*, trans. James Harkness, University of California Press, Berkeley and Los Angeles

Fowler, Roger, 1981 *Literature as Social Discourse: the practice of linguistic criticism*, Batsford, London

——1991 *Language in the News: discourse and ideology in the press*, Routledge, London and New York

Fowler, Roger and Kress, Gunther, 1979 'Critical Linguistics', *Language and Control*, eds Roger Fowler, Bob Hodge, Gunther Kress and Tony Trew, Routledge & Kegan Paul, London, pp. 185–213

Fromkin, Victoria and Rodman, Robert, 1978 *An Introduction to Language*, Holt, Rinehart and Winston, New York

Frow, John and Morris, Meaghan, eds 1993 *Australian Cultural Studies: a reader*, Allen & Unwin, Sydney

Frug, Mary Jo, 1985 'Re-reading Contracts: a feminist analysis of a contracts casebook', *Postmodern Legal Feminism*, Routledge, New York and London, pp. 53–110

Fuller, Gillian, 1995 *Engaging Cultures: negotiating discourse in popular science*, unpub. PhD thesis, University of Sydney

Gallop, Jane, 1988 *Thinking Through the Body*, Columbia University Press, New York

Game, Ann, 1991 *Undoing the Social: towards a deconstructive sociology*, Open University Press, Milton Keynes

Game, Ann and Metcalfe, Andrew, 1996 *Passionate Sociology*, Sage, London

Garfinkel, Harold, 1967 *Studies in Ethnomethodology*, Polity, Cambridge

Garfinkel, Harold and Sacks, Harvey, 1970 'On Formal Structures of Practical Actions', *Theoretical Sociology*, eds J. C. McKinney and E. A. Tiryakian, Appleton-Century-Crofts, New York, pp. 337–366

Gasche, Rodolphe, 1995 *Inventions of Difference*, Cambridge University Press, Cambridge

Gatens, Moira, 1992 'Power, Bodies and Difference', *Destabilizing Theory*, eds Michele Barrett and Anne Phillips, Polity Press, Cambridge, pp. 120–137

——1996 *Imaginary Bodies: ethics, power, corporeality*, Routledge, London and New York

Gates, H. L., 1986 *'Race',Writing and Difference*, University of Chicago Press, Chicago

Gee, James, Hull, Glenda and Lankshear, Colin, 1996 *The New Work Order: behind the language of the new capitalism*, Allen & Unwin, Sydney

Geertz, Clifford, 1983 'Blurred Genres: the refiguration of social thought', *Local Knowledge: further essays on interpretive anthropology*, ed. Clifford Geertz, Basic Books, New York, pp. 19–35

Georgakopoulou, Alexandra and Goutsos, Dionysis, 1997 *Discourse Analysis: an introduction*, Edinburgh University Press, Edinburgh

Gibson-Graham, J. K., 1996, *The End of Capitalism (As We Knew It): a feminist critique of political economy*, Basil Blackwell, Oxford

Giddens, Anthony, 1986 *The Constitution of Society: outline of the theory of structuration*, University of California Press, Berkeley and Los Angeles

Goffman, Erving, 1981 *Forms of Talk*, Basil Blackwell, Oxford

Goodrich, Peter, 1990 *Languages of Law: from logics of memory to nomadic masks*, Weidenfield and Nicholson, London

——1991 *Reading the Law: a critical introduction to legal method and techniques*, Basil Blackwell, Oxford

——1996 *Law in the Courts of Love: literature and other minor jurisprudences*, Routledge, London and New York

Gore, Jennifer, 1995a 'Foucault's Poststructuralism and Observational Research: a study of power relations', *After Postmodernism: education, politics and identity*, eds Richard Smith and Philip Wexler, Falmer Press, London, pp. 98–111

——1995b 'On the Continuity of Power Relations in Pedagogy', *International Studies in the Sociology of Education* vol. 5, no. 2, pp. 165–188

Graff, Gerald, 1981 'Literature as Assertions', *American Criticism in the Poststructuralist Age*, ed I. Konigsberg, University of Michigan Press, Ann Arbor, pp. 58–85

Gray, Genevieve and Pratt, Rosalie, eds 1991 *Towards a Discipline of Nursing*, Churchill Livingstone, Melbourne

——1995 *Scholarship in the Discipline of Nursing*, Churchill Livingstone, Melbourne

Graycar, Regina and Morgan, Jenny, 1990 *The Hidden Gender of Law*, Federation Press, Sydney

Groppe, Maureen, 1994 'Talk-Radio Hosts Decide to Go Off the Air and On the Ballot', *Congressional Quarterly*, 9 April 1994, pp. 852–854

Grosz Elizabeth, 1989 *Sexual Subversions*, Allen & Unwin, Sydney

——1994 *Volatile Bodies: towards a corporeal feminism*, Allen & Unwin, Sydney

——1995 *Space, Time and Perversion*, Allen & Unwin, Sydney

Gunew, Sneja and Yeatman, Anna, eds 1993 *Feminism and the Politics of Difference*, Allen & Unwin, Sydney

Gupta, Akhil and Ferguson, James, 1992 'Beyond "Culture": space, identity, and the politics of difference', *Cultural Anthropology* vol. 7, no. 1, pp. 6–23

Hall, Stuart, 1980 'Encoding/Decoding', *Culture, Media, Language: working papers in cultural studies, 1972–79*, eds Stuart Hall, Dorothy Hobson, Andrew Lowe and Paul Willis, Routledge in association with the Centre for Contemporary Cultural Studies, University of Birmingham, London and New York, pp. 128–138

——1996 *Stuart Hall: critical dialogues in cultural studies*, eds David Morley and Kuan-Hsing Chen, Routledge, London and New York

Halliday, M.A.K., 1979 'Modes of Meaning and Modes of Expression: types of grammatical structure, and their determination by different semantic functions', *Function and Context in Linguistic Analysis: essays offered to William Haas*, eds D.J. Allerton, Edward Carney and David Holdcroft, Cambridge University Press, Cambridge, pp. 57–79

——1985 *Spoken and Written Language*, Deakin University Press, Geelong (reprinted Oxford University Press 1989)

——1994 *Introduction to Functional Grammar*, 2nd edn, Edward Arnold, London

Halliday, M.A.K. and Hasan, Ruqaiya, 1976 *Cohesion in English*, Longman, London

——1985 *Language, Context and Text: aspects of language in a social-semiotic perspective*, Deakin University Press, Geelong (reprinted Oxford University Press 1989)

Halliday, M.A.K. and Martin, J.R., 1993 *Writing Science: literacy and discursive power*, Falmer Press, London

Haraway, Donna, 1981 'In the Beginning Was the Word: the genesis of biological theory', *Signs: journal of women and culture in society* vol. 6, no. 31, pp. 469–481

——1988 'Situated Knowledges: the science question in feminism as a site of discourse on the privilege of partial perspective', *Feminist Studies*, vol. 14, no. 3, pp. 575–600

——1992 *Primate Visions: gender, race and nature in the world of modern science*, Verso, New York

Harding, Sandra, 1986 *The Science Question in Feminism*, Cornell University Press, Ithaca, New York

——ed. 1987 *Feminism and Methodology: social science issues*, Indiana University Press, Bloomington and Open University Press, Milton Keynes

Hargreaves, John, 1986 *Sport, Power and Culture*, Polity Press, Cambridge

Harré, Rom, 1990 'Some Narrative Conventions of Scientific Discourse', *Narrative in Culture: the uses of storytelling in the sciences, philosophy and literature*, ed. Cristopher Nash, Routledge, London and New York, pp. 81–101

Harris, Roy, 1987 *Reading Saussure: a critical commentary on the Cours de Linguistique Générale*, Duckworth, London

Hasan, Ruqaiya and Martin, J.R., eds. 1989 'Introduction', *Language Development: learning language, learning culture* (Meaning and Choice in Language: Studies for Michael Halliday), Ablex, Norwood, New Jersey, pp. 1–17

Hatzimanolis, Efi, 1993 'Timing Differences and Investing in Futures in Multicultural (Women's) Writing', *Feminism and the Politics of Difference*, eds Sneja Gunew and Anna Yeatman, Allen & Unwin, Sydney, pp. 128–142

Haviland, John B., 1979 'How to Talk to your Brother-in-Law in Guugu Yimidhirr', *Languages and Their Speakers*, ed. Timothy Shopen, Winthrop, Cambridge, pp. 161–239

Hays, Samuel P., 1987 *Beauty, Health, and Permanence: environmental politics in the United States, 1955–1985*, Cambridge University Press, Cambridge

Hekman, Susan J, ed. 1996 *Feminist Interpretations of Michel Foucault*, University of Pennsylvania Press, Pennsylvania

Hester, Stephen and Eglin, Peter, eds 1997 *Culture in Action: studies in membership categorisation analysis*, International Institute for Ethnomethodology and Conversation Analysis and The University Press of America, Washington, DC

Higgins, C. S. and Moss, P. D., 1982 *Sounds Real: radio in everyday life*, University of Queensland Press, Brisbane

Hilmes, Michele, 1997 *Radio Voices*, University of Minnesota Press, Minneapolis

Hjelmslev, Louis, 1961 *Prolegomena to a Theory of Language*, trans. F. J. Whitfield, University of Wisconsin Press, Madison, Wisconsin

Hobson, Dorothy, 1980 'Housewives and the Mass Media', *Culture, Media, Language: working papers in cultural studies, 1972–79*, eds Stuart Hall, Dorothy Hobson, Andrew

Lowe and Paul Willis, Routledge in association with the Centre for Contemporary Cultural Studies, University of Birmingham, London and New York, pp. 105–114

Hodge, Robert and Kress, Gunther, 1988 *Social Semiotics*, Polity Press, Cambridge

Hodge, Robert and McHoul, Alec, 1992 'The Politics of Text and Commentary', *Textual Practice* vol. 6, no. 2, pp. 189–209

Horvath, Barbara, 1985 *Variation in Australian English: the sociolects of Sydney*, Cambridge University Press, Cambridge

Hutchby, Ian, 1996 *Confrontation Talk: arguments, asymmetries and power on talk radio*, Lawrence Erlbaum, Hillsdale, New Jersey

Hutchby, Ian, and Wooffitt, Robin, 1998 *Conversation Analysis: principles, practices and applications*, Polity Press, Cambridge

Iedema, Rick, Feez, Susan and White, Peter, 1994 *Write-It-Right—Literacy in Industry Research Project. Stage 2: media literacy*, (Issues in Education for the Socially & Educationally Disadvantaged Monograph 6), Disadvantaged Schools Program, Metropolitan East Region, NSW Department of School Education, Sydney

Jakobson, Roman, 1960 'Concluding Statement: linguistics and poetics', *Style in Language*, ed. Thomas A. Sebeok, MIT Press, Cambridge, pp. 350–377

——1981 *Selected Writings, Vol. III: poetry of grammar and grammar of poetry*, Mouton, The Hague, Paris and New York

James, Alison, Hockey, Jenny and Dawson, Andrew, eds 1997 *After Writing Culture: epistemology and praxis in contemporary anthropology*, Routledge, London and New York

Jayyusi, Lena, 1984 *Categorisation and the Moral Order*, Routledge, London

Joseph, John E. and Taylor, Talbot J., eds 1990 *Ideologies of Language*, Routledge, London and New York

Josephides, Lisette, 1997 'Representing the Anthropologist's Predicament', *After Writing Culture: epistemology and praxis in contemporary anthropology*, eds Alison James, Jenny Hockey and Andrew Dawson, Routledge, London and New York, pp. 17–33

Joyce, Helen, Nesbitt, Christopher, Scheeres, Hermine, Slade, Diana and Solomon, Nicky, 1995 *Effective Communication in the Restructured Workplace*, The Australian National Food Industry Training Council, Victoria

Kamler, Barbara, 1997 'An Interview with Terry Threadgold on Critical Discourse Analysis', *Discourse: studies in the cultural politics of education* vol. 18, no. 3, pp. 437–445.

Kendall, Gavin and Wickham, Gary, 1999 *Using Foucault's Methods*, Sage, London, Thousand Oaks and New Delhi

Kendon, Adam, 1988 *Sign Languages of Central Australia*, Cambridge University Press, Cambridge

Killingsworth, M. Jimmie and Palmer, Jacqueline S., 1992 *Ecospeak: rhetoric and environmental politics in America* , Southern Illinois University Press, Carbondale

Kirby, Vicki, 1997 *Telling Flesh: the substance of the corporeal*, Routledge, London and New York

Kirk, David, 1990 'Knowledge, Science and the Rise and Rise of Human Movement Studies', *ACHPER National Journal* vol. 127, pp. 8–11

——1992 *Defining Physical Education: the social construction of a subject in postwar Britain*, Falmer Press, London

Kline, Stephen Jay, 1995 *Conceptual Foundations for Multidisciplinary Thinking*, Stanford University Press, Stanford

Knudtson, Peter and Suzuki, David, 1992 *Wisdom of the Elders*, Allen & Unwin, Sydney

Kress, Gunther, 1985 *Linguistic Processes in Sociocultural Practice*, Deakin University Press, Melbourne (reprinted Oxford University Press 1989)

——1988 'Language as Social Practice', *Communication and Culture: an introduction*, University of New South Wales Press, Sydney, pp. 79–129

——1994 'Text and Grammar as Explanation', *Text, Discourse and Context: representations of poverty in Britain*, eds Ulrike Meinhof and Kay Richardson, Longman, London and New York, pp. 24–46

——1996 'Representational Resources and the Production of Subjectivity: questions for the theoretical development of critical discourse analysis in a multi-cultural society', *Texts and Practices: readings in critical discourse analysis*, eds Carmen Rosa Caldas-Coulthard and Malcolm Coulthard, Routledge, London and New York, pp. 15–31

Kress, Gunther and Hodge, Robert, 1979 *Language as Ideology*, Routledge and Kegan Paul, London (2nd edn Hodge and Kress, 1993 Routledge, London and New York)

Kress, Gunther and van Leeuwen, Theo, 1990 *Reading Images*, Deakin University Press, Geelong

——1996 *Reading Images: the grammar of visual design*, Routledge, London

Kristeva, Julia, 1969 *Semiotike: recherches pour un sémanalyse*, Seuil, Paris

——1970 *Le Texte du Roman*, Mouton, The Hague

——1984 *Revolution in Poetic Language*, trans. Margaret Waller, introduction by Leon S. Roudiez, Columbia University Press, New York

——1988/91, *Strangers to Ourselves*, trans. Leon S. Roudiez, Harvester Wheatsheaf, New York and London

——1998 'Logics of the Sacred and Revolt', trans. John Lechte, *After the Revolution: on Kristeva*, eds John Lechte and Mary Zournazi, Artspace, Sydney, pp. 19–30

Labov, William, 1972a *Sociolinguistic Patterns*, University of Pennsylvania Press, Philadelphia

——1972b *Language in the Inner City*, University of Pennsylvania Press, Philadelphia

Lather, Patti, 1991 *Getting Smart: feminist research and pedagogy with/in the postmodern*, Routledge, New York and London

——1993 'Fertile Obsession: validity after poststructuralism', *Sociological Quarterly* vol. 34, no. 4, pp. 63–69

Lattas, Andrew, 1990 'Aborigines and Contemporary Australian Nationalism', *Social Analysis, no. 27. Writing Australian Culture: text, society and national identity*, ed. Julie Marcus, pp. 58–63

Laughren, Mary, 1982 'Warlpiri Kinship Structure', *Languages of Kinship in Aboriginal Australia*, eds Jeffrey Heath, Francesca Merlan and Alan Rumsey, Oceania Linguistic Monographs No. 24, University of Sydney, pp. 72–85

Lee, Alison, 1995 'Gender and Text in Educational Research', *Australian Educational Researcher* vol. 21, no. 3, pp. 35–46

——1996 *Gender, Literacy, Curriculum: re-writing school geography*, Taylor & Francis, London

Lemke, Jay, 1995 *Textual Politics*, Taylor & Francis, London

Lévi-Strauss, Claude, 1972 *The Savage Mind*, Weidenfield and Nicolson, London

Levinson, Marjorie, 1986 'Insight and Oversight: reading tintern abbey', *Wordsworth's Great Period Poems: four essays*, Cambridge University Press, London and New York, pp. 14–57

Levinson, Stephen C., 1983 *Pragmatics*, Cambridge University Press, Cambridge

Li, Charles, ed. 1976 *Subject and Topic*, Academic Press, New York

Liberman, K, 1982 'Some Linguistic Features of Congenial Fellowship Among the Pitjanjatjara', *International Journal for the Sociology of Language, vol. 36: Australian Aborigines: sociolinguistic studies*, ed. Graeme MacKay, pp. 35–51.

Lock, Graham, 1996 *Functional English Grammar: an introduction for second language teachers*, Cambridge University Press, Cambridge

Loughlan, Patricia, 1996 'The Historical Role of the Equitable Jurisdiction', *The Principles of Equity*, ed. Patrick Parkinson, Law Book Company Information Services, Sydney, pp. 3–27

Luke, Allan, 1995 'Getting Our Hands Dirty: provisional politics in postmodern conditions' *After Post-Modernism: education, politics and identity*, eds. Richard Smith and Philip Wexler, Falmer Press, London, pp. 83–87

——1997 'The Material Effects of the Word: apologies, "stolen children" and public discourse', *Discourse: studies in the cultural politics of education* vol. 18, no. 3, pp. 343–368

Lyons, John, 1968 *Introduction to Theoretical Linguistics*, Cambridge University Press, Cambridge

Lyotard, François, 1984 *The Postmodern Condition: a report on knowledge*, Manchester University Press, Manchester

Macdonell, Diane, 1986 *Theories of Discourse: an introduction*, Basil Blackwell, Oxford

Malinowski, Bronislaw, 1923 'The problem of meaning in primitive languages', Supplement 1 in *The Meaning of Meaning*, eds C.K. Ogden and I.A. Richards, Kegan Paul, London, pp. 451–510

Maltz, Daniel N. and Borker, Ruth A., 1982 'A Cultural Approach to Male–Female Miscommunication', *Language and Social Identity*, ed. John Gumperz, Cambridge University Press, Cambridge, pp. 196–216

Martin, J.R., 1992 *English Text: system and structure*, Benjamins, Amsterdam

Martin, J.R., Matthiessen, Christian M.I.M. and Painter, Clare, 1997 *Working with Functional Grammar*, Arnold, London

Mason, Sir Anthony, 1996 'Foreword', *The Principles of Equity*, ed. Ian Patrick Parkinson, Law Book Company Information Services, Sydney

Mauro, Tullio de, 1972 *Edition Critique du Cours de Linguistique Générale de F. de Saussure*, Payot, Paris

McHoul, Alec, 1990 'Discourse', *The Encyclopedia of Language and Linguistics, Volume 2*, ed. R. E. Asher, Pergamon, Oxford, pp. 940–949

McHoul, Alec and Grace, Wendy, 1993 *A Foucault Primer: discourse, power and the subject*, Melbourne University Press, Melbourne

McHoul, Alec and Luke, Allan, 1989 'Discourse as Language and Politics: an introduction to the philology of political culture in Australia', *Journal of Pragmatics* vol. 13, pp. 323–332

McInnes, David, 1998 *Attending to the Instance: towards a systemic based dynamic and responsive analysis of composite performance text*, unpub. PhD thesis, University of Sydney

McNay, Lois, 1992 *Feminism and Foucault: power, gender and the self*, Polity Press, Cambridge

McWilliam, Erica, 1996 'Introduction: pedagogies, technologies, bodies', in *Pedagogy, Technology and the Body*, eds E. McWilliam and P.G. Taylor, Peter Lang, New York, pp. 1–23

Meggitt, Mervyn J., 1962 *Desert People: a study of the Walbiri Aborigines of Central Australia*, Angus & Robertson, Sydney

Meinhof, Ulrike H. and Richardson, Kay, eds 1994 *Text, Discourse and Context: representations of poverty in Britain*, Longman, London

Miller, Toby, 1993 'The Media Industries: radio', *The Media in Australia: industries, texts, audiences*, eds Stuart Cunningham and Graeme Turner, Allen & Unwin, Sydney, pp. 41–45

Miller, Toby, Lucy, Niall and Turner, Graeme, 1993 'The Production Process: radio', *The Media in Australia: industries, texts, audiences*, eds Stuart Cunningham and Graeme Turner, Allen & Unwin, Sydney, pp. 156–170

Mitchell, A.G. and Delbridge, Arthur, 1965 *The Pronunciation of English in Australia* (rev. edn), Angus & Robertson, Sydney

Mohanty, Chandra Talpade, 1992 'Feminist Encounters: locating the politics of experience', *Destabilising Theory: Contemporary Feminist Debates*, eds Michele Barrett and Anne Phillips, Polity Press, London, pp. 74–92

Montgomery, Martin, 1986 'DJ Talk', *Media, Culture and Society* vol. 8, pp. 421–440

Napaljarri, Peggy Rockman and Cataldi, Lee, collectors, eds and trans, 1994 *Yimikirli: Warlpiri dreamings and histories*, HarperCollins, San Francisco, London and Sydney

Nash, David, 1980 *Topics in Warlpiri Grammar*, unpub. PhD dissertation, Massachusetts Institute of Technology

——1982 'An Etymological Note on Warlpiri *Kurdungurlu*', *Languages of Kinship in Aboriginal Australia*, eds Jeffrey Heath, Francesca Merlan and Alan Rumsey, *Oceania Linguistic Monographs* no. 24, Oceania Publications, Sydney, pp. 141–159

Nash, David and Simpson, Jane, 1981 ' "No-name" in Central Australia', *Papers from the Parasession on Language and Behaviour*, eds Carrie Masek, Roberta A. Hendrick and Mary Frances Miller, University of Chicago Press, Chicago, pp. 165–177

Nast, Heidi J. and Pile, Steve, eds 1998 *Places Through the Body*, Routledge, London and New York

NBEET (National Board for Employment, Education and Training), 1996 *Literacy at Work: incorporating English language and literacy competencies into industry/enterprise standards*, Australian Government Publishing Service, Canberra

Niranjana, T., 1992 *Siting Translations: history, post-structuralism and the colonial context*, University of California Press, Los Angeles

Norris, Christopher, 1982 *Deconstruction: theory and practice*, Methuen, London and New York

Painter, Clare and Martin, J.R., eds 1986 *Writing to Mean: teaching genres across the curriculum*, Applied Linguistics Association of Australia, Occasional Papers No. 9

Parker, Andrew and Sedgewick, Eve Kosofsky, eds 1995 *Performativity and Performance*, Routledge, London

Patterson, Annette, 1997 'Critical Discourse Analysis: a condition of doubt', *Discourse: studies in the cultural politics of education* vol. 18, no. 3, pp. 425–435

Pennycook, Alastair, 1994a 'Incommensurable Discourses?', *Applied Linguistics* vol. 15, no. 2, pp. 115–138

——1994b *The Cultural Politics of English as an International Language*, Longman, London and New York

Pether, Penny, 1991 'Fiduciary Duties: Congreve's *The Way of the World*', *Australian Journal of Law and Society* vol. 7, pp. 71–82

——1997 'Pursuing the Unspeakable: towards a critical theory of power, ethics, and the interpreting subject in Australian Constitutional Law', invited paper, *Critical Perspectives on Australian Constitutional Law Seminar*, Annual Public Law Weekend, Centre for International and Public Law, Australian National University, November 1997 (forthcoming in *Federal Law Review*)

——1998 'Principles or Skeletons? Mabo and the discursive constitution of the Australian nation', *Law/Text/Culture* vol. 4, pp. 115–145

Pheng, Cheah, 1994, 'Sexual Difference, Cultural Difference: body and history in Gallop', *Jane Gallop Seminar Papers*, ed. Jill Julius Matthews, (Humanities Research Centre Monograph 7), Australian National University, Canberra

Plant, Sadie with RosieX, 1995 'Dr Sadie Plant—doyenne of cyberfeminism up close and unmanned', *geekgirl* issue one, stick, www.geekgirl.com.au/geekgirl/001stick/index.html

Potter, Jonathan, 1996 *Representing Reality: discourse, rhetoric and social construction*, Sage, London, Thousand Oaks and New Delhi

Potts, John, 1989 *Radio in Australia*, University of New South Wales Press, Sydney

Poynton, Cate, 1985 *Language and Gender: making the difference*, Deakin University Press, Melbourne (reprinted Oxford University Press 1989)

——1993 'Grammar, Language and the Social: poststructuralism and systemic-functional linguistics', *Social Semiotics* vol. 3, no. 1, pp. 1–21

——1997 'Language, Difference and Identity: three perspectives' *Literacy and Numeracy Studies* vol. 7, no. 1, pp. 7–24

——1999 'Talking like a girl', *Musics and Feminisms*, eds Sally Macarthur and Cate Poynton, Australian Music Centre, Sydney, pp. 119–128

——in prep. *A Civilisation of Speech: voice, modernity and the speaking subject*

Psathas, George, 1995 *Conversation Analysis: the study of talk-in-interaction*, Sage, Thousand Oaks, London and New Delhi

Rabinow, Paul, 1986 'Representations are Social Facts: modernity and postmodernity in anthropology', *Writing Culture: the poetics and politics of ethnography*, eds James Clifford and George Marcus, University of California Press, Berkeley, pp. 234–261

Roberts, James C., 1991 'The Power of Talk Radio', *The American Enterprise*, May–June, pp. 56–61

Rooney, Ellen, 1986 'Who's Left Out? a rose by any other name is still red; or the politics of pluralism', *Critical Inquiry* vol. 12, Spring, pp. 550–563

Rumsey, Alan 1982 'Gun-Gunma: an Australian Aboriginal avoidance language and its social functions', *Languages of Kinship in Aboriginal Australia*, eds Jeffrey Heath, Francesca Merlan and Alan Rumsey, Oceania Linguistic Monographs No. 24, University of Sydney, pp. 160–181

——1984 'Meaning and Use in Ngarinyin Kin Classification: a rejoinder to Scheffler', *Oceania* vol. 54, no., 4, pp. 323–331

——1994 'The Dreaming, Human Agency and Inscriptive Practice' (draft paper)

Ryan, Judith, 1989 *Mythscapes: Aboriginal art of the desert*, National Gallery of Victoria, Melbourne

——1990 *Paint Up Big: Warlpiri women's art of Lajamanu*, National Gallery of Victoria, Melbourne

Sacks, Harvey, 1974 'On the Analysability of Stories by Children', *Ethnomethodology: selected readings*, ed. Roy Turner, Penguin Education, Harmondsworth, pp. 216–232

——1992 *Lectures on Conversation*, ed. Gail. Jefferson, Polity Press, Oxford

Sacks, Harvey, Schegloff, Emmanuel and Jefferson, Gail, 1974 'A Simplest Systematics for the Organization of Turn-Taking for Conversation', *Language*, vol. 50, pp. 696–735

Saussure, Ferdinand de, 1959 *Course in General Linguistics*, ed. Charles Bally and Albert Sechehaye in collaboration with Albert Riedlinger, trans. with introduction and notes by Wade Baskin, McGraw-Hill, New York

——1983 *Course in General Linguistics*, ed. Charles Bally and Albert Sechehaye in collaboration with Albert Riedlinger, trans. and annotated by Roy Harris, Duckworth, London

Scannell, Paddy, ed. 1991 *Broadcast Talk*, Sage, London, Thousand Oaks and New Delhi

——1992 'Public Service Broadcasting and Modern Public Life', *Culture and Power: a media, culture and society reader*, eds Paddy Scannell, Philip Schlesinger and Colin Sparks, Sage, London, Thousand Oaks and New Delhi, pp. 317–348

Scheffler, Harold W., 1978 *Australian Kin Classification*, Cambridge University Press, Cambridge

Schegloff, Emanuel, 1968 'Sequencing in Conversational Openings', *American Anthropologist* vol. 70, pp. 1075–1095

Schegloff, Emanuel and Sacks, Harvey, 1973 'Opening up Closings' *Semiotica* vol. 7, pp. 289–327

Schiffrin, Deborah, 1987 *Discourse Markers*, Cambridge University Press, Cambridge

——1994 *Approaches to Discourse*, Blackwell, Oxford and Cambridge, Massachusetts

Schirato, Tony and Yell, Susan, 1996 *Communication and Cultural Literacy: an introduction*, Allen & Unwin, Sydney

Scott, Peter, 1995 *The Meanings of Mass Higher Education*, Society for Research in Higher Education and Open University Press, Buckingham

Scutt, Jocelyn, 1990 *Women and the Law: commentary and materials*, Law Book Company, Sydney

Searle, John R., 1969 *Speech Acts: an essay in the philosophy of language*, Cambridge University Press, Cambridge

——1979 *Expression and Meaning: studies in the theory of speech acts*, Cambridge University Press, Cambridge

Shilling, Chris, 1993 *The Body and Social Theory*, Sage, London

Sinclair, J. McH. and Coulthard R.M., 1975 *Towards an Analysis of Discourse: the English used by teachers and pupils*, Oxford University Press, London

Skinner, B.F. 1957 *Verbal Behaviour*, Appleton-Century-Crofts, New York

Smith, Dorothy E., 1987 *The Everyday World as Problematic: a feminist sociology*, Open University Press, Milton Keynes

——1990 *Texts, Facts, and Femininity: exploring the relations of ruling*, Routledge, London and New York

——1999 *Writing the Social: critique, theory, and investigation*, University of Toronto Press, Toronto

Spivak, Gayatri Chakrovorty, 1976 'Translator's Preface', *Of Grammatology*, Jacques Derrida, Johns Hopkins University Press, Baltimore, pp. ix–lxxxvii

——1987 *In Other Worlds: essays in cultural politics*, Methuen, New York

——1988, 'Can the Subaltern Speak?', *Marxism and the Interpretation of Culture*, eds Cary Nelson and Lawrence Grossberg, MacMillan Education, London, pp. 271–316

Stanner, W.E.H., 1937 'Aboriginal Modes of Address and Reference in the North-West of the Northern Territory', *Oceania* vol. 7, pp. 300–315

Steiner, Peter, 1984 *Russian Formalism: a metapoetics*, Cornell University Press, Ithaca and London

Stewart, Colin, 1990 'Format Music on Radio', *Metro* vol. 83, Winter, pp. 44–47

Stoler, Ann Laura, 1997 *Race and the Education of Desire: Foucault's history of sexuality and the colonial order of things*, Duke University Press, Durham and London

Street, Annette Fay, 1992 *Inside Nursing: a critical ethnography of clinical nursing practice*, State University of New York, Albany

Stronach, Ian and MacLure, Maggie, 1997 *Educational Research Undone: the postmodern embrace*, Open University Press, Buckingham and Philadelphia

Stubbs, Michael, 1983 *Discourse Analysis: the sociolinguistic analysis of natural language*, Basil Blackwell, Oxford

Sutton, Peter, 1982 'Personal Power, Kin Classification and Speech Etiquette', *Languages of Kinship in Aboriginal Australia*, eds Jeffrey Heath, Francesca Merlan and Alan Rumsey, Oceania Linguistic Monographs No. 24, University of Sydney, pp. 182–200

Suzuki, David, 1990 *Inventing the Future*, Allen & Unwin, Sydney

Tannen, Deborah, 1994 *Gender and Discourse*, Oxford University Press, New York and Oxford

Taussig, Michael, 1993 *Mimesis and Alterity: a particular history of the senses*, Routledge, New York and London

Taylor, Talbot J. and Cameron, Deborah, 1987 *Analysing Conversation: rules and units in the structure of talk*, Pergamon, Oxford

ten Have, Paul, 1999 *Doing Conversation Analysis: a practical guide*, Sage, London, Thousand Oaks and New Delhi

Thibault, Paul J., 1997 *Re-reading Saussure: the dynamics of signs in social life*, Routledge, London and New York

Thompson, John B., 1990 *Ideology and Modern Culture: critical social theory in the era of mass communication*, Polity Press, Cambridge in association with Blackwell Publishers, Oxford

Thorne, Barrie and Henley, Nancy, eds, 1975 *Language and Sex: difference and dominance*, Newbury House, Rowley, Massachusetts

Thorne, Barrie, Kramarae, Cheris and Henley, Nancy, eds 1983 *Language, Gender and Society*, Newbury House, Rowley, Massachusetts

Threadgold, Terry, 1986 'Semiotics, Ideology, Language', *Semiotics, Ideology, Language*, eds Terry Threadgold, E. A. Grosz, Gunther Kress and M.A.K. Halliday, Sydney Association for Studies in Society and Culture, no. 3, Sydney, pp. 15–60

——1988 'Language and Gender', *Australian Feminist Studies* vol. 6, pp. 41–70

——1997a *Feminist Poetics: poiesis, performance, histories*, Routledge, London and New York

——1997b 'Narrative and Legal Texts: telling stories about women who kill', *UTS Review: cultural studies and new writing* vol. 3, no. 1, pp. 56–73

——1997c 'Performativity, Regulative Fictions, Huge Stabilities—Framing Battered Woman's Syndrome', *Law/Text/Culture* vol. 3, pp. 210–231

Tinning, Richard, 1990 *Ideology and Physical Education*, Deakin University Press, Geelong

Todorov, Tzvetan, 1984 *Mikhail Bakhtin: the dialogic principle*, trans. Vlad Godzich, Manchester University Press, Manchester

Tolson, Andrew, 1991 'Televised Chat and the Synthetic Personality', *Broadcast Talk*, ed. Paddy Scannell, Sage, London, Newbury Park and New Delhi, pp. 117–200

Trew, Tony, 1979 '"What the Papers Say": linguistic variation and ideological difference', Roger Fowler, Bob Hodge, Gunther Kress and Tony Trew, *Language and Control*, Routledge and Kegan Paul, London, pp. 117–156

Trinh, T. Minh-ha, 1989 *Woman, Native, Other*, Indiana University Press, Bloomington

Trudgill, Peter, 1974 *The Social Differentiation of English in Norwich*, Cambridge University Press, Cambridge

Turner, Roy, ed. 1974 *Ethnomethodology: selected readings*, Penguin, Harmondsworth

Usher, Robin, 1996 'A Critique of the Neglected Epistemological Assumptions of Educational Research', *Understanding Educational Research*, eds David Scott and Robin Usher, Routledge, London, pp. 9–32

——1997 'Seductive Texts: competence, power and knowledge in postmodernity', *The End of Knowledge in Higher Education*, eds Ronald Barnett and Anne Griffin, Institute of Education, University of London, London, pp. 99–111

van Dijk, Teun A., 1977 *Text and Context: explorations in the semantics and pragmatics of discourse*, Longman, London and New York

——1987a *News as Discourse*, Laurence Erlbaum, Hillsdale, NJ

——ed. 1987b *News Analysis*, Laurence Erlbaum, Hillsdale, NJ

——ed. 1997 *Discourse Studies: a multidisciplinary introduction*, vol. 1: *Discourse as Structure and Process*; vol. 2: *Discourse as Social Interaction*, Sage, London, Thousand Oaks and New Delhi van Maanen, John, 1995 'Style as Theory', *Organization Science* vol. 6, pp. 133–143

Vestergaard, Torben and Schroder, Kim, 1985 *The Language of Advertising*, Basil Blackwell, Oxford

Voloshinov, Valentin N., 1973 *Marxism and the Philosophy of Language*, trans. Ladislav Mateka and I.R. Titunik, Seminar Press, New York and London (orig. pub. 1930 as *Marksizm I Filosofija Jazyka*, Leningrad)

von Sturmer, John, 1981 'Talking with Aborigines', *Australian Institute of Aboriginal Studies Newsletter* no. 15, pp. 13–30

Walkerdine, Valerie, 1985 'On the Regulation of Speaking and Silence: subjectivity, class and gender in contemporary schooling', *Language, Gender and Childhood*, eds Carolyn Steedman, Cathy Urwin and Valerie Walkerdine, Routledge and Kegan Paul, London, pp. 203–241

——1988 *The Mastery of Reason: cognitive development and the production of rationality*, Methuen, London

——1990 *Schoolgirl Fictions*, Verso, London and New York

Walkerdine, Valerie and Lucey, Helen, 1989 *Democracy in the Kitchen: regulating mothers and socialising daughters*, Virago, London

Watkins, Megan, 1997 'Textual Recipes: language pedagogy and classroom discourse', *Southern Review* vol. 30, no. 3, pp. 287–301

Weedon, Chris, 1997, *Feminist Practice and Poststructuralist Theory*, 2nd edn, Blackwell, Oxford and Cambridge, Massachusetts

Wierzbicka, Anna, 1992 *Semantics, Culture and Cognition*, Oxford University Press, Oxford

Wilkinson, Sue and Kitzinger, Celia, eds 1995 *Feminism and Discourse: psychological perspectives*, Sage, London, Thousand Oaks and New Delhi

Williams, Glyn, 1992 *Sociolinguistics: a sociological critique*, Routledge, London and New York

Wilson, Elizabeth, 1998 *Neural Geographies: feminism and the microstructure of cognition*, Routledge, New York and London

Wright, Georg Henrik von, 1971 *Explanation and Understanding*, Cornell University Press, Ithaca, New York

Wright, Janice, 1996 'Mapping the Discourses in Physical Education', *Journal of Curriculum Studies* vol. 28, no. 3, pp. 331–351

Index